My definition of personal success is "Having those who know me best respect me the most, and finishing well." This book, by my close friend, Bob Buford, shows how to accomplish this goal. Read it and be changed!

— Rick Warren, author, *The Purpose Driven Life*®

A motivating set of believable best practices for those who are seeking to re-define the journey.

— Steve Reinemund, chairman and CEO, PepsiCo

Finishing Well is an inspirational guide for the journey through Life II. It unveils the depth of choices that are available in our second lifetime. It dem-onstrates in a meaningful way how easy it is to find and follow a repositioned power of purpose. All we have to do is listen to ourselves, embrace our enthu-siasm, and get involved. Bob Buford makes us realize we all have the potential to be code breakers.

— Roger Staubach, chairman and CEO, the Staubach Company; Hall of Fame NFL quarterback

Most of us feel fortunate to get one person's wisdom in a book. Bob Buford has brought us insights and thought-provoking ideas from more than fifty leaders from diverse backgrounds on finishing well. Each chapter has unique takeaways that can ensure a more productive direction in your life. If there was one book to read about what to do next, this is it. *Finishing Well* is a guide that should be read and reread.

— Wally Hawley, cofounder, Interwest Partners

The experiences and words of advice found in *Finishing Well* can be of enormous value to anyone wishing to enhance both their personal and professional lives.

— Dr. Kenneth Cooper, founder, the Cooper Clinic

Demographics will be the most important factor in the next society. "Second Career" and "second half of one's life" have become buzz words in America. Increasingly men and women take early retirement but they do not stop working. These "second careers" will often take unconventional forms. Bob Buford's new book breaks new ground in interviewing the exemplars and pathfinders who are living on this new frontier. *Finishing Well* is an important book. It reads extremely well.

— Peter F. Drucker, "Father of modern management"

FINISHING WELL

Congratulations on taking
your first step towards
"finishing well".
JD, Rob & Bob

Men's Fraternity
Feb 2009

Is.40:28-31

FINISHING WELL

What People Who REALLY Live Do Differently!

BOB BUFORD

THOMAS NELSON
Since 1798

NASHVILLE   DALLAS   MEXICO CITY   RIO DE JANEIRO   BEIJING

Published in Nashville, Tennessee, by Thomas Nelson. Thomas Nelson is a registered trademark of Thomas Nelson, Inc.

Thomas Nelson, Inc., titles may be purchased in bulk for educational, business, fund-raising, or sales promotional use. For information, please e-mail SpecialMarkets@ThomasNelson.com.

Cover design: Anderson Thomas Design
Cover Image: Getty Images
Interior Design: Susan Browne Design

Library of Congress Cataloging-in-Publication Data

Buford, Bob.
  Finishing well / by Bob Buford.
     p. cm.
  Includes bibliographical references.
  ISBN 978-1-59145-395-6 (TP)
  ISBN 978-1-59145-110-5 (HC)
  ISBN 978-1-59145-233-1 (IE)
  1. Older Christians—Religious life. 2. Success—Religious aspects—Christianity. I. Title.
  BV4580.B83 2004
  248.8'4—dc22

                                                                              2004008236

Printed in the United States of America

08 09 10 11 12 QW 9 8 7 6 5

Contents

Foreword

For years I have been asking people, "Would you like the world to be a better place for your having been here?" Everyone is quick to say, "Yes!" But when I ask them, "What's your plan?" they smile and laugh, because they don't have a clue. As Bob Buford found in his research for his book *Halftime,* most people, as they approach the magic ages of forty-five or fifty, would like to move from success to significance. They want to move from a time in their lives when they felt they had to prove themselves—what Bob calls in this book Life I—to a time when they can give back and make a difference—what Bob calls Life II. Life I is what happens before halftime and Life II is what comes afterward.

As Bob found in writing *Stuck in Halftime,* many of us don't know how to make the transition from Life I to Life II—from success to significance. Without a strategy or role models, we often get drawn back into Life I. I don't have to look far for an example.

When Bob first asked me if I would write the foreword to *Finishing Well,* I was reluctant. After all, Peter Drucker had written the foreword to *Halftime* and *Stuck in Halftime,* and Peter Drucker is my guru as a management thinker. He's forgotten more than most people ever knew. Add to that the fact that Bob thinks Peter is the wisest man alive. How could I ever write a foreword that could match words of wisdom from Peter Drucker? When I realized what was happening, I had to laugh. Here I was in a ridiculous competition reminiscent of Life I, concerned about proving myself.

How do we keep from reverting back to old ways and stay on Life II's path to significance? The answers are in this book. Bob went on an interview odyssey. He talked to 120 exceptional people—folks he called "code breakers"

—who were venturing into the Life II frontier and "shouting back" learnings. About half of those people are quoted in this book, including me.

After grappling with this foreword, I suggested that Bob take me out of the book itself. He refused. I guess he feels that sometimes the best way to learn is to teach. And did I ever learn from reading this book! I think you will too. You'll discover a pearl of wisdom on every page. Life II is uncharted territory. In the past most people thought you "retired and then died." That's no longer a given today. We have choices we've never had before. In many ways we can make the *best* of our life the *rest* of our life. Enjoy! Thanks again, Bob, for challenging our thinking and way of being.

—Ken Blanchard
Coauthor of *The One Minute Manager*® and *The Servant Leader*

Introduction: Life II

THE STRONGEST INSIGHT YOU HAD IN *Halftime* WAS THAT THERE IS MORE THAN ONE LIFETIME.
— PETER F. DRUCKER

"I HAVE RECEIVED A SECOND LIFE!"
— SHAKESPEARE, *The Tempest*

This is a book about a life that didn't used to exist. It's what I call Life II.

Odds are, you'll live a whole adult lifetime that wasn't available to your parents and grandparents. Their life expectancy at birth was fifty years. We have two lifetimes now. Life I is what occurs before halftime, and Life II comes afterward. Most people have a pretty good plan for Life I, but few can see their way forward into Life II. Life I has a multitude of clear role models and consists of fairly simple steps. You grow up somewhere, go to school somewhere, form your own family, and go to work somewhere. Then you retire and you _____. (You fill in the blank.)

Halftime is the in-between season that occurs at about age forty-five, plus or minus a few years, the time I described in my first book.¹ It's the season of "now what?" In our time, halftime really marks the end of Life I and the beginning of a whole new second adult season that I've identified as Life II. Halftime used to be the beginning of the end. Now it is the beginning of a whole new beginning—a season that for me and many others has turned out to be the richest and most meaning-filled season of all.

We have few role models for Life II, because until recently we thought of life past the age of sixty as the end of productivity. Regardless of the euphemisms used to describe them, these were the "senior" years—time to head off into senior living, which certainly wasn't thought of as any kind of new beginning, more like *the long good-bye*.

Not long ago I was invited to speak to a group who ministered to what they called senior adults. In the course of several side conversations, I asked people what was meant by that term, and they weren't quite sure. A banner outside proclaimed "Over 50," but the exhibits were for hospices and for cruises with happy old folks looking off into the sunset. Displays offered flyers for senior living facilities—what used to be called "old folks homes." But when I asked these eagerly listening individuals how many of them would like to be referred to as "seniors," only four or five hands out of 280 went up, and those were at a tentative half-mast. When I read them the Life I sequence with the "fill in the blank," a roomful of people unanimously and simultaneously finished my sentence "you retire and you *die*."

The new territory we discover in Life II is what Magellan and other explorers called *terra incognita*, or unknown territory, someplace off the map of the known world. We're not quite sure what's out there. Having listened to hundreds of halftime stories, I can say with some conviction that most people feel this way. An expression I heard verbatim more times than I can count is: "I'm in halftime and I don't have a clue where to go from here." I went through a time when I wasn't sure myself. I faced hard questions I couldn't answer.

In order to come to grips with these questions, I did what I've done the last twenty years of my life whenever I didn't know: I went to the mountaintop; I went to see Peter.

Peter Drucker is my wisdom figure, my go-to source for understanding. He has over four million words in print! Not long ago, *The Economist* magazine commissioned Peter to write a twenty-seven-page section on "the Next Society." They picked a ninety-two-year-old to write about what's next for the world! And if it's good enough for them, it's certainly good enough for me. So, in my quest for answers, and filled with anticipation, I went to see him.

I found Peter at home in Claremont, California. He lives in a surprisingly unassuming suburban house near the Business School at Claremont Graduate University that bears his name. He was relaxed, fit, and characteristically warm and gracious. I had sent a letter ahead to get him thinking, and he was more than ready.

"What now, Peter?" I asked. "I'm sixty-four. I still have plenty of gas in the tank, but where to drive?"

"The most important thing you're working on is halftime," he began. "You've identified a need, and you've started a lot of people asking the right questions and put them on a quest for significance. Now it's time for you to go find the lessons for what makes the second half of life work.[2] But," he warned me, "don't write a book for old people. Find the lessons for the forty-five-year-olds. By sixty-five it's too late."

THINKING AHEAD

The lessons for the forty-five-year-olds? That's become my primary quest over the course of the past year, and what this book is about. Peter calls it my "third career." After thirty years in the television business, and now almost twenty years in a parallel career as a social entrepreneur, working through the organization I founded, Leadership Network,[3] I've taken this new adventure very seriously.

One thing I've noticed in my quest is that Life II takes most people by surprise. It's as if they wake up one day in a new world. Suddenly the landmarks are different. Thanks to cutting-edge technologies and the rapid advance of science, we've explored all the geographic frontiers. From microbiology to outer space, we've seen some amazing things. But now, it turns out, the most challenging frontiers are human and demographic. Here's how Peter Drucker put it in the foreword to my third book, which sought to explore why so many capable people were "stuck in halftime" and having a hard time getting traction on their second halves:

> In a few hundred years, when the history of our time will be written from a long-term perspective, I think it is very probable that the most important event these historians will see is not technology, it is not the Internet, it is not e-commerce. It is an unprecedented change in the human condition. For the first time—and I mean that literally— substantial and rapidly growing numbers of people have choices. For the first time, they will have to *manage themselves*.

Unfortunately, as Peter also observed, we are totally unprepared for it.

Up until maybe 1900, even in the most highly developed countries, the overwhelming majority followed their father—if they were lucky. If your father was a peasant farmer, you were a peasant farmer. If he was a craftsman, you were a craftsman. There was no such thing as upward mobility.

And now suddenly, a very large number of people choose what they want to be. And what's more, they will have more than one career. The average working life span is now close to sixty years. You got twenty years in 1900.

In a very short time, we will no longer believe that retirement means the end of working life. Retirement may even come much earlier than ever, but working life will continue if only out of economic necessity. For many, however, working well beyond retirement will be a choice based on preference. They will either tire of luxury or desire to use their knowledge and experience to contribute to society.[4]

Most people *are* unprepared and they are searching for meaning in midlife. They are seeking. This is a midlife demographic wave. The good news is that it's up to us. It's the bad news too, for choice brings with it uncertainty and a burden of responsibility. Two books that have been perpetually on the bestseller lists indicate that the search is shared by many, many people who have found that success in life is not the final answer: Po Bronson's, *What Should I Do with My Life?*[5] (a totally secular book of more than fifty stories of people who really don't know the answer beyond "find a good job") and Rick Warren's *The Purpose Driven Life®*[6] (15 million copies sold in just over a year, Christian from cover to cover with over 1,500 biblical references). The book you hold in your hand occupies a middle ground—more answers than Bronson's lost wanderers and less theological than Warren's excellent book.

Most people don't really have plans or role models for Life II. It comes as a surprise to most, but not to the group I call the "code breakers."

I set out a year ago on what I would call an interview odyssey for people seeking to crack the code on Life II. I wanted to find the pioneers, the pathfinders, the leaders ahead of us in this new territory. These code breakers redefine what it means to be fifty and beyond. I wanted to find out what they were thinking and, more importantly, what they were *doing* to find meaning in Life II. Over a period of time I interviewed over 120 exceptional people—those making a meaningful difference in the lives of others and, as a by-product, living with passion and contagious enthusiasm. About half of them are quoted at length in the pages of this book. They have punched through the demographic frontier that seems to impose real limits for most of us, and they have lessons to teach us.

So let's get started. Most of the words in the following chapters are boiled down from more than a thousand pages of single-spaced dialogue with the code breakers, the pathfinders. I want you to have a sense of the tone and atmosphere of these interviews, so I invite you to think of reading this book as going to lunch with me and some of the smartest people on the planet . . . people who have "cracked the code" on how to be effective and fulfilled in Life II.

By the time I spoke to Peter Drucker, I had already conducted about twenty interviews. As I described my early findings for his reaction, he said, "You are interviewing the exemplars, the heroes of this next life. They may not be smarter than the others, but the main difference between them and the nonheroes is that they *think ahead*. The nonheroes aren't introspective. They don't think ahead. They let life surprise them. They are not aware. But if you tell them, they're receptive." In other words, like most of us nonhero types, they get it when they see it, and once they get it they can implement it in their lives. That's what I have been doing all my life: finding out how the heroes think and act differently, then implementing it in my life.

A HIGHER PURPOSE

That's my format—take an exemplar to lunch.[7] Find out how he or she is doing life. Follow the lessons. Expect to learn from what follows, exploring what these pioneers are doing to make Life II richer and more meaningful than the rest of us.

This is not, however, nor is it meant to be, a random sample of American life. Most of these code breakers are like Tom Luce, with whose story I begin. Born into modest means, Tom's mother worked in a dress shop and lived in a strategically located duplex so he could go to the best public schools in Dallas. Graduating from SMU, then night law school, Tom went on to a career as a superlawyer and founder of a big law firm. Now he's changing the world for millions of schoolkids, the kids with working moms whose breakthrough into the middle class comes through their education, just as it did for Tom.

You'll meet some celebrities in these pages—a Heisman Trophy winner, a White House chief of staff, a best-selling author, a winner of six Grammy awards—but most are products of the so-called American Dream: modest means, good education, finding and building on a core strength, and a sense of calling to serve others in Life II. They are all multipliers who are making a lot of what they've been given to work with. Far from just wasting away by themselves, they are deeply engaged in contributing to the lives of others. That's where the legacy of their lives live on. It's what I call *socially productive aging*. Most, but not all, are people of committed Christian faith, as I am. Some are Jewish. Some are seekers. The *difference* in their faith dynamic is that *they act on it;* they step out. They are willingly at risk and often in harm's way. Most of them set a course for Life II in their forties and fifties, well before their "retirement threshold" arrives.

And they will finish well, running through the tape. As Dr. Kenneth Cooper puts it, "I want to work on Friday and die a quick death on Monday." Most aren't superrich. Though some are, they redeploy their wealth voluntarily to build and support ministries and social enterprises that will make the world a better place.

All are interesting. There's not a one I wouldn't like to spend more time with and introduce my friends to. I think you will find them interesting too.

And if you follow the lessons they teach with their lives, you will go a long way toward cracking the code for your own Life II. Maybe not like they did, for their examples are both exceptional and diverse, but I believe what you discover from them may help guide you to ways that express your own core and your own life's calling. You'll find a list of the "cast of protagonists" in the table of contents and their background information in Appendix 1, and then we'll get started with our learning-over-lunch adventure.

But please know this: *You are the protagonist of your own life.* That's the "free" in free society and free enterprise. You are a composite of many influences. My aim is that you see yourself, and the choices you will make to guide your own Life II experience, in the mirror of these accomplished people. As Peter Drucker said, we may not be inventors, innovators, and pioneers, but once we see it, we can do it. We are up to it. What we need is the will to live more for meaning than for money, status, or applause. We need the intention to serve a higher purpose than fulfilling our own selfish wants and needs.

If we have the "want to," the people in this book can show us the "how to." So come with me now and let's see what we find. I encourage you to mark this book up as you read, and in so doing, join the conversation. Underline what resonates with you. Write your reactions in the margins. Think of it as if you and I were at a quiet table together with a code breaker.

Get involved. Learn the lessons.

SECTION I
Is There Something More?

CHAPTER ONE

Let's Do Lunch

Visualize this. You and I are having lunch at your favorite place. It's comfortable, a good place for going to talk. You've come to a point in your life where you're asking, *What now? What's next?* You feel a new season in the air. I've invited a wise friend who seems to have some answers to the questions you've been asking, someone who seems to be ahead of us in this season I call Life II.

Certainly, all of the hundred-plus interviews I did for this book weren't over lunch, but it's a good way to think of the conversations you will find in these pages. Organic, personal, each one unique. We're in the company of wise and caring friends talking about things that matter. I followed whatever paths our conversations led us down, and I listened to what was said.

Lesson one: Just listen.

Today I've invited Tom Luce because he's a friend, a wise counselor, and someone whose own life models many of the lessons we seek to learn. Many of the themes we'll explore in this book are present in this one particular interview, so it's a good place to start.

LUNCH WITH A WISE FRIEND

Tom Luce had just wrapped up a long session working on public education issues when we spoke. He had been in a conference room full of people who were helping an eighty-five-year-old client from West Texas decide how to deploy his resources. Tom's a superachiever, passionate about public education, and knee-deep in a program to help fix it.

Tom's faith and the biblically oriented class he's attended faithfully for more than thirty years are at the center of his motivation to give his life to public service. But the choice hasn't always been easy: Tom also has medical conditions that cause him to live with continual pain and prevent him from getting a good night's sleep. But he refuses to let such things impede his work.

TOM LUCE

As we sat down, I asked Tom to tell me what parts of his life's work had given him the most satisfaction.

"When I started the law firm," he said, "my goal was to build an institution that would outlast me. From the very beginning, my goal was to build something strong enough to survive my departure, and doing that allowed me to be free, because I knew I could step down without regrets when the time came. I could leave because I'd know I'd accomplished my goals, and others would take it from there.

"The other thing that I feel good about," he said, "is the wonderful friendships I've developed over the years. God gave me the ability to be a good counselor, to put myself in the clients' shoes, and that has led to many rewarding relationships." Friendships are important to Tom. He and I have known each other for fifteen years.

"Tom, I know how much these friendships mean to you," I said, "but obviously you also have a passion for a variety of projects. For example, you were the key guy in implementing billion-dollar-plus mergers, bringing a Magna Carta to this country, and building a nationally recognized law firm."

"Yes," he said, "all of that was very satisfying to me, and being able to step out of my normal role in situations like that has made practicing law even more of a pleasure. But the real reason I'm drawn to institution building, Bob, is that I never really had a burning desire to be a lawyer. My first interest was always business, and I never really intended to practice law. If I hadn't gone into law, more than likely I would have been an entrepreneur, a builder of businesses. That's where my gifts are, but as it turned out, I took those skills and applied them to other things."

"Most of us have different seasons in life," I said. "Our passions change.

Was there a point at which you felt the law firm was becoming more institutional than entrepreneurial?"

"It was entrepreneurial for a number of years," he said. "We worked very hard at establishing our practice and acquiring clients, but I never wanted to be a managing partner, even though I was for many years. I felt that job demanded different skills, and I was more of an entrepreneur, not an institution runner. I wanted to use my entrepreneurial gifts, so turning the job of managing partner over to someone else was an easy step for me."

"Was there a halftime period?" I asked. "Did you come to a point when you felt you'd been there and done that? Or did you decide there was still more to do?"

"I think it was a little of both," he said. "I reached halftime in '88 or '89, when I decided to run for governor. I'd built a law firm and achieved some success, and I felt that the political arena might be the best way to make the move to significance."

"Running for governor turned out to be a firebreak for you, didn't it?" I asked.

"Yes, it did," he said, "and it was very difficult for me to go back to practicing law after I lost. It wasn't what I felt I was supposed to do in the next stage of my life. I was searching for what to do next, but obviously the door I thought was open had been closed."

"So, with a little perspective on all that, how do you feel about the experience now?"

"I'm really glad I ran for governor," he said. "If I hadn't taken the risk I think I would have always wondered if it was something I should have pursued. It was disappointing to lose, but I'm still glad I did it. The hard part was that I didn't just lose the race; I also lost a lot of my financial security. I'd spent so much on the governor's race that it took years to restore my assets.

"I eventually went on the board of Dell, Inc.," Tom continued, "which helped me rebuild my financial base and allowed me to focus again on public education. That led me to Just for the Kids. But basically I had to go back to ground zero before I could move on to what I was meant to do next."

"But at some point you got involved in Ross Perot's presidential campaign," I responded. "When was that?"

"That was the spring of '92," he said, "and I felt I owed a debt to Ross for his early confidence in me that launched my career as a lawyer and helped me build my law firm. I discharged that obligation but was still wondering, *Wait a minute, Lord! What did I misunderstand?* I was seriously in need of some answers."

THE PAST AS PROLOGUE

It's often surprising how unexpected changes of direction can lead us back to the things we're supposed to discover. In Tom's case, he realized that what had given him his start in life—education—was really where he wanted to focus his service. He was the son of a single mother who worked as a salesclerk in a small shop in an upscale community. They lived in a modest apartment, but because they were in the Highland Park school district, Tom had the opportunity to go to some of the finest schools in the country.

Good schooling made Tom's upward mobility possible, and he never forgot that. "I first got involved in education reform," he told me, "because Ross Perot asked me to. Ross was our biggest client, and he volunteered me for a couple of projects, so that's why I did it. Once I got involved, I was overwhelmed by a sense of gratitude for the education I'd received. But in the background was this sense of righteous anger because I'd had such a good education, and here were kids who were being crippled for life by the very schools that should be helping them succeed.

"The fact that my mother sacrificed her own interests for my sake," he explained, "enabled me to do all the things I've done. But suddenly I was seeing kids who weren't getting any help at all, and that really made me angry.

"You've often talked about finding your passion, Bob, and what got me out of being stuck in halftime, and over the hump of being involved in making a difference for others, was stepping out and hiring someone to come in and help me solve the problems. It was a critical first step, and it turned out to be the step that helped me move beyond my halftime experience. Something about committing to another person forces you to make a serious decision to do something."

"And that was when you hired Brad?" I asked.

"That's right," he said. "I first met Brad Duggan in 1983. He'd been president of the Texas Elementary School Principal Association. Only two education organizations out of about eighty had backed the 1983 education reform bill, and Brad's group was one of them. I knew he was dedicated to reform, and I had a vision to form an organization to help make changes. That was the basis of Just for the Kids.[1] I asked Brad if he'd join me and help build the organization, and fortunately he said yes.

"I remember the conversation well. Brad said he'd love to do it, but he wanted to know if I was serious or just dabbling. So he said, 'Tom, I'd be making a big jump to come with you. How long will you be committed to this?' So I told him I was in it for three to five years at least. And if it worked out as we hoped, I was in for the long run. It was a critical decision for both of us. I'd committed for a certain number of years, and that was the big step in making Just for the Kids happen.

"Since that time," Tom continued, "Just for the Kids has found a unique specialization—collecting data on school performance all over the country. Statistics are collected on every phase of the education process, segmented by social and economic factors. From that analysis it's possible to identify the best schools by grade and subject with every type of student population, and then determine how they achieved superior results. Most importantly, we then make those 'best practices' available to educators and parents on the Internet.

"When parents see the performance of their kids' schools, they're better equipped to judge how well the schools are doing and what kind of education their kids are getting. In fact, the No Child Left Behind program implemented by the Bush administration mandates that performance data be collected on every school in the country.

"Administrators may say, 'If you had the kids I have, coming from single-parent homes, who move around a lot or are on the free-lunch program, your kids wouldn't perform well either.' But Just for the Kids gives parents the facts, showing how other schools with the same problems are performing. It gives them objective standards, so principals, administrators, and parents can see what's really happening. And principals who are trying to make excuses for their shoddy performance can be held accountable."

GETTING OUTSIDE YOURSELF

"Tom, you've created an incredible program," I said, "but how did you go from your law practice to creating an institute for education reform?"

"My first concept was to follow the model of the nonprofit organization you founded, Leadership Network,"[2] he said. "You've used Peter Drucker's expression to 'go to the islands of health and strength' to convene them, let them talk to each other and learn from each other. I knew twenty or thirty talented school principals, so I convened them. The problem was that I wanted to change 6,500 schools in the state of Texas. I didn't have the personal knowledge to go that far, so one thing led to another. We learned how to measure success, how to replicate it, and how to create a best-practices scenario. The essence of what we're about today is measuring success, figuring out how those schools do it, and then convincing others to do the same."

"From 1994 until today," I said, "Just for the Kids has had some amazing results."

"You could say that," Tom said. "We're now in sixteen states and just got a grant that will help us go to all fifty. We've trained 7,000 principals and teachers in Texas, and we're beginning to see the payback in terms of quality and classroom results. So I couldn't be happier."

"You're in your early sixties now," I said. "What does the future hold? Imagine that we're meeting here twelve years from now, and let's assume you've finished well, and life has worked out just as you'd hoped. What would all this look like to you then?"

"I'd like to know that I've helped a million kids achieve their God-given potential," he said. "I think that's what public education is all about, helping children maximize their God-given talents. Everyone has a bundle of gifts, and the schools can help each child maximize his or her talents. They can't do it alone; our children are vulnerable to so many influences, many of them not good. But schools can help kids choose the right ones and act on them. I'd like to know I've helped a lot of kids."

"I like the sound of that," I said. "But what will you need to do in the intervening years for that to happen?"

"Well, I will need to take Just for the Kids to all fifty states," he said, "and teach 'best practices' to 100,000 principals and teachers. They're the ones who will change the lives of the kids."

"How many kids are you talking about?" I asked.

"About sixty-five million," he said. "You remember the old line about the bank robber Willie Sutton? Somebody asked him why he robbed banks, and he said, 'Because that's where the money is.' Well, we go into the public schools because that's where the most kids are, and we want to impact those kids with habits and knowledge that will change their lives. The ones who have the hardest time maximizing their human potential are those in public schools. I want those kids to have an education as good as the one I had."

"What effect do you think that will have on the broader culture?" I asked.

"Outside of the faith component, a good education does more than anything to help people maximize their human potential. Christ can do it better than the public schools, but the public schools can do so much more than they're doing now, and that's my passion."

"Earlier you said you were looking for whatever it is that you were called to do. Is this it?" I asked.

"My desire was to know I'd performed a public service, which I think I was called to do. Time will tell how much value these things will have, but I believe this is what I'm supposed to be doing. To the best of my judgment, I'm doing God's will."

"How do you know God's will?" I asked.

"I don't know for sure," he said, "but I pray a lot, and I try to do what I believe is right. The hard thing is to pray for God's will to be done in your life, that you'll know it when it comes, and that you'll be strong enough to go out and follow it."

"You've had some health problems that caused you to think about the long term and finishing well," I said. "Do you think most people finish well?"

"As a lawyer, I've had occasion to counsel a lot of people, in all stages of their life," he said. "Based on my experience, I don't think many of them finish well unless they've found some new mountains to climb. I think that's what determines if a person is truly successful in life. It's important to feel as if you're making a difference, and I think it's probably pretty good medicine as well."

What Tom found was something my friend and best-selling author Jim Collins calls a BHAG—"Big Hairy Audacious Goal"—a goal that demanded commitment of time and resources and would remain challenging for years to come. And it was a challenge that required Tom to look outside the box for answers and whose impact would be felt for years after his lifetime.

"I think an important part of finishing well," he told me, "is curiosity, wanting to learn more. Curiosity is very important, because it involves thinking outside yourself."

CHAPTER TWO

Is There
Something More?

THE GREATEST CASE OF MISTAKEN IDENTITY IN MODERN SOCIETY RELATES TO THE FOUR MARKS OF PUBLIC SUCCESS: MONEY, POWER, FAME, AND STATUS.

SUCCESS SHOULD NEVER BE CONFUSED WITH WEALTH OR POWER. RATHER, SUCCESS SHOULD BE LINKED TO EXCELLENCE AND FULFILLMENT. . . .

I HAVE NO PROBLEM WITH MONEY, POWER, FAME, OR STATUS—AS LONG AS THEY'RE TREATED AS RESOURCES, RATHER THAN AS GOALS IN THEM-SELVES. BUT THAT'S PRECISELY THE PROBLEM FOR MOST PEOPLE—AND WHY? IT'S SO HARD FOR PEOPLE TO ANSWER THE QUESTION "HOW MUCH IS ENOUGH?" IF ACQUIRING MONEY OR FAME IS YOUR GOAL, HOW DO YOU KNOW WHEN YOU HAVE ENOUGH? EVERYONE I KNOW WHO HAS A LITTLE WANTS MORE. BUT EVERYONE I KNOW WHO HAS A LOT ALSO WANTS MORE.
— TOM MORRIS [1]

Success in midlife is a paradox.

Success seems to make more demands than it satisfies. Over and over I heard successful people at the peak of their power say they'd gotten much further along in life than they ever dared hope, only to discover that it still wasn't quite enough.

Gabriel Garcia Marquez, Latin America's greatest writer, describes in a *New Yorker* magazine article his life of scraping by as an aspiring young writer in Columbia on borrowed food, borrowed books, and free drinks. Finally he gets a piece published in *El Espectador*, a leading literary supplement in Bogata.

Uneasy about how well he did, he seeks out a "chance" encounter with a leading critic. Instead of talking to Gabriel about his story, the critic speaks of his audacity: "I suppose you realize the trouble you have got your-self into," he said, fixing his green king-cobra eyes on mine. "Now you're in the showcase of recognized writers, and there is a lot you have to do to deserve it. In any case, that story already belongs to the past," he concluded. "What matters now is the next one."

The quest for success allows no rest. Our sense of accomplishment seems to evaporate with the achievement of each goal, and immediately the need arises to find another goal. Is there a way off this treadmill? Are we doomed to have every achievement disappear like a soap bubble the moment we grasp it? Success doesn't seem to produce significance, causing us to wonder: Can we find a goal that really satisfies, so that we are not continually compelled to drop each accomplishment in the dust and plunge after the next one?

What Matters Now Is the Next One

While the primary focus of this book is not faith or philosophy, who could better answer questions about goals and purpose and the search for mean-ing than a philosopher? Dr. Dallas Willard understands as well as anyone I know the ever-increasing demands of success achieved on our own terms.

DALLAS WILLARD

He is on the faculty at the University of Southern California, in Los Angeles, where he has been a pro-fessor of philosophy for nearly forty years. In addi-tion to his work there, he has taught at the University of Wisconsin and held visiting appointments at UCLA and the University of Colorado. His books, including *Renovation of the Heart* and *The Spirit of the Disciplines*, are wisely written and widely read.

Dallas has had a profound impact on my faith and approach to life. I find him both deep and approachable—at heart he's a plaid-shirt type of guy. If I could pick one person to ride along with me as a coach on the deeper things in life, it would be Dallas Willard.

During our conversation, we discussed the idea that faith, far from being irrelevant, really gives life its purpose and meaning. "Dallas, you've said that meaningfulness always requires a context. People feel meaningless if they don't have either heaven for a context, or a meaningful set of relationships, or a meaningful purpose in life that might relate to their work. Is that right?" I asked him.

"Yes, exactly," he said. "And if we don't have some larger context than just the dreary day-to-day facts of life, negative feelings take over our lives, and that will eventually lead to some kind of crash."

What he described, I've seen recently in people past the age of fifty who haven't come to grips either with faith or issues of life and death. They often go into a long, slow, downward slide, and develop emotional problems that can even be fatal. So I asked Dallas, "What's the impact of all this on someone who is at or near retirement age?"

"Those who are not necessarily at retirement but let's say in their forties or fifties," he replied, "often come to realize that they're never going to achieve what they had hoped to achieve in life. Or in some cases they may achieve it but realize that it wasn't worth achieving after all. Both of these things happen, and that's when people who don't have a larger frame of reference tend to be overwhelmed by their emotions. The sense of having missed out on love, for example, may afflict them. Some people may fall prey to sexual desire—they become obsessed with it. Or they become fixated on revenge, and the feeling that they really need to get back at those who hurt them in some way. In other cases, they simply fall prey to a sense of despair and hopelessness.

"There's a section in my book *Renovation of the Heart* where I deal with this issue using real-life examples. Without this background of meaningful lives, by which I mean looking forward to a glorious future in the presence of God, people's feelings can overwhelm them. And as they grow older, they find themselves more and more depressed, and sometimes even suicidal. These kinds of negative feelings really devastate their souls."

"One might argue," I said, "that the disease of hopelessness may bring on premature mental and physical decline that can't be alleviated by all the physical things—technology, creature comforts, man-made kinds of happiness, and so on—that our culture spends trillions of dollars pursuing."

"I would be willing to say," Dallas answered, "that you could empirically verify the causation flowing from the hopelessness and the disappointment to many of the physical effects we see in people in their later years. We know, for example, that thoughts and experiences impact and shape the brain in physical ways; and of course, the brain is the chemical factory from which the rest of the body gets its life, through the glandular system and other mental and emotional controls."

"Have you written on this?" I asked.

"Yes, I have, but there's an expert in this exact subject at UCLA, Dr. Jeffery Schwartz, and he has years of experience in this field. His book *The Mind and the Brain: Neuroplasticity and the Power of Mental Force* demonstrates how emotions of all kinds can change physiology and contribute both to health and to the onset of physical and emotional diseases. You can spend months studying this subject, but the general idea is that the brain responds to desires, thoughts, and experiences, and as it does so, it reforms itself in certain ways. So there is, as scientists have known for decades, a two-way interaction between the brain and the mind."

"I suspect this would be a very powerful factor for people in the second half," I said.

"Oh, yes," he replied. "This certainly affects the aging process. We've heard forever that attitude makes a difference, and that's an empirical fact. People with a hopeful, forward-looking, confident attitude will find that things are different in their lives. They're upbeat, they're more physically fit, they're generally happier; and of course, this goes hand in hand with research into the effects of prayer on well-being, which is now empirically established. We've always said, 'Prayer changes things,' and it really does, both emotional and physical things."

A STARTLING CORRELATION

"You know, it's ironic, Bob," Dallas continued, "but this actually scares a lot of people. They don't have a problem with prayer as some sort of abstract or religious practice, but they don't know what to make of it when they discover that prayer really changes things in their lives. But it's an undeniable fact, and a number of double-blind controlled studies by empirical researchers who were not religious people have demonstrated the effects of prayer on everything from heart patients to the germination of wheat. There is a clear impact when people pray.

"I'm reminded," he added, "of a medical doctor who was raised in Texas, Larry Dossey, who once said that if your doctor doesn't lay hands on you and pray for you, you should sue him for malpractice. Well, that may be a little extreme! But the reason, he said, was because the evidence is so great that prayer makes a huge difference in the outcome, that to overlook the power of prayer amounts to medical malpractice."

"I know what you're saying," I responded. "I sometimes think a lot of people would be horrified to think that God actually hears and acts on their prayers! But, as you say, it's not just that the Bible assures us of the effects of prayer; science today has confirmed it."

"If we truly understood the Bible," Dallas said, "we would understand the effect of prayer in our lives, and the impact of that could be tremendous in the physical as well as the social realm. Knowing God and believing that there is a plan and a purpose for our lives should fill us with joy, and I think that's the right attitude for anyone approaching the second half of life. It used to be a common expression that the devil has no happy old people."

"Let me focus on that," I said. "Let's say I'm a typical forty-five-year-old, and I'm coming to what I call halftime. I'm feeling a bit anxious about how I've been spending my time, and one day I look up from my desk and wonder what it's going to be like to be sixty-five, seventy-five, or eighty-five. Retirement and old age loom out there somewhere, and I'm nervous about that. So what's your advice, doctor?"

"Very simple," he said. "My prescription is that you should devote the rest of your life to doing those things which you know to be good and profitable for humanity, and that means especially for the human beings who live around you. You should devote yourself to advancing their well-being."

"Let me ask you about something Henri Nouwen said to me several years ago," I replied. "When he endorsed my first book *Halftime*, he said, 'I think there is a stage beyond significance, and that is surrender.' But he also went on to say that he didn't think most people could make it from success to surrender in one step, because they'd be too angry about what they lost.

"What I've concluded," I continued, "is that there are really four steps in this process. The first is struggle, which is trying to be successful. The second is success, which means you've reached that point, and I believe that in today's world most people can achieve a level of success if they have focus and determination. Third is significance, which I define almost in the same words you've used—using your experience and knowledge to help others. And finally comes surrender, which means being fully aligned with a higher purpose for your life."

"Well," Dallas said, "I would offer two comments. I believe the third step you've described, that of *significance*, actually requires surrender. I don't think you can really manage surrender within the parameters of success; you have to give up. You have to surrender yourself to this other good before you can achieve the kind of significance you're talking about. The other point is that you don't have to worry about that now. If you set your sights on attaining that final step of surrender and give yourself up to being a blessing to others, which is the source of significance, then I think the rest will come naturally. Christians should be able to do that naturally. But frankly, Bob, they don't know how."

THE KNOWING/DOING GAP

I found Dr. Willard's statement quite provocative, and I paused to reflect on it. The church has always taught the importance of surrender, yet we don't (perhaps can't) let go of our own desires and ambition in order to let God take control of our lives. The mere thought of that gives all of us pause.

I said, "What you seem to be describing, Dallas, is a *knowing/doing gap*, that even what we know, what we've been taught, what we've heard in sermons, what we've read in books, doesn't seem to be a viable reality for most Christians. There seems to be a chasm between our knowledge and our ability or willingness to do it."

"That's very true," he said, "and I would even put it in these terms: *We know about these things but we do not believe them.* Too many Christians profess to believe them because they're expected to, but *profession* of belief doesn't carry the action. Only *real* belief carries action. We live in a context where millions and millions of professing Christians do not believe what they profess because they've been taught that the important thing is to profess it whether you believe it or not. Just think of the words of the apostle James: 'You do not have because you do not ask God.'[2] Our faith is not strong enough to believe and to expect God to answer. Consequently, this gap between faith and action creates a severe problem."

"That's very troubling, isn't it?" I said. "It's obviously true, just as you said. But it's such a strong indictment of the modern church."

"Unfortunately," he said, "historically we have emphasized professing certain things, and sometimes people died for not professing them. The religious wars were all about this. In more recent times, evangelicals have stressed professing faith—not necessarily having it but professing it. As a result, many people don't think of death as a joyous trip to a world that is so much better than this one. Most Christians are terrified by the thought of dying."

THINKING ABOUT LIFE FROM THE PERSPECTIVE OF LIFE III, THE LIFE BEYOND THIS LIFE

"It makes a tremendous difference to me," I replied. "The way I think about the work I'm doing is that even if I don't get rewards on earth, there will be reward in heaven, and that makes an awfully big difference to me."

"That's because you believe this, Bob, and you're ready to act as if it were true. You *do* act as if it were true. We live pale and empty lives here on earth because we're ignorant about what lies ahead, and we need to see that the dimensions of life are so much greater than what we can see, hear, and touch today. I know from what you've said, Bob, and certainly from your previous books, that you really do understand this bigger dimension. I know that you are looking forward to being with your son and the others who have preceded you to heaven; this is very real for you. I wish everyone could feel that connection."

"When I sold my company in 1999," I said, "I began to redeploy my assets into kingdom projects because I believe that there is a kingdom. Ultimately I moved a great deal of money into more productive work because I believe life here on earth isn't the whole show, or even the main event."

"That's right," Dallas said. "I remember hearing about your fellow Texan, R. G. LeTourneau, who gave 90 percent of his wealth away and kept just 10 percent for his own needs. People thought he was crazy, but he was crazy like a fox. He understood reality. The more he gave, the more his business boomed, and he was paying hundreds of millions of dollars into his kingdom account. I think that's the crux of our problem with the whole issue of finishing well. We see the headlines about ministers and priests falling into sexual sin, and I believe these people are genuinely heartbroken and disappointed by what they've done. But it isn't just the sin that hurts them. What really troubles them is that they probably achieved what they believed was success, and it didn't satisfy them.

"One of my favorite stories," Dallas continued, "is about the dog races in Florida. They train these dogs to chase an electric rabbit, and one night the rabbit broke down and the dogs caught it. But they didn't know what to do with it. They were just leaping around, yelping and biting one another, totally confused about what was happening. I think that's a picture of what happens to all sorts of people who catch the rabbit in their life. Whether it's wealth or fame or beauty or a bigger house, or whatever, the prize isn't what they thought it would be. And when they finally get it, they don't know what to do with their lives. This is a huge factor in finishing badly: *People need a rabbit that won't break down.* But that's not something the superficial values of this world can really give them."

"What are the characteristics of a rabbit that won't break down?" I asked.

"First of all," he said, "it has to be tied to something that transcends the individual life. For some people it used to be just being a member of a family, or someone saying, 'I want to leave the world a better place.' Maybe you heard the story about the guy up in the Northeast whose textile factory burned down, and he continued to pay his workers because he knew they wouldn't be able to make it otherwise. That's a beautiful story. This man had a sense of a rabbit that wouldn't break down, at least in this life. And then, of course, I believe that people ought to have an understanding of eternal life, a context so much greater than this life alone. That's the rabbit that will never break down."

I replied, "People sometimes say to me, 'Bob, you'll never know the effect of what you're doing in this lifetime,' and I take a lot of comfort from that.

The implication is that there is another life where all those things will matter so much more."

"Yes," Dallas said, "I believe that."

"That's a rabbit that won't break down."

"Absolutely! The effects of what you're doing are so much greater than what you can ever comprehend that we can't begin to get our minds around it. This work touches every dimension of human life, and has an inexhaustible future."

"You know," I said, "your rabbit metaphor works so well! You always want to have that rabbit out ahead of you. You never want to catch the rabbit!"

"That's exactly right. Just think about what Paul wrote in Philippians; he's got a rabbit: 'Not that I have already attained, or am already perfected; but I press on.'[3] That's where we want to be living, and I'd want to be living there if I lived to be ninety years of age. I want to be living there when I step from this world into the next one."

"That's a very visual image," I said. "Stepping across in one brief moment into that other life, which is eternal."

"Yes, indeed," he said. "And it's something we should be looking ahead to with confidence, the knowledge that *paradise is actually in session right now*. When Jesus spoke to the thief on the cross, he said, 'Today you'll be with me in paradise.' Just as you've expressed it, Bob, your son has been living in paradise for many years now; and paradise is in session now. It isn't something that's going to start later. It's ongoing."

"Do you think of it as just passing through a membrane," I asked, "stepping through an invisible barrier into that other existence?"

"Yes," he replied, "I think what Jesus was teaching about death is that you will not experience it, and I really think what that means is that it will probably take you awhile to realize you're actually dead. You'll finally recognize it when you notice that what you're experiencing now is very different from what you felt earlier. In John 8:51, Jesus says, 'Most assuredly, I say to you, if anyone keeps My word he shall never see death.'[4] What that means is that for the person who is dying, once they step through they're not going to have an experience of death."

"What a wonderful image," I said. "Just after my son died, I remember writing to a man who is mature in these matters to ask if he thought Ross could see what we're doing here on earth. And when he wrote back, he said, 'Well, he probably has the capacity to see what you're doing, but he's so busy doing what he's doing now that he probably doesn't spend much time with that.'"

"Yes," Dallas said, "I think that's exactly right. A young man in my class last year lost his mother who was killed in an automobile accident. He wanted to know if she would be worrying about him. I said I believe that she is aware of so many different things now that she will see him in the light of eternity, and not in the light of his temporary troubles. And while she still loves and cares for him as much as ever, she's got a lot of things to occupy her now. I do believe that people who have gone on can know what's happening to us, but they're not going to be worried about us because they have a much broader understanding of life than we can begin to imagine."

Christians often use the term *worldview* to describe the philosophy and life-context we live by; but in the terms Dallas was using, worldview may not be a big enough concept. For the life of the believer reaches beyond this world into time, space, and eternity. What a wonderful idea! "Dallas, I'm grateful for your comments," I said. "You've certainly helped expand my own thinking on these issues, and I think I'm beginning to see the connection between success and significance in a new way."

The Distance between Success and Significance

"Well, I'm glad if I've helped," he said. "I think the critical difference between success and significance is that success has more to do with outcomes I'm in charge of, while significance has more to do with outcomes I'm not in charge of. The beautiful thing about significance is that we resign the outcomes to God, and we let a power beyond ourselves take care of them. Success is focused on my action, my control, my outcomes, whereas significance is found in a much larger context. I'm not running that context, and the step of surrender is crucial because surrender allows me to release the outcome."

"Let me tell you a story," I said, "about a man I interviewed last week—Lawrence Dutton, a member of the Emerson String Quartet, which is a wonderful classical music ensemble. He did all the right things—started playing early, went to Julliard, and had all the right accomplishments along the way. One year he and the quartet won two Grammy awards. It was a remarkable achievement, but Lawrence said that after the initial euphoria of the awards, he was deeply depressed for a time because he felt he'd done it all. How much higher could he jump?"

Dallas said, "He caught the rabbit, didn't he?"

"Yes," I replied, "I think you're right. He caught the rabbit."

"He caught it and found out it wasn't so hot after all."

"That's right," I said. "Today he's a serious Christian, and he's now caught the rabbit four more times. He's won six Grammy awards, but he doesn't seem to be as troubled by it now."

"Well," Dallas said, "he's got a different rabbit."

"Exactly," I said. "His model for his career is Isaac Stern, a violinist who achieved the highest possible celebrity in his career. But he dedicated himself to saving Carnegie Hall, to mentoring young artists like Yo Yo Ma, and other things with real significance. There were no guarantees. Mr. Stern wasn't certain he could save Carnegie Hall, or that any of the young performers he mentored would go on to achieve success. So he accepted an element of uncertainty. And for him that *was* the rabbit that wouldn't break down."

"Isaac Stern had confidence," Dallas added, "because he knew he was committing himself to something that had a life of its own—something that was good. That's where faith in God, and in the presence of his kingdom, becomes so important."[5]

"Let me ask one more question," I said. "What would finishing well mean to you?"

"It would mean that I would stay with the objectives that I believe have been placed before me by my family, my God, and my country," he said. "I really believe there is a unity in those objectives, and they have to do, in my case, with teaching. Now I don't just mean in the classroom; I mean talking, writing, and so on in a way that would actually help people deal with their lives before God. I would like to keep my strength and carry on with this, and die in the presence of my loved ones with the manifest presence of the other world around me. That would be finishing well."

"And what will you be doing the week before you die?" I asked.

"My idea of bliss is to carry on with my work and be in the presence of my loved ones until the day I step through that membrane you described earlier."

"That strikes me as the three things you've been talking about: *context, purpose,* and *worldview*. Keeping the faith until the end, being engaged in your purpose right through the tape, and making a seamless transition into the world that you know comes next."

"Right," he said. "And at the time of passage, for the other world to intrude into this world and just take over. I would like for those around me to see that take place."

> I believe that it is not dying that people are afraid of. Something else. Something more unsettling and more tragic than dying frightens us. We're afraid of never having lived. Of coming to the end of our days with the sense that we were never really alive. That we never figured out what life was for.
> — *Harold Kushner*

I wrote the following poem after my conversation with Dallas Willard:

CATCHING THE RABBIT
The Night the Rabbit Broke Down

It's a false thing
     and all the yelping dogs must know it.
     But they're caught up in the pure
     thrill of the chase,
     doing what they have been trained to do.

The starting bell clangs.
>The gates smash open,
>and out they come in hot pursuit.
>Adrenalin pumping.
>Eyes on the prize.

The mechanical rabbit bobbing ahead
>always pursued, never caught.
>The pell mell energy of the other
>dogs, all in a rush!

The vibrant, muscular pulse has a
>visceral charge to it that is more compelling
>than cool reason. The training
>takes over—not thinking,
>but raw action in response to
>known stimuli.

Like a middle linebacker when
the ball is snapped—all instinct.

But one day—
>The bell rings,
>the gates open,
>the same mad rush down the track.

But then . . . something new, something unexpected
>and unprepared for happens—
>The dogs catch the rabbit!

Yecch! Is this what I've been
>chasing all these years?
>Surely this isn't *it!*

Confusion reigns. The dogs don't
        know what to do. They're just
        leaping around, yelping,
        and biting one another.

What now? What next?
        No habit pattern to replace
        the instinctive logic of the
        race that has made unthinking
        sense of this mad dash.

The race itself was the thing.
The hot pursuit that has given
        form and forward momentum to
        day after day.

Tomorrow and tomorrow and tomorrow
        Got to eat
        Got to sleep
        Got to stay in shape.

Another season, another race,
        another chance to win,
        a plane to catch,
        a pitch to make,
        people to impress,
        a risk to take.

Another rabbit to chase,
        another trophy to win,
        it's all momentum!

But what if the rabbit breaks down?
>then what?
>*then* what?
>Silence . . .
even in the midst of pandemonium.

Silence . . .
>and God who inhabits the silence . . .
God who has
>been there all along.

God, help me I pray.
>Give me another rabbit to chase,
>a new problem to solve,
>only this time:
>a rabbit that won't break down,
>a rabbit that always stays ahead of me.

Give me a rabbit that's
>*worth* chasing!

CHAPTER THREE

It's about Redefining What Makes You Get Up in the Morning

THE VALUE OF THINGS IS THE AMOUNT OF LIFE YOU HAVE TO PUT INTO HAVING THEM.
— HENRY DAVID THOREAU

As successful people come to halftime, they begin to ask themselves, *What causes me to get up each morning with renewed enthusiasm? What's in the box? What's the main thing, the pearl of great price? What's central to my life?* And they often ask, *Do I want to look back ten years from now and find myself with more of the same?*

Many are waking up at halftime and answering that question, "No! I don't want to fill the rest of my life with more of the same kind of success I've been achieving. I've chased the mechanical rabbit long enough. I've caught it many times only to find myself looking for another rabbit. The quest is endless and meaningless. I'm ready for the real rabbit. It's dawning on me that I want more than just success; I want a more meaning-rich life now."

Success and significance are similar in terms of what you actually do day-to-day. But which of these you pursue makes a difference in *why* you get up in the morning, because the endgame changes. Success commonly means using your knowledge and experience to satisfy yourself with fame and fortune. Significance, however, means using the same knowledge and experience to serve others—that is, to change lives. The outcome defines the difference and changes your attitude toward what you do.

Sooner or later, you come to a fork in the road. Down one road you find more of the same. The first sentence of *The American Idea of Success* by Richard Huber pretty well summarizes all 450 pages of his extensive research: "What is success? In America, success has meant making money and translating it into status, or becoming famous."[1]

Pretty stark, but correct.

Down the other road—what Scott Peck called "the road less traveled"[2] in another well-known book, the outcome is entirely different. The process of travel on either road may be much the same, but each will lead to different outcomes. Here's how Peter Drucker contrasts the outcome of same-ol', same-ol' success with the outcome of significance:

> *Business* supplies . . . either goods or services. *Government* controls. A business has discharged its task when the customer buys the product, pays for it, and is satisfied with it. Government has discharged its function when its policies are effective. The *"nonprofit" institution* neither supplies goods or services nor controls. Its "product" is neither a pair of shoes nor an effective regulation. Its product is a changed human being. The nonprofit institutions are human-change agents. Their "product" is a cured patient, a child that learns, a young man or woman grown into a self-respecting adult; a changed human life altogether.[3]

Down one road there's more money, status, and power. Down the other there's the opportunity to change lives—in many cases for eternity. It's not an easy choice. What do you choose? What's in your box? You can't put both in first place. Sooner or later you must choose. What is your primary loyalty in life? To which do you want to devote the day when you get up each morning?

Several of the people I interviewed gave up more money and status for the opportunity to change people's lives forever. Let's sit down with two of them to hear in their own words what drew them forward in Life II. Also, listen for the not-so-hidden clues that reveal the downside that each person sought to avoid.

THE CONNECTOR

In his best-selling book *The Tipping Point*, Malcolm Gladwell describes three types of people: "the Maven" (wizard/expert/mentor), "the Connector" (networker), and "the Salesman" (someone who can get an idea across). It's hard to fit my Silicon Valley friend, Wally Hawley, into any one of these categories because he is consummately skillful in all three. But most of all, I see Wally as a Connector.

From the moment I met Wally, it was apparent that he had a passion for making a difference, and especially for bringing together groups of highly accomplished people, showing them how to get involved in the nonprofit sector. I have seen Wally at work, and I'm an admirer of his skill and tenacity. So when we got together for our interview, I asked him to fill in the picture for me with a little background on how he moved from capital investments to investing himself in changing lives.

WALLY HAWLEY

First, as I often do in interviews, I asked about his Life I motives. "Wally," I said, "tell me about your business career. How did you get started?"

"I attended Stanford and Harvard Business School, and then went to work for McKinsey & Company in San Francisco," he told me. "I spent four years in the Netherlands, working with their European operations, and by age thirty-two I was hired as the U.S. president for a large privately held Dutch company that was one of our McKinsey clients in Holland. In addition to running the holding company and buying companies for them in the United States, I formed a venture fund to make minority investments in companies. That introduced me to the concept of venture capital, and I found it fun. It was challenging to get involved in smaller projects and help them grow."

"So how did you go from that high-energy world to halftime?" I asked.

"Well, I formed InterWest Partners in 1979," he said. "I launched it with a colleague from the Dutch company, and the rest is history. InterWest is now twenty-three years old, controls eight funds and a lot of capital. But somewhere along the way I ran into your book *Halftime*, which changed everything for me. Suddenly I realized that making a lot of money wasn't all there was to life. From a worldly point of view, everything was going pretty well. Finances, health, family—I was doing fine and had no serious problems. I didn't come to faith until I was fifty, but faith was becoming more important to me; reading your book then forced me to ask myself if I was neglecting another part of my life.

"At that point more than ten years ago," Wally said, "I moved out of venture capital, and today I'm only marginally involved in that world. I devote most of my time now to nonprofit. One of my reactions to this whole process is that I have too many friends who say they're retiring, but they don't know what to do. They're frustrated or bored because what they're doing is meaningless. If you ask me how I define the stage of life that you call "finishing well," I'd say I'm redeploying. *I didn't retire; I've just redeployed.* For me, that's what it means to finish well."

"Sounds like your work actually set you up to do all these other things," I said.

I found this to be true in many interviews. The incentive that drew people forward had played out and no longer produced stimulation and excitement. It was no longer what made them want to get up in the morning. As Wally put it, "One day I realized *something was missing*. I had this feeling that *I'd been there and done that*. But there was also something else regarding my faith: I had a sort of gnawing inside me. When I look back now, I realize that God was directing me, leading me along. I was starting to pick up books about characters in the Bible, or reading certain books in the Bible with no particular purpose in mind. Then at one point I joined a Bible study and started going to church. That's when I discovered the *missing piece*—faith and putting my faith to work.

"Faith is your guidance system now," I said, "but what was your guidance system before that?"

"Good question," he said. "Good ethics, maybe, but that hasn't changed. What really changed was that it went from being *about me* to being *about others*. I've always felt I treated people well, but the measure was what I got out of it personally. Was I growing? Was I making more money? It was always I, I, I. Now it's about other people."

"As you grew deeper in your faith," I said, "you began to turn toward more significance-oriented things. But I take it you didn't have a Damascus Road experience. It wasn't as if within two weeks you came to faith, quit your business, gave up all your old friends, and became a monk!"

"No, nothing of the kind," Wally said with a smile. "I left my monk's robe at home! I was beginning to do some work in the nonprofit area but without a lot of direction. I began to explore working with faith-based activities. That's when I got involved with Young Life, which, as you know, is a large Christian youth organization. Then I met you and got involved in FaithWorks.[4] I also got involved in my local church because it has a wide outreach. Over time I began to replace my substantial interests in the secular world with comparable interests oriented to maturing in my faith."

"Would it be fair to say," I asked, "that you were the same person you were before, but you just moved into a new venue?"

"That's what my wife says," Wally answered. "She tells me I'm basically the same person, but I don't really think you can be the same person once you've given your life over to God. When you're becoming a servant, your heart is in a very different place. Sure, I have the same name and the same skill sets. The difference is that I'm not thinking about me all the time but am more concerned with helping other people. I'd contend that I'm not really the same person anymore. A passage in Luke 12 says, 'To whom much is given, much is expected.'[5] I used to think about that only in the context of finances. What's expected goes far beyond finances. Much is expected in using your time, your talent, and your abilities for God's purposes."

PUTTING FAITH INTO ACTION

"Through your work with programs like FaithWorks and Time Out, which is one of your programs to reach out to high achievers, you've played an important role in your part of the country," I continued. "Tell me about that."

"Well, I could tell you many stories, Bob, but let me give you just one example. Early on we brought some business leaders together with a group of faith-based organizations to test the Drucker Foundation Self-Assessment Tool[6] and match people up as partners. Not only did the tool work, but people in that first group met each other, liked each other, and almost all of them started joining boards of directors to help them improve their work.

"I remember one case where one of those businessmen began working with City Team, a well-known group that works in low-income neighborhoods. He liked it so much he left his job to become chief financial officer of City Team. He based his decision entirely on what he learned in that one-day assessment event. Others from that first group have gone on boards or on staffs and become major supporters of these groups. Today we have a database of over four hundred leaders that we've brought together, and my guess is that we've impacted between fifty and a hundred highly successful and influential people whose lives have been significantly changed."

"Is there a way to measure that kind of change?" I asked.

"The common denominator," he said, "is that it's *putting faith into action*, and committing one's time. A lot of these people are keeping their day jobs, but suddenly they're doing a lot more. They're involved in new things, and making a difference in the world not only for themselves but for a lot of other people as well."

"Wally, tell me what you think of when I say the word *retirement?*"

"It could mean one of several things," he said, "none of which I want to do. The first is to go play golf and just tune out. Another is just sort of dropping out, hanging around, gardening, or watching television. But the common denominator is that in every case you're not doing anything purposeful or beneficial."

"How long are you going to live?" I asked.

"As long as the Lord lets me," he replied. "You know, I had a good friend who was very successful in the real estate business, and he was just beginning to put his faith to work, getting involved in Young Life. He really had wonderful intentions. We were fishing with a group of guys up in Colorado last summer, talking about all this stuff at dinner one night. He was so excited. Ten hours later he was dead—a massive heart attack. That was a wake-up call for me, Bob. We don't know how long we have, so the answer is to get going today.

"After my friend's funeral, some of the guests gathered at a club to socialize, but I decided to take a walk out on the mountain. I was thinking, *What if that had been me? Would I have to apologize for my life?* I concluded that I wouldn't have to apologize, but I knew that if I hadn't redeployed my time and assets, and if I'd just continued in my search for personal wealth and success, it could have been a very different story."

"One last question, Wally," I said. "You've said that when you redeployed yourself, you realized it was important to be aligned with whatever the Lord would have you do. Is that a fair way to put it?"

"Yes, that's right," he said.

"How do you know God's will?" I asked.

"Simplistically, Bob," he said, "the Lord did many things for me long before I was communicating with him and really acknowledging him. And when I look back at my life, including the circumstances of meeting my wife, I can see how he was leading me all along the way. So I say, if God can guide my life when I'm not even trying to listen to him, how much more can he do when I'm really trying? I'm just attempting to learn more about what God is doing in the world, and he directs my footsteps along the way."

A Changed Heart

Wally's story is powerful because he's put a lot of the pieces of a great Life II together. I found another compelling perspective on the halftime change from success to significance in Jay Bennett, a high achiever who is a found-ing partner with the law firm of Dunkley, Bennett, Christensen & Madigan PA in Minneapolis. After graduating from Dartmouth in 1971, Jay com-pleted his law degree at William Mitchell College in Minneapolis. He tested his wings with a large metropolitan firm before he and a friend decided to launch the practice he now heads.

Jay Bennett

Today Jay serves as general counsel for a variety of for-profit and nonprofit organizations, working with business formation, capitalization, operations, and succession planning. In addition, he oversees two foundations that serve the cities of Minneapolis and St. Paul. One of those, a ministry called Kingdom Oil, has become a dynamic outreach to men and women in the business community, bridging them to high-yield nonprofit initiatives in the Twin Cities.

When I spoke to Jay, I was curious to know how a high-powered corporate lawyer came to be so intensely focused on ministry, so I asked him for a little background. "I was raised in a high-expectations, high-performance household," he told me, "by parents who positioned me for success. In high school I thought I wanted to be a doctor, but organic chemistry pretty well killed that idea! So I decided law school was a good alternative, and I changed directions."

"You gave up your dream of a career in medicine?" I said.

"Yes," he said. "Or, you might say it gave up on me! Anyway, after graduating from law school, I went to work for a big national firm. It was good experience, but I was basically a slave of the firm: I was killing myself, working extremely long hours, and I sensed that it was probably never going to change. I stayed there five years, getting some great training along the way, but I knew that if I wanted to be a husband and a father, or have enough freedom or independence of my own, I'd have to do something else."

"First you gave up medicine; then you decided to give up law too?" I asked.

"No," Jay laughed. "But at age thirty I did jump from that big, secure ship, and along with my best buddy from law school, started a new firm. Our strategy was to use our little law office as a platform for 'success,' meaning running a solid legal practice while pursuing other interests at the same time. The plans we made back in 1979 paid off, and despite some bumps and bruises along the way, business has been good ever since."

"And all those silly lawyer jokes don't bother you?" I asked.

"No," he laughed again. "We hear them and we tell them, like everybody else. But despite the jokes, I truly believe that the practice of law is an honorable profession. The old saying, 'It's better to give than receive,' is really true, and my colleagues and I have tried hard to be first-class lawyers and still maintain a servant's heart.

"The most satisfying thing for me," he said, "is the relationships. I love meeting people and hearing what's on their hearts. You talk to them, share their concerns, and look for ways to help them achieve their goals. To be trusted like that, and then to be trustworthy as a partner and a servant in that situation, is a tremendous honor. I've been blessed to achieve a measure of financial freedom, and I have a great team around me. Knowing that the business is strong and secure has given me the opportunity to reach out beyond the law practice and help people in the community on a more personal and more spiritual level."

"Jay," I said, "you said your parents instilled a lot of drive and determination in you during your growing-up years; but somewhere along the way, you redefined the balance in your life between success and significance. How did that happen?"

"Well, that would be 1981," he said, "which was a big year for me. My little law firm was two years old, and in May my wife, Sally, and I attended a Christian weekend retreat known as Cursillo. During that retreat both of us had a powerful reawakening as to who Jesus was and what he had done for us. The spiritual transformation lifted us to another level. In June of that year I made an offer to purchase the house owned by my best client, and he looked at me like I was crazy. He said, 'Jay, you're just starting out. You've got a new business, two little boys, and not much money. How are you going to buy this house?' He knew I couldn't afford that big house and he didn't want to take all my money. So he said, 'Look, Jay, just go out that door, then come back in and offer less.' Well, I was obedient. He looked at my new offer, then smiled and said, 'Okay, I've made bad deals before. Sold!'"

"Sounds like you hit the jackpot!" I said.

"Well, as you can imagine, Sally and I were pretty excited," Jay said. "But then, in August, tragedy struck. My law partner, Bill Dunkley, with whom I had risked everything, was in a horrific boat accident. The twin 260 horsepower inboard he was racing in hit a wave. He was thrown out of the boat, which then turned and ran over him, almost completely severing his arm near the shoulder and ripping him open. Two teenage boys in an adjoining boat raced over to Bill. They jumped in the water and dragged him to shore. Miraculously, an ambulance was driving by at that exact moment, so they rushed Bill to the hospital. And after something like fourteen hours of reconstructive surgery, they had him patched back together, barely.

"After that," Jay said, "our little law firm went through a couple of difficult years. Bill was recovering, and I put in a lot of hours trying to keep it going. But the combination of the Cursillo awakening, the house deal we had made, and Bill's accident was like a pot just bubbling on the fire, and ultimately led to my halftime experience."

"How did that happen for you, Jay?" I asked.

"I look at life sort of like a rheostat—an adjustable light switch on the wall. When you turn the dial, through service or compassion or worship or just walking with God, you get more light. When you turn away from God or turn your back on the people around you, the light dims. For me, that rheostat was installed on my heart back in 1981. As I learned to adjust the dial, issues like *success* and *significance* began to take on a whole new meaning for me.

"In fact," he continued, "I came to see my life as a tug-of-war between opposing forces. The world's values tell you that it's how you look, what titles you hold, or how much money you make that matters most. But that's a fraud. God is saying that how you live your life is what really matters. In that still, small voice, he invites us to live a transformed life, a life that transcends the dominant themes of this planet. I was really drawn toward the light when I began practicing the spiritual disciplines, starting each day a little more slowly, and making a clear space in my life to hear the voice of God."

"That's a nice metaphor," I said. "We sometimes feel that spiritual things are out of our control—like some mystical force out there somewhere—but what you found is that your own attitudes, habits, and behaviors helped bring you into a closer relationship with God."

"Exactly," he said. "When you turn the rheostat and the light increases, that still, small voice becomes more audible. It tickles and then lures and then compels. If you have eyes to see and ears to hear, as Jesus said it, then God lets you know you're his. And the sense of his presence flowing through your spirit, soul, and body is really awesome. It's unlike anything else.

"The sweet spots in my life," Jay continued, "are those moments of revelation when I get little bits of truth that are relevant to my particular circumstances. It happens sometimes when I pray. Or it happens when I'm reading the Bible pursuing a relationship with the Lord and seeking answers to life's issues. It happens when I'm with others, and it happens especially when I'm being still in his presence. Thoughts just pass through my mind, words are processed in my heart, and sometimes I can see the sweet spot that God wants me to see."

"That's a powerful description," I said. "But how has that sense of God's presence worked itself out in your life?"

"The events of 1981 led me to go back to my best client—the same guy who sold me the house—and I told him I was feeling a nudge to set up a foundation to help Christian ministries. I had a five-year business plan that projected what we could reasonably expect to contribute and how we could give away the earnings. To make a long story short, he loved the idea, and together we built that foundation from the ground up. Five years later, we had accumulated ten times the amount in assets that we'd projected. And that's how my parallel career was launched."

Obviously Jay's halftime experience has been very productive. In addition to the highly successful foundation and the good work he does through the law firm, he's involved in a wide range of civic and charitable activities, and he and his family are active in their church. So I asked him, "Jay, tell me what finishing well means to you."

"Finishing well," he said, "is a continuous process of becoming a better vessel for God's purposes. I just want to improve continuously in my effectiveness for kingdom things. I think the apostle Paul was probably the ultimate halftimer. As Saul of Tarsus he was a successful guy. He was educated; he had position and authority. He was self-confident and knew the law. He certainly had a high sense of his own righteousness. But then he took that trip to Damascus, and along the way he had spiritual angioplasty—a major change of heart. After that, he pursued a parallel career. He made tents, he preached, and he wrote letters to the churches about kingdom things. But in everything, he gave all the credit to God."

"I really like that," I said. "Sounds like Paul was the working model for what we all ought to be. But tell me, how do you want to be remembered?"

"When I think about being remembered," Jay said, "I think about how short obituaries are. Everything in your résumé gets boiled down to a couple of sentences of gray newsprint, and the memorial service wears off in a couple of hours. I just want to be remembered as a man who passionately loved God. Hopefully the by-products of that will be obvious."

"What's your advice to someone who might want to follow that kind of model?" I asked.

"My advice," he replied, "is to make sure you die in battle. It's good to know what your desired outcomes and objectives are, but you never know what's going to happen in your life. The key is to live intentionally, with passion, for a cause that's worthy of your life. And then die bloody. I plan to go down swinging. I want to die in battle."

ACHIEVING BALANCE

Harvard Business School professor Laura Nash, who I have known and admired for twenty years, has written a terrific new book. She and her HBS

DR. LAURA NASH

colleague, Howard Stevenson, did a series of interviews with high achievers who attended HBS graduate and executive programs. The book, which reports their findings, is titled *Just Enough*. What they found has a lot of similarities to what I found with Wally, Jay, and others in this book.

Dr. Nash has had a varied career in and around Harvard as a classics professor and business school professor, as well as a term or two teaching at the divinity school, and is now starting over as a researcher and writer at age fifty-four. When I talked with Laura I asked, "Is halftime and finishing well different for women?"

She responded, "I've noticed that many women tend not to measure life in such linear fashion as men. Their first questions are more likely to be, 'What's the state of the relationship? What's the state of the family? What's the state of my working life?' And those things don't tend to come in chunks. You're struggling with them at eighteen; you're struggling with them at thirty. And then many women I know at my age right now are just beginning careers. I notice when I interview people that women tend to answer questions differently than men, partly because they've delayed, they've juggled, they've subordinated career to family and family to self in ways that don't fall into neat patterns."

"They're not so locked on a single target?" I asked.

She responded, "Yes, many women don't get started in the same way, and they keep starting over and over again with more openness in the environment but less direction. Women just aren't the same kind of linear thinkers, and so a constant renewal of targets goes on in a responsive way. Then as roles change, children grow up, marriages develop, spouses have more or less time as they progress in their careers. Some people get divorces and then have a sense of starting over, partly because what they do each time is different. It's not a one-target track."

"Tell me about your new book," I asked.

"The premise is that there are four components to success that people seek in their lives—achievement, happiness, significance, and legacy."

"Sounds like an ongoing balancing act between one good thing and another where women have some distinct advantage," I said.

"Yes," she responded, "and I think that's where this organic and more feminine model comes in. It's only taken me fifty-four years to see a pattern. It's not toward some single end; it's an openness to change. And that's been exciting. I've had a funny career in the sense of moving from classics into business ethics, from business ethics into organizational structures, leadership, and then into religion and business and so on."

Laura Nash has redefined what makes her get up in the morning over and over. We wrapped up our conversation with her describing her kaleidoscopic life this way: "My impression is that there is no end to it. It's ongoing transformations. You keep starting over."

A Portfolio Person

John Castle is another friend, raised in the small East Texas town of Mount Pleasant, who has rebalanced his portfolio for Life II. The highlight of my interview with John was the sage advice he offers to those deciding how to rebalance their portfolios for Life II. Number one in his law school class, he was one of the founders of Hughes & Luce.[7] John went on to become general counsel and then executive vice president of EDS, the firm's largest client.

John played a pivotal role in EDS's separation from General Motors and its transition to a new board and management team. He took a generous

JOHN CASTLE

package and "retired." John represents a whole category of people who work on several projects simultaneously in Life II. He's what I call a *portfolio person*. In the same way he handled a portfolio of various initiatives as a lawyer, he now works with nonprofits. These include strategic planning for his Episcopal diocese and serving on several nonprofit boards. He is a great advisor and counselor.

"One thing that's a lot more important to me now that I've turned sixty is aging well," John told me. "My friend Bill Brice was a good example. As I watched him in his later years, he became more philosophical, more thoughtful, and more relational. Here's a guy who had spent his whole life doing big things, but as he grew older there was a subtleness about him, a good spirit, and a good sense of humor.

"Unfortunately," John said, "I've seen other people who weren't aging well. They became increasingly critical, judgmental, and bitter—a better word might be *cranky*. All sorts of influences can move you in one direction or the other. But I want to see myself becoming more like Bill Brice, with more time for people—upbeat, positive, thoughtful, and cheerful. And I plan to be more intentional about that." There's the rheostat idea again.

John is, by nature, intentional in most things. And when he gets involved in nonprofit activities, he looks for three things: "The first thing I look for," he told me, "is clarity about the mission. I think that's essential. Second, I look for people I respect who are practical-minded. Third, I want to be sure that it's the sort of project that I can bring something of value to, and in which I'm being involved in a meaningful way. So I always ask myself: *Is it a mission I believe in? Do I believe in the people who are in it?* and *Does it use my talents and gifts in a way that engages me?*"

I believe John Castle just handed us the keys to defining exactly what to look for that will make getting up in the morning worthwhile in Life II.

CHAPTER FOUR

It's about Finding Your Core

To find my home in one sentence,
Concise, as if hammered in metal.
Not to enchant anybody.
Not to earn a lasting name in posterity.
An unnamed need for order, for rhythm, for form,
Which three words
Are opposed to chaos and nothingness.
— Czeslaw Milosz

Once you accept the idea that you want the second half of your life to major on significance, the next step is to focus on finding the core of your personality—the immovable center of who you really are. You can't use equipment that hasn't been issued by your Creator and shaped by your experiences. A great benefit of being in halftime or the second half is that you know what you've got to work with, and that helps you find where you belong.

Peter Drucker helped me see my own core. He told me in 1991, at the Biltmore Hotel in Los Angeles, that my mission for the second half of my life was to work on "transforming the latent energy in American Christianity into active energy." That's his phrase, but I believe it's right for me. The form of the work may turn out to be a book, a speech, or a contribution of time, talent, or money to Leadership Network or some other organization, he said. But whatever the form, it would be an expression that would grow out of the core of my being.

We all have an essential core, and I believe that the great majority of people I've interviewed for this book are aware of that. Whenever they're in doubt or in crisis of one sort or another, they can always return to that essential core.

WHAT TO DO IN A MIDAIR COLLISION

With the idea of finding that core in mind, I went to the EDS headquarters in Dallas to interview Jeff Heller. Jeff and I graduated from high school to-

JEFF HELLER

gether in Tyler, Texas. We used to walk down the hill to O'Neal's Ice Cream after school and swap stories. I was on the football team and Jeff was on the swim team. He went on to become a champion swimmer at both the high school and collegiate levels.

The EDS headquarters complex in North Dallas is spectacular, a giant hub for the high-tech outsourcing business, and it looks it in every way—like a spaceship rising out of the prairie. The company employs more than 140,000 professionals in sixty countries and serves 9,000 customers worldwide. Jeff was brought back from early retirement to rescue the company and restore the confidence of a demoralized workforce. EDS became a huge company under Jeff's leadership as president. When he first joined the staff, EDS was just a $5 million company. Its revenue is over $21 billion today. He was just wrapping up a meeting when I arrived.

When Jeff came out of his meeting, we went into the conference room where box lunches were waiting for us. Suddenly, there we were, two old high school buddies catching up on what had been happening in our lives since high school.

Finally I got to the point and asked if he'd gone through halftime. "Yes," he answered. "I've had several." And he proceeded to tell me about two specific ones.

Jeff didn't go into business straight out of college. Instead, he joined the Marine Corps, went to flight school, and flew combat missions over Vietnam where he put his life on the line every day, never knowing when it might be his turn. On one later occasion, flying over Norfolk, Virginia, he was involved in a midair collision that sheared a wing off his airplane. "Five hundred knots, about five hundred feet off the ground," he told me, "and bang, I've got no control of the plane. I'm gyrating through the sky. The training just took over at that stage."

In the sheer terror of that moment, Jeff remembered his flight instructor's words: "When you know you've got uncontrollable problems, look up. Wait for the airplane to roll and when you see blue, hit the release." Jeff said that when he grabbed the airplane's face curtain and looked up, he was looking straight at the ground and it was getting closer very fast. But then the plane flipped back around. "As soon as I saw blue," he said, "I punched out, and the sound of being thrust into the airstream at five hundred knots was just horrendous."

Jeff ejected successfully, then just as he was wondering whether or not his parachute would work, it snapped open. The canopy shot straight up, he swung *once* in the harness, then immediately hit the ground. It was that close. If any step in the process had taken even a second longer, Jeff wouldn't be here today. It was a miracle. But that wasn't the last time he was to be tested. The next time was an unexpected wake-up call when he was working at the GM headquarters in Detroit. GM owned EDS for a time, and Jeff spent part of his career there. One day he began to experience serious chest pains. He went to see his doctor, who did a CT scan and immediately put Jeff on the operating table for a seven-way bypass.

"A seven-way bypass?" I said. "How many ways are there?"

"I'm not sure," he said, "but I'm pretty sure they got them all!"

The surgery lasted over ten hours. "When I woke up I wasn't all that happy that I'd done it," said Jeff. "It leaves you sore and brutalized for a while. But I quickly focused on the idea that I might not be around forever, and I thought about all the things you always know you should do but don't because you think you've got more time."

In the hospital, Jeff had time to deal with those issues and settle his mind. He needed to know that he was taking care of his family, so he wrote out a will and instructed his attorneys on how to handle his finances in case anything went wrong. During those few short seconds in the midst of his mid-air collision, however, he had no such luxury. It was do or die. "But still," he said, "it was enough time to realize that it really wasn't in my hands; it was in somebody's hands but not mine."

He described those two life-changing events as his halftime experiences, and he said, "They defocused me." This was a term that had special meaning for Jeff. As you'd expect with a former Marine pilot, he's a very focused individual. But in light of two near-death experiences, he had to step back from the things that claimed all his waking hours and concentrate on the ultimate questions he'd been ignoring. He had to find his core.

He said he knows there's a reason why he's still alive today. I asked him what he thought that reason might be and he answered, "You know, relationships are the long-term force that holds this company together—what you're doing, who you're doing it with. My meaningful work is to reconstruct this company around its relationships."

Jeff Heller discovered that relationships are his core. More than cash flow and computers, relationships define his business style and explain his remarkable longevity in an extremely competitive industry. People trust Jeff.

As a person who has already made enough money to take care of his family, educate his children, and do just about anything he sets his mind to, Jeff is no longer working for his own sake but for the sake of the people he serves. His mission now is to rebuild the company that has been his whole working life, for the benefit of his people and his customers. I have defined significance as using your knowledge and experience to serve others, and that can happen in virtually any environment. Not all the *significance* careers are in nonprofits.

ALWAYS COME BACK TO YOUR CORE

Your core is what you never give away. The core of Winston Churchill was his belief in Britain and his absolute resolve in the face of the life-and-death challenge that Hitler posed to the British Isles. He followed Neville Chamberlain, who had dealt with the same situation by appeasement. Churchill is famous for saying, "Never give in!" and one could say that he was born for that moment. His iron will may have prevented Hitler from destroying Western civilization. In that one shining series of moments, thank God, Churchill was up to the task; he went back to his core.

Another man who knows his core and sticks to it is Wilson Goode, a majestic black man who some would say did everything wrong but it turned out right. His father was an illiterate sharecropper in North Carolina and a hopeless alcoholic. The family moved twelve times in Wilson's first twelve years of life. His father eventually went to prison for beating up his mother with a garden hoe, and the family had to struggle along without him.

WILSON GOODE

When Wilson went to junior high and high school, his teachers told him, "You ought to be in the industrial arts program so you can get a job when you leave school." The counselor told him not to waste his time on academics. So of course he took academics, because he believed that was what God wanted him to do. His most compelling statement in our interview was, "If I listened to man and not God, I would be nowhere." So I asked him, "How do you figure out what God's telling you?" And he said, "I listen."

I asked, "How do you do that?" And Wilson replied, "I think that most of us are so noisy we can't hear God's will. We're so busy talking, and listening to ourselves, and listening to other people's advice that we don't get quiet long enough to let God speak to us, and know that God is speaking to us. Consequently, we end up very unhappy. I know that it's God's will when I'm directed to something, because I listen."

His point was well-taken. To hear anything in today's noise-saturated culture, you have to get to a place where you can hear God's still, small voice. "Sometimes I just go to my living room," Wilson told me, "and I just listen. Early in the morning while the sun is coming up, I listen to God speak. And even while I'm sleeping sometimes, God is speaking, and I know it. Sometimes it's hard to put into words, but you just know when you're in sync with God's way and with God's will for your life. You know because it works, and there's harmony between you and God when that happens."

There was genuine excitement in his words. But it struck me that there were two sides to that coin, so I asked him, "Do you know when you're out of sync?" And he didn't hesitate. "Oh yes," he said. "It feels like punishment.

God will pull you back in a minute. Sometimes that little human in you takes control, and you think that you can do it all by yourself, and then God just pulls you right back."

After high school, his counselor told him, "Don't go to college, Wilson; you'll just embarrass yourself." So of course he went to college and graduated in the top 10 percent of his class. Every step of his journey, people kept telling him what he couldn't do. Then sometime later, after he'd moved to Pennsylvania, gained leadership experience in the community, and done a lot of good work there, he decided to run for mayor of Philadelphia where he could make a real difference. But, once again, people said, "Wilson, don't even think about that! You can never be mayor of Philadelphia."

First of all, they told him, there's never been a black mayor in Philadelphia. Second, he would be running against Frank Rizzo, a two-time mayor and former chief of police. So Wilson ran for mayor because he was convinced it was what God wanted him to do, and was elected the first black mayor of the city. Later, after he finished his term of office, he felt God was calling him to recruit mentors for some of the toughest kids in the country. Approximately 70 percent of inmates' kids end up in lives of crime, and Wilson wanted to do something about that.

So I asked him, "Wilson, what was the size of your budget when you were mayor?"

He said, "Two billion dollars with 30,000 employees."

"So now you're just going from church to church recruiting mentors? How does that make any sense in terms of what you were doing before?"

He said, very simply, "It's what God wants me to do." And that is Wilson Goode's core, whatever form it takes.

The thing that excites people when they get to a certain tipping point in their lives (a point where people reach halftime and realize they must choose how to spend Life II) is not another stock option or another million dollars; it's doing something that truly matters. For a man like Wilson Goode to go from serving as mayor of Philadelphia with 30,000 employees and a $2 billion budget to recruiting mentors, one by one, for at-risk teenagers and children of prisoners is a remarkable change. I asked him, "How many employees do you have now, Wilson?"

"None," he said.

"Who is doing all your recruiting?"

He replied, "I do it myself. I go from church to church telling people about the need and recruiting folks who are willing to mentor these children, one by one."

Wilson was the child of a prisoner, himself, so he understands the need. Like so many of the people in this book, and so many of those who begin this process of "repurposing" in order to discover a life of true significance, the old measures and standards no longer apply. What matters is how the work they do now will impact other people, and how it will contribute to the spiritual and emotional health of the communities they serve. For the first time in their lives, in most cases, people discover that they're doing a job for the sheer joy of it—they've found the *work that isn't work at all.* Whether paid (Jeff Heller gets paid a lot) or unpaid (Wilson Goode gets paid much less, if any), it's the meaning that makes the difference, not the money.

SUCCESS THAT MATTERS

Another man I know and admire is one of the most effective philanthropists in the country—he has given away hundreds of millions of dollars—but he declined to do a taped interview with me because he wants to do everything anonymously. He and his wife were featured in a newspaper article a few years ago and I was so moved by their story, I thought, *Now that's what I'd like to be doing when I'm his age!* He plans to give his considerable fortune away in his lifetime. And now that he's in his late seventies, he's very aware of time.

He's vigorous about his giving but determined to do it without fanfare. I told him that I understood and wouldn't violate his principles. Here's an example of a man who has found his core, and all he does springs from it. He knows who he is at the center of his being, and he doesn't need recognition, praise, or fame for the good he does. What he does springs from who he is at the core.

Peter Drucker says that people don't change the *me* that they are. In other words, you can change the venue in which you express yourself but you never change the core of who you are. What you do when you decide to make important life changes, he says, is to *reposition* yourself for a new role. You find your core, and then you find the most significant way to express it.

SIXTY YEARS—ONE CORE IDEA

Peter told me, "Basically my last career change was when I was about thirty years old—around 1939, back before World War II. That's when I began

PETER DRUCKER

doing what I do now. I've changed locations, but not my job."

Born in Vienna, Peter grew up in comfortable circumstances. His mother had studied medicine; his father was a high civil servant, and later, a banker. Peter started as a business writer for a major German newspaper. But when he saw the threat of Adolf Hitler in the early thirties, he said, "It's time for a change!" So he repositioned himself, first as an investment banker in London, then to New York as an American feature writer for a group of British newspapers. Peter was the first to see fully that management would be a major factor in the twentieth century. In fact, management would be the main factor that propelled the United States to become the most prosperous nation on earth. So Peter spent his next sixty years developing principles of management and making them useful, first for the business sector and then for nonprofits and churches. It became the core idea around which his work revolved.

Knowing your strengths and weaknesses, he told me, is an essential part of the process. When you know who you are, you can be comfortable making decisions about what you want to do, and where. "Let me use myself as an example," Peter said. "The two most attractive offers I got in my life, I turned down, because *I knew what not to do*. One was when I was offered the job of economist at Goldman Sachs. I had no hesitation to say no. I knew I was good at it because I had already done it, but I also knew the job wasn't right for me. Then a few years later, I was offered a deanship at Emory University in Atlanta, and it was a very attractive, well-paid job. I knew that my days at Bennington, where I was at the time, were numbered," he said, "but I didn't have any hesitation to say no, because I knew I couldn't live in the segregated South of the 1940s.

"It's better there now, of course," he continued, "but I knew what to say no to. And, you know, I have never regretted saying no to either offer. I would have been miserable in those jobs. But here's my point: One has to learn what to say no to." Peter could say yes and no without hesitation because he knew his core—writing about management and society.

A Life of Meaning and Purpose

Dan Sullivan has developed a simple but effective way to help Life II people find their core. Dan leads The Strategic Coach Program, which has been helping entrepreneurs achieve greater simplicity, focus, balance, and confidence in their lives since 1988. Essentially, he leads them to discard everything that is not a core value. When we talked about finishing well, I asked Dan, "What kind of conversations do you have with your clients in midlife? What kind of questions do you ask them?"

Dan Sullivan

"Whenever I speak to people about their plans," Dan told me, "sooner or later the question comes up, *What are you trying to do with your life?* My purpose is to reconnect the practical, day-to-day decisions they're making with the bigger picture, which is what they want to accomplish over the long term with their lives. I've always believed that it's much more important to have really great questions than really great answers. Really great answers tend to close things down, while really great questions open things up.

"So my basic approach to life," he said, "is to collect really great questions. I tend to go for questions that force people to think about what they're doing. Do they even know who they are? Do they have a game plan or a sense of purpose in their life? Is there a big contribution they'd like to make? I've found it very comfortable over the years just to ask people those kinds of questions, and it always opens up extraordinarily interesting conversations."

The real problem is that most of us tend to focus on the practical, the immediate, the here and now, when the most important questions are much broader than that. This is especially true for those of us in Life II who are learning to overcome the old stereotypes about retirement and growing older. But Dan Sullivan isn't after those stereotypes. "I'm not going to buy into the conventional notions of what being sixty years old actually means," he said.

"When I started planning for my second half, I made a twenty-five-year plan, and I have a pretty good idea what I want to be doing for the next quarter century. How I look at myself right now, from a motivational standpoint and in terms of having large goals ahead, is what you might expect to see in someone in their mid- to early-forties. I've been acutely aware over the last twenty-five years that I'm in a state of training. I've been honing my skills, and now I have to perform.

"I've sketched out the next twenty-five years as the period of my major contribution and impact on this planet. And when I get there, at age eighty-four, I'll think about what lies beyond that. My father worked until he was eighty-four. He was a landscaper, and he had his best business year when he was eighty-three. So I have a role model in my own family of someone who was very productive in his eighties."

"That's a compelling vision," I said. "Obviously, most people haven't thought that far ahead. Which makes me wonder, what do you say to people who are moving into midlife and beginning to think they're near the end?"

"I have about 3,000 entrepreneurial business owners in The Strategic Coach Program right now," he replied, "and this is a constant conversation topic that I have with those in their late fifties and early sixties. A lot of them will say, 'Well, I think I'm going to wind down now.' When I ask why they'd want to do that, they say, 'Oh, I'm just getting tired.'"

Dan talks to these executives about physical fitness and purpose, but he doesn't let them think seriously about becoming perpetual golfers and snowbirds. He said that he tells them, "Simply checking out and coasting is not an option. In order to restore some vitality and excitement in your life, you must have a higher purpose. You've got to pour yourself into a larger, overriding goal that will occupy your time and talents."

REACTIVE VS. CREATIVE RETIREMENT

Now and then Dan meets hard cases who can't imagine making that kind of change. "I ask these guys, 'Have you accomplished everything you wanted in life?' And they answer, 'Yes, pretty well.' So I say, 'You mean all your biggest goals in life are really in the past now? There's nothing much in the future for you?' And they reply, 'Yes, that sounds about right.' The next question is much more to the point. I say, 'How long do you think you're going to last if the most important things in your life are all in the past?'

"The fact is," Dan continued, "if that's your attitude, you're not going to last very long. So I ask them questions. I want to help them examine the implications of the things they're thinking. They're buying into ideas they haven't consciously thought through. Most of these people still have an extraordinary amount to contribute, and I would like to get them excited about that fact so that all of us can benefit from those wonderful entrepreneurial resources."

What's the benefit of that? Dan explained, "If I can turn on a whole bunch of sixty-year-olds to the idea that they have another twenty-five or thirty years of high productivity and contributions to make, revolutionary things could begin to happen. If you just think about the kinds of people they are, and the impact they've had on thousands of lives during their careers, it's amazing to think what kind of contribution they could make from here on out. I want every one of them to succeed at that. But you know what? It's also a matter of self-preservation for me, because I don't want to buy into lack of hope or vision for the future.

"In The Strategic Coach Program," Dan said, "we make a sharp distinction between what we call *reactive retirement* and *creative retirement*. Reactive retirement is buying into the whole notion that your active time on this planet is really up after about sixty or so. So you leave the real world, and then you live off of your investments. You're no longer building; you're living 'off of,' and you just hope that you die before you run out of assets.

"Well," he said, "that doesn't fly in my book. If you look up the word *retire* in the dictionary, one of the prominent definitions is 'to take out of use.' When you retire, you're taken out of use, which is a pretty sad statement. Psychologically, that idea has a profound effect on people. What does it mean to be useless? That's *reactive retirement*."

"Then what do you recommend?" I asked.

"What I call *creative retirement*. At The Strategic Coach we say, '*We want you to decide to retire today*. Begin a new life after today. We want you to retire from everything you dislike doing, and focus your attention totally on what you love doing.' We get people to make a list of everything they would no longer do if they were retired. This includes people they would no longer associate with and activities they would no longer involve themselves in. After they make their list we say, 'Okay, now we want you to focus on everything you would continue doing, things you would like to do more of, and things you would be willing to start doing now.

"'For the rest of your life,' I tell them, 'you're going to get rid of the things on that first list, and you're going to continually enlarge the things on the second list.' Well, that has an enormous impact on people because they realize that there's a great deal in their life that they love doing. But one of the great tragedies—and I think it's one of the reasons why people decline so fast after they retire—is that retirement means giving up a lot of the things that they loved doing.

"What I want to do," Dan said, "is to challenge everyone who has an ounce of energy left to get rid of all notions of reactive retirement. The answer to finishing well is *creative retirement*, which, if you do it right, isn't retirement at all but plunging into some of the most important work you'll ever do."

A twenty-five-year high-productivity plan at age sixty built entirely around the core of the things you love to do struck me as a great strategy for finishing well.

CHAPTER FIVE

It's Been in Your Life
a Long, Long Time

THE PAST IS PROLOGUE.
— INSCRIPTION AT THE NATIONAL ARCHIVES IN WASHINGTON, D.C.

If you're looking for your core and you can't find it, look in your history.

Most people don't know what their core is. When we do Halftime work-shops around the country, we ask for a show of hands. "How many of you have a corporate mission statement at the place you work?" Instantly, a roomful of hands shoot up in the air. Then we ask, "How many of you have a mission statement for you, personally, a mission statement for your life?" Only a few hands go up this time, and some of them at half-mast. The gap, I've decided, is because many people don't take their lives as seriously as they take their jobs.

In the previous chapter we defined core as the immovable center of who you really are. It's the equipment your Creator has issued to you—the mental, physical, and emotional tools you've got to work with, as well as your experiences and deepest passions. At halftime you have an abundance of life experiences that point the way to what will work for you in the next season of your life. You change the venue. You probably change the objectives, but you don't change the basic core of "you."

The ever-insightful Margie Blanchard (wife of Ken and, for a long while, president of Blanchard Training and Development) loves to help people find their core. Here's the way she put it when we talked: "The biggest joy in my life," she said, "is, and has been for a long time, within the idea of career development, helping people find what I call the *secret sauce*, or the leverage factor, that was in their lives all along. You didn't create it, but you can discover it and make sure in this next stage of your life (when it's going to be a little harder, possibly) that the leverage factor is there. And then I think the next part is leverage in service of other people.

"So I think the two things have to come together," Margie said. "The first is discovering that secret sauce, and the special part about you that God created, and that you've been using since you were eight years old. The second is deciding how to use it: Toward what end? Toward making the world a better place? Toward something with a much larger purpose?"

"I like the image," I said, "but how does this work? I don't think it's an instinctive process, is it?"

"No, I don't think people are particularly good at sitting back and watching themselves and seeing what they have done over and over again. I especially don't think they're good at describing it with words. We live our life in language. Without the words to describe it, I think it's difficult for someone to get it out there. If you can get it out there, what you'd like to see happen, the world cooperates."

What Marge is telling us is that the "it" you're looking for is already part of you. You don't manufacture it in midlife. It's more like doing archaeology on your life, brushing the debris away to bring into view what's been buried there all along. She's saying, *Listen to your life!* It might be helpful to enlist a professional like Marge to whom you tell your story, so you can ask, "What do you see there? What is my life telling me? How can I discover the 'it' that has been in my life all along? How do I find a word or a phrase to name it?" Believe me, it's there.

In Halftime workshops, within the space of a morning and an afternoon, we help people find the phrase that describes their core. Peter Drucker told me long ago, "You ought to be able to get your mission statement on the front of a T-shirt." My personal mission statement is "100X," which comes from Jesus' parable of the sower. I want to be the "good soil" in which the seed reproduces a hundredfold. At my core, I'm a multiplier—whether it was the television business, my significance work, or just lunch conversations with friends—that's what I'm compelled and emotionally suited to do.

Last fall, Leadership Network hosted a workshop at a country club in Greenwich, Connecticut, for friends of Rick and Jill Woolworth. That night at dinner, Jill (a supermom of three who is pursuing a graduate degree in counseling now that she has an empty nest) told me, "My T-shirt would have one word on it." I asked, "What is it?" She said, "Relationships, and the 'T' is a cross."

A RADICAL TRANSFORMATION

As chairman of the Trammell Crow Companies, Don Williams has been a deal maker and connector of the first order, managing some of the largest real estate negotiations and mega-building projects in the country. For at least two decades, Don has pursued a parallel career—his passion for serving the inner city and the ethnic ministry community in Dallas. Don was chairman of the Dallas Citizens Council, composed of heads of the city's largest corporations. Through that work he's been able to help direct public attention and substantial capital and other resources into many important urban projects and public issues. Basically, you can't do something like that unless you're CEO of a big outfit, and Don hasn't wasted his entrée.

DON WILLIAMS

So how did a hard-charging, no-nonsense corporate executive like Don Williams discover his passion for service? Not the way you'd expect. As he told it to me, he had been on a long and exhausting business trip to the Middle East, making financial connections from Paris to Tehran, and from Brussels back to Riyadh, Saudi Arabia. By the end of that marathon, he had planned to fly straight back to Paris, change planes in New York, and return home to Dallas. But thanks to delays of many kinds—political intrigues, news of a war in Cyprus, and a myriad of schedule changes—he was bounced from Cairo to Moscow and ports in between before returning to Paris. By the time he finally got to New York, he was exhausted and running to make his connection.

"It was snowing and sleeting when I got to JFK Airport," he said, "and to make matters worse, those little buses that come around didn't come around. I could see I was going to miss my flight, so I took off running between terminals to get to my gate on time, and suddenly I slipped on the ice on the circular driveway outside the building. I just went down, full force, spread eagle on the pavement. I tore the knees off my suit; my knees were bleeding, my hands were bleeding. I've still got the scars on my hands from that spill. I was just lying there, facedown on the sidewalk, and I had an epiphany . . . literally.

"*God*," I said, "*what am I doing with my life? What's happening to me?* It was an epiphany in the truest sense of the word. I suddenly saw that all this striving, workaholism, or whatever it was that was pushing me was just taking all the energy I had and then some. I'd never relied on God, or anyone else for that matter. Fundamentally, my attitude was, *It's us against the world*.

"Well, I finally got up off the ground," Don told me, "and I just stood there, and I didn't even try to make that flight. Instead, I got a bus back into the city. I spent the night in a nice hotel and came home the next day, and from that moment on I began to change my habits. I was determined to change my thinking and behavior, the best way I could."

"That's an amazing story," I said. "You're lying there on the pavement— it almost sounds like a near-death experience—and your life flashes before your eyes."

"That's a good way to put it," he replied. "In biblical terms, I think you'd call it a *chronos/kairos* moment—an instant in which everything came together for me and I could finally see the truth. I'd lived my life on the clock—get this done, accomplish that, here are the deadlines, here are my markers. That's *chronos*, or the clock. But there was something of eternity in that moment too, which was the *kairos*. It was an extremely powerful moment for me.

"I'm not sure even now," he said, "that I know the full implications of that experience, but it gave me a fresh new look at myself. The most important result, I think, was that I really began to change my behavior, and I was prepared to pay the price for that if I had to. If I wanted to be successful in business, that was one thing. I could do that. But what I needed most of all was to get back in touch with my wife and my boys. So I got involved in their lives, coaching the boys' teams. We started taking family trips; I started teaching Sunday school again. I wanted to get centered with my family, my faith, and the community."

"That must have seemed like an impossible task at times," I said. "You were the top guy at Trammell Crow, involved in major projects all over the world."

"That's right," he said. "We were the largest developer in the United States, and one of the largest private property owners anywhere."

"How did you continue to manage these worldwide holdings and projects while finding time for church and family?" I asked.

Don told me that to make his life manageable under his newfound priorities, he came up with the idea of forming business partnerships with highly qualified, highly motivated people who would participate with Trammell Crow in their projects. This plan called for a minimal amount of hierarchy, and it enabled the creative people they partnered with. The partnership helped bring out the best in them, and helped them do their best in whatever they hoped to accomplish. "That mode of doing business is a guiding principle for me now," said Don. "If you hire the best and brightest, give them some mentoring and training, and then let them do their thing, that environment can lead to tremendous growth."

"How many partnerships were you involved in?" I asked.

"At the peak, I was probably a general partner in at least 2,500 partnerships, many of which did more than one project. Those partnerships probably owned at least 6,000 real estate projects, mostly domestic."

MOTIVATED TO SERVE

On that miserable but enlightening day in JFK Airport, Don found his core. The thing deep inside that made him tick had been there all the time, but it took the epiphany for him to uncover it. However, his discovery didn't end there. When Don looked into his life, he found certain attitudes and deeply held beliefs that had been there all along. He identified these and built on them to begin his own transition from success to significance.

Don's understanding of social issues, as he has shared with me on several occasions, began when he was growing up in Roswell, New Mexico. One memorable incident happened when his baseball team, which included whites, blacks, and Hispanics, stopped for lunch at a roadside cafe. Just as the boys were placing their orders, the owner came over and said the black players couldn't eat inside the cafe; they would have to eat in the back room.

"Our coach just looked at that man and said, 'Mister, this is a baseball team. We travel as a team, we play as a team, and we eat as a team.' An argument ensued, so the coach just turned to us and said, 'Guys, we got here together, and we're leaving together. Let's go.' The whole team got up and walked out of the restaurant.

"That was an important lesson for me," Don said. "It's not just a head thing but a heart thing. I've always had a profound sense of equality with all human beings, and an anti-class-structure attitude. I've enjoyed being part of the wealthy class, but distinction based on those things is immoral. I was involved in the civil rights movement in college. After law school, I came to Dallas and volunteered to work in the housing projects. I gave free legal service to the poor, and somehow the idea of equality of opportunity, not based on race or class, was a major concern for me from the beginning."

Building bridges between people of different social or ethnic backgrounds is about as important to Don today as building office towers or shopping centers. "At times," I said, "you seem to have a righteous anger about social injustice."

"Few things will set me off as quickly as violation of a person because of race, ethnicity, class, or whatever. We're all the same before Christ. How dare anyone discriminate against another person on the basis of class when Christ wouldn't do it! If you study the Bible or the philosophical roots of freedom and democracy, you'll find a compelling case for equality and our duty to do something about it. It's not an abstraction."

Don felt a strong compulsion to "engage the issues of the least among us," as he put it. He had no knowledge of how to go about it, but that didn't stop him for a minute. He made the plunge. He used the Dallas Citizens Council to put his calling into action—what I call a "parallel career"— while continuing as managing partner at the Trammell Crow Companies. When I think of a parallel career, including my own, it's like pouring two barrels of buckshot into a barrel of apples. It fills up the natural empty spaces in your life until you have "just enough" of each of several competing values.[1] "I had no idea what I was doing," he said. "It's not like I'd read all the literature or anything. But there was a kind of clarity urging me to take a leap of faith. I didn't know enough, but a knowing exists beyond our conscious ability to articulate it. I knew what I was supposed to be doing, and I knew it was a calling. And that decision has been confirmed for me over the last eight years."

"How so?" I asked. "I'd be curious to know what that confirmation looked like."

"One key moment came in my meeting with Dr. Napoleon Lewis, a renowned thirty-year principal of an inner-city high school in Dallas. I went to see him at his office at Lincoln High School, and I was telling him what we in the Dallas Citizens Council wanted to do—that we were interested in working with the schools and community organizations, just to be useful to them. But Dr. Lewis wasn't taking anything I said seriously. He certainly wasn't paying court to me as a big shot, or as a downtown white business leader. I was polite, but I was offended by his obvious disregard and disinterest, so I finally said, 'Well, Dr. Lewis, I guess what we're doing doesn't fit what you're doing. If I can ever be useful to you, let me know.'

"Then, as I stood up to go, Dr. Lewis said, 'Oh, sit down, boy. You know what I've been trying to figure out is: What's your hustle?' I said, 'Sir?' And he said, 'I don't think you've got a hustle, do you?' I said, 'No sir, I don't. No Trammell Crow projects, no political program, no nothing. What you see is what you get.'

"And he said, 'Well, if you don't have a hustle, we can work with you. But you have to know that you're the first white businessman to come into this community in the last twenty years that didn't have a hustle.' That was key for me. One of my earliest illumination points was seeing the need first to understand and then to listen."

"He wasn't impressed by your money or influence," I said. "Dr. Lewis wanted to know if your heart was in it before he signed on."

"That's right," Don said. "The currency I had to spend was time, and everything changed when he knew that's what I meant."

"Tell me about your view of longevity, Don," I said. "What does the future hold for you?"

"I love this life," he said, "and I hope I'll be all right in the afterlife too. But, honestly, I don't think much about the afterlife. I love life, and I just can't wait for each day with all there is to do."

As Don spoke these words, I thought of his airport epiphany and realized he had truly found the core value that had been in his life from boyhood. "Have the changes that came into your life after your epiphany on a New York sidewalk changed your thinking about how you use your wealth?"

"I decided I'm going to die dead broke," he said. "I want to go broke on the day I die, so there's nothing in my will for any of my children, or anything else. There will be funding to take care of my wife for her lifetime, but even that's in a trust, so at the end of her time the money goes to charity.

"I've been greatly blessed by God, and I'm very fortunate," he continued. "I see myself as a steward of what he has given me. Whatever resources I have in terms of time or wealth ought to be directed toward the good of others, and I choose to place it with the poor. That's what motivates me."

BEING PREPARED

A few fortunate souls don't have to stop at halftime and redefine their core. From the outset they find their core asset and use it to build a career that's both successful and significant. They step into a suit that's already their size and never need to be refitted. Dr. Kenneth Cooper is one of these men.

DR. KENNETH COOPER

He has been my personal physician for several years. More importantly, he's founder and CEO of the Cooper Clinic in Dallas, perhaps the world leader in preventive medicine. Executives from all over the planet come to the Cooper Clinic for a full head-to-toe physical examination, and its staff is the best I've ever seen.

Health matters are, of course, an important part of finishing well. I wouldn't go a year without having a physical at the clinic. My brother, Jeff, found out he had lung cancer during his exam two years ago. He's alive and well today, thanks in large part to prompt diagnosis and surgery. The survival rate for lung cancer patients is about 20 percent, so I'm deeply grateful to the Cooper Clinic for their expert intervention on Jeff's behalf.

Ken Cooper grew up in Oklahoma City. His father was a dentist and Ken briefly considered dentistry as a profession, but watching his dad perform oral surgery, he says, cured him of that idea. He was active in sports in school and lettered in track, basketball, and football. His ability to focus helped him win the state championship in the mile his senior year. He also earned all-state honors in basketball and graduated second in his class. Ken was a fitness addict when he was young, and he grew up to write nineteen books and countless articles on fitness.

Ken's father instilled qualities of lifelong importance in his son: a work ethic that won't quit, a love for medicine, and an enthusiastic and highly committed faith. "My father was born and raised in Alabama," he told me. "His father was an itinerant pastor who would go out and speak on Sunday and be gone for weeks at a time, traveling around the country in a horse and buggy. He'd get paid twenty-five dollars for speaking, and he'd give twenty dollars of it back to the church.

"Being the oldest of five kids, my father had to support the family while his father traveled. He started at fourteen years of age and did all sorts of things. When he went to dental school, the pastor of a Baptist church in Nashville befriended him and helped support him financially to get through school. He had a little apartment with no windows above the auditorium at Vanderbilt University, and that's where he lived while he went through his dental training. He made great grades."

Clearly, Ken inherited his father's discipline and determination. His father became a dedicated family dentist and practiced until age seventy-seven. When I asked Ken if he thought his father had finished well, he said, "He practiced dentistry all day on Friday and died on Monday. What a way to go! I hope I finish as well as he did."

Ken has had a rich faith since childhood, and once considered a career as a missionary to China. "I was active in Trinity Baptist Church in Oklahoma City," he told me. "As an eighteen-year-old I dedicated my life to full-time Christian service. I was convinced I was going into medicine, so I thought I'd become a medical missionary in China. But I never really felt the strong sense of calling I needed. Then in 1988, when I finally went to China for the first time, I had a chance to speak at medical schools, and they accepted me with open arms.

"I've been invited back many times since," he said, "and on several occasions I've had the opportunity to give my Christian testimony. And one day, when I was doing this, I realized, *Wow! I am a missionary in China!* That really gave me a good feeling.

"It wasn't at the level I thought I'd be doing it when I was eighteen," he said, "but thanks to the work I'd accomplished in medicine over the intervening years, I made front-page headlines in the *Beijing News*—'Dr. Cooper Comes to China'—and the response to my visits was fantastic. So after all those years of feeling that I hadn't fulfilled my calling, the Lord showed me a way to combine my professional work and my interest in ministry."

We can see in Ken's story how three things that existed early in his life combined to form his core: his inherited interest in medicine, his strong commitment to mental and physical health, and his zeal for Christian service. Ken is one of the lucky ones whose core found significant expression from the outset with no need for a halftime adjustment. Since the founding of his clinic, he has been able to focus these three beams of light into a brilliant point that burns ever brighter as he continues his work.

HEALTHY HABITS

Clearly Ken Cooper has done a lot of things right. Thirty-four years after stepping out on his own, he's the best-known specialist in his field, in the world. "But," I told him, "you're seventy-two years old now, Ken. Surely you must have thought about what comes next. So what comes to mind when I say the word *retirement?*"

"It may be okay for somebody else," he said. "But I'd be *bored sick*. If I just go away for a vacation eight or ten days, I'm ready to come back and get to work. Plus, I stay on the telephone. I have a high-pressure life right now, at least seventy hours a week. I get to bed most nights around midnight. I'm up by 5:30, here at 6:30 in the morning, I have my prayer time and Bible study, and then I'm on the go the rest of the day."

Bored sick? That's an interesting phrase, I thought. Probably more literally true than Dr. Cooper realized. I wondered if people get sick from boredom?

"Let's take it a step further," I said. "When you look at people in the age bracket of, say, sixty to eighty years of age, what's the value of retirement for them?"

"Financially, physically, emotionally, they're not prepared for it," he said. "That's why there's a retirement syndrome that brings depression, anxieties, frustrations, suicide, all of the above. I've seen it happen in so many cases in my own practice. You have a really successful executive who has reached the top of his career, then at age sixty-five he's forced into retirement. In the meantime, he and his wife have led completely separate lives to the extent that when they suddenly get back together at age sixty-five, they have almost nothing in common. In many of the cases I've seen, they end up getting divorced. Or when the tensions are simply too much, the man may even end up putting a bullet in his head."

"That's pretty extreme," I said. "Is that really common?"

"I'm afraid this is not the exception," he said. "When two people have gone separate routes for a long time, retirement completely disrupts their lives. That's why I say that a marriage requires work, perseverance, and attention, just like a job. We spend so much time trying to be successful in business, and so little time trying to be successful in our marriage or with our kids."

Later in the conversation I asked Ken if he expected to have a long life. "I don't know how long I'm going to live," he told me. "It doesn't make any difference to me. If I die tomorrow, that's fine. I'm ready to go. But I want to live until that last moment. I want to live a long, healthy life and die suddenly. I don't want to be flat on my back with Alzheimer's for five years before I pass away. That's my goal, and I think I'm doing the best possible things I can do to achieve that goal."

"Take me to the next step," I said. "What would you say to those at halftime and beyond who are looking at retirement, considering the implications for their own lives?"

"Keep these things in mind: Death is universal, everyone dies, but not everyone lives. Proverbs 13:18 says, 'Poverty and shame will come to him who disdains correction, but he who regards a rebuke will be honored.'[2] In other words, shame and poverty come to those who are not disciplined. I have often been asked what factors cause you to be successful in your profession. Is it professionalism, physical stamina, or something else? I've thought about that for some time, and I finally decided that success is being highly *disciplined*, just as my father was.

"Next," he said, "it's important to know that you can grow healthier as you grow older. Who determines that? You do. The philosopher Charles Peguy said that when a man dies, he dies not so much from the disease he has, but from the life he has lived. In Genesis we're told that a man should live 120 years. We don't live that long, not because of design deficiency, but because of the way we treat our bodies.

"If you want to slow down aging, live a long, healthy life to the fullest, and then die suddenly." He added, "You have to eliminate the three things that are working against you: smoking, inactivity, and obesity. As we grow older our bodies change, not so much because we're older, but because we do less physically.

"In other words," he continued, "a lot of the physiological effects of aging are not really physiological at all; they're adaptive responses. We're seeing performance now in people in their advanced years—seventy-five, eighty, ninety years of age—that we never dreamed possible thirty or forty years ago. These are people who have heard the message, improved their lifestyles, and are now reaping the dividends."

Ken's father was passionate about prevention and nutrition, but he had little interest in physical fitness and didn't exercise enough to benefit from it. "In retrospect," Ken added, "if I'd had the privilege of working with my father, he might have lived longer. We did have the chance to work with my mother, and she lived to be eighty-two. She voted in the presidential elections in 1984, the day before she died."

To add a telling postscript to Ken's story, the good work he's done doesn't end with his clinical practice or his mission trips. In recent months he's helped formulate nutrition plans that could affect all of us.

Not long ago Steve Reinemund,[3] chairman of PepsiCo, the parent company of Frito-Lay, formed with Ken Cooper a joint research project aimed at addressing the growing national problem of obesity. Their partnership set out to reduce the high fat content of all those chips and dips.

At the end of the project, Frito-Lay announced their new "Better for You" snack line, which includes products such as Lays Potato Chips, Doritos, Tostitos, and Ruffles. Each package displays a printed label identifying it as a "Cooper Class One" product. The products contain zero percent trans fats, less than 150 calories, no more than five grams of fat, less than one gram of saturated fat, and less than 240 mg of sodium per one ounce serving.

Today Ken is using the passion and focus that were at the core of his life from the beginning in a new venue that will benefit untold millions of people. And in many ways, it resembles the missionary calling he once feared he'd left behind. His message on the back of millions of bags of chips is a proclamation of his significant contribution to the health of a nation!

CHAPTER SIX

It's about Finding the Significance Potential in Your Everyday Work

OUR GRAND BUSINESS IS NOT TO SEE WHAT LIES DIMLY AT A DISTANCE, BUT
TO DO WHAT LIES CLEARLY AT HAND.
— THOMAS CARLYLE

You don't have to leave home or leave work to develop the significance potential in your life. Good ideas for how to achieve significance are everywhere for those with eyes to see. They are right in front of you "hidden in plain sight." You don't have to be rich or obtain special credentials. I define significance as "using your knowledge and experience to add value to the lives of others," as the three interviews in this chapter demonstrate. Like Ken Cooper whom we met in the previous chapter, you stay where you are, use what you've got. You build on what you have found works for you. The difference is that you turn it outward instead of inward, achieving significance in using what you have to benefit others.

After graduating from business school at the University of Virginia, Steve Reinemund went to work for the Marriott Corporation, where he proved himself to be a leader and a promoter of good ideas. When I asked Steve to fill me in on his journey, over breakfast at Sea Island, Georgia, he told me, "When I came out of school, Bill Marriott was just starting an MBA Management Development Program, and I was in the first group. After I completed that course, I went to work full-time and got my start in the restaurant business."

His first assignment, he said, was with Roy Rogers Restaurants. "We were making a run to become a national player, so it was a good time to be there. I was able to develop the business, and I got some tremendous coaching along the way. At one point we bought a chain of restaurants that was about three times our size. My boss went out and made the deal, then

STEVE REINEMUND

came to me and said, 'Okay, Steve, I did the deal; now it's yours. Make it happen!'

"I was thirty-two, and that's where I cut my teeth," he said. "Eventually we got out of that business, and in 1984 I left to go to PepsiCo as head of operations for Pizza Hut. I did that for a year and a half, then became CEO in '86, and stayed until '92. From there I went to Frito-Lay until '99, then to corporate as CEO of PepsiCo in 2001."

FINDING THE RIGHT OPPORTUNITY

Clearly Steve was on a fast track, and some of his accomplishments as a marketing wunderkind are legendary. The example that really got my attention, however, was a promotion he created for the Salvation Army. Over the years, Steve served on the local Salvation Army board for two years, then on the national board for six. Eventually he was asked to serve as chairman of the all-volunteer board, which he did for two more years, another example of a parallel career.

"That experience," Steve told me, "gave me a chance to be who I am, and to bring some of my skills to an organization that could benefit from them. As board members, our role was to help Salvation Army officers understand the significance of the army's national reputation, and to do whatever we could to help protect that reputation. People knew what the army stood for, and we wanted to strengthen its positive image."

Steve was looking for ways to bring greater attention to the annual "kettle campaign," which produces about a fourth of the charity's annual revenue. The opportunity came in "over the transom" at a football game. As Steve told me, "I was CEO of Frito-Lay at the time and my family and I had made the move to Dallas. We were at Texas Stadium for the annual Thanksgiving Day game, and when I looked down at the field during halftime, I noticed a high school band marching, but there was really nothing special going on.

"It occurred to me," he said, "that this would be an ideal place to have an official kickoff for the kettle campaign. In those days the highest rated TV spot on Thanksgiving weekend was the Dallas Cowboys game, and that's probably still true. So when I got back to my office, I called Jerry Jones, spent some time talking to his daughter, Charlotte, who was absolutely terrific, and I laid out my idea. She took the idea to Jerry and the Cowboys organization, and they liked it. We got together and compared notes, and about nine months later we held the first-ever national kickoff for the Salvation Army winter campaign."

Thanks to Steve's original idea, the Salvation Army landed eight minutes of prime coverage on national TV. "We had the national commander tell the story," Steve said. "We had the headliner, Reba McEntire, tell the story. We had Jerry Jones tell a very personal story about his involvement in the army. Jerry had been a great supporter of the army before, but he's an even bigger supporter now. That first kickoff was really a terrific event—more than the money it generated, which is obviously important, it allowed us to present the message of the Salvation Army to the public."

And as I reported in the last chapter, Steve also cooperated with Dr. Kenneth Cooper to dramatically improve the nutritional content of Frito-Lay snack foods. He found his calling for service right in the midst of his leadership role at PepsiCo.

Beginning with the End in Mind

Steve drew on his superb marketing skills—the tools innate to him and which made him so successful in business—to create a promotion of untold significance that would benefit others for decades to come.

At the end of our interview, I asked Steve the same question I've asked everybody in these pages: *If you were at the end of your life, looking back at where you are now, what would have to have happened for you to feel good personally and professionally about your life?* He answered instantly. "First, my kids' lives would have worked out," he said. "Second, I would have left my mark on some other men."

"That's it?" I said.

"That's it," he said.

"There's a notable omission there, Steve," I said. "There's nothing about PepsiCo."

He smiled. "No, there isn't. I adjust my work to those other realities."

Steve has a lot of capacity and drive, but he never lets business keep him from the things that matter most. "When I left Frito-Lay to go to PepsiCo," he told me, "it meant that I had to move to the corporate headquarters in Purchase, New York. The problem was that my kids were still in Dallas, finishing up high school, playing football, and involved in many other things.

"My wife and I talked it over, and I decided I wasn't going to uproot them and wreck their lives. I had a corporate jet at my disposal at the time, so I decided to spend four days each week in New York, then jet back to Dallas to be with my family for the weekends." It just so happened that Pepsi's largest division and Steve's former home were both in Dallas, so the trip was well within the lines of business. But the bottom line was that Steve worked it out to fit his deepest priorities. "In all that time," he told me, "I never missed even one of my son's football games." A great example of "just enough."

THE ONE MINUTE MANAGER MEETS THE WORLD'S GREATEST LEADER

At age sixty, Ken and Margie Blanchard, equally brilliant in different ways, discovered their *calling* in plain sight in the center of their corporate lead-

KEN & MARGIE BLANCHARD

ership training and consulting business. I've known these two utterly magnetic people for twenty years. Ken's first half led him to become perhaps the best known trainer in the world. He credits the Young President's Organization (YPO) for his breakthrough.

They both went to Cornell University in upstate New York and set out to become college professors. While on sabbatical from the University of Massachusetts in 1977, they were invited to speak at a YPO university in Hawaii. That's where Linda and I first met Margie and Ken. Ken had been asked to make three presentations during the week. During every class period, YPOers can choose between three or four different classes. Ken wasn't well-known at that point, so just a handful of people, including me, attended his first session, but it was a huge success. Ken is an astonishing communicator.

During coffee breaks at YPO universities, people talk about which speakers are best, and everyone from Ken's first group was saying, "You gotta go hear this guy!" So the second session was double the size of the first, and virtually everybody attended the third and final one. Since Ken was the hit of the university, a number of the YPOers came up to them and said, "Why are you returning to the University of Massachusetts at the end of the year? When you're hot, you're hot. You should start your own company." Margie and Ken appreciated their enthusiasm, but laughed. "We can't even balance our own checkbook. How are we going to start our own company?" Their response was quick. "We'll help you!" In no time, Ken and Margie had five volunteers for an advisory board. They knew a good idea when they saw it, and they helped the Blanchards begin a new phase—and the beginning of the legend.

A short time later, Ken took the basic concepts he had been teaching to corporations and together with Spencer Johnson—who was working on a book on parenting—created a small, easy-to-read book called *The One Minute Manager*®. With the help of YPOers, they originally self-published the book and sold over 20,000 copies with little advertising. When they went to New York and got it published, *The One Minute Manager* took off like a rocket, eventually selling more than thirteen million copies. Once that book hit the bestseller lists, Ken Blanchard's name became a household word.

Ken and Margie have gone through several transitions in life since then. From the university campus to the training and consulting business, now Ken has cofounded the Center for FaithWalk Leadership, a nonprofit ministry that brings leadership principles modeled by Jesus to the problems of the church and business world. Ken continues to serve as the chief spiritual officer of the Ken Blanchard Companies. Margie currently heads up the firm's Office of the Future, a think tank that keeps them innovative and constantly changing to meet new marketplace demands. Both organizations are committed to helping people in the profit and nonprofit worlds to lead at a higher level around the globe. But I'm getting ahead of the story. When

Ken reached halftime in his own life, he realized that, just like everyone in his parable books, he needed to deal with some essentials if he was to have real peace of mind. He describes his spiritual journey in his book *We Are the Beloved.*

"In 1985 my journey got a boost when Margie and I met Bob and Linda Buford," he writes. "I had met Bob casually before at some YPO events where Margie and I had been asked to speak, so I knew of his commitment to a personal ministry to help ministers at large churches and be a special coach for many business leaders." Ken then goes on to say:

> On the way to a YPO conference in Mexico City, we saw the Bufords between flights in the Admirals Club at Dallas-Fort Worth Airport. When we got on the plane, I discovered that Bob's seat was across the aisle from mine. Earlier in the day, I had found tucked away among the bills in my wallet a little booklet about the spiritual laws of Christianity that Phil Hodges had given to me. His daughter LeeAnne had gotten it at Sunday school. I don't recall putting it in my wallet, but there it was! Now that Bob Buford was sitting next to me, that booklet took on new meaning.[1]

When we found our seats on the plane, I was very surprised to see that Ken and I wound up sitting right across the aisle from each other. Coincidence? I wonder. But once we were in the air, I prayed silently, "Lord, if you want me to say anything to this man about spiritual things, I'm game, but now I think I will take a nap." At that point I just put my head back on the headrest and closed my eyes.

A KAIROS MOMENT

The next thing I remember, Ken was leaning across the aisle with a little book in his hand. On the cover it said, "The Four Spiritual Laws," a pamphlet I knew very well. Written by Campus Crusade founder Bill Bright, it explained the plan of salvation. As Ken recounts the story in his narrative:

"Bob, this booklet is in my wallet for some reason. Maybe it means we should talk about Christianity. I have a few questions I'd like to ask you."

"I'll do my best, Ken," said Bob. "But remember, I'm only a layman."

So there in the sky we started going over the booklet together. The first spiritual law stated: God loves you and offers a wonderful plan for your life.

I could buy that one all right, but the second law was where my questions started. It contended that we are all sinners. That had always bothered me. From my standpoint, the concept of original sin was too negative. I'd always thought that people should be considered to have "original potentiality." That is, as human beings we have the potential to be either good or bad.

When I asked Bob about original sin he said, "Let me ask you a question, Ken. Do you think you're as good as God?"

"Of course not," I answered. "The concept of God has to do with perfection."

"Okay. On a scale of 1 to 100, let's give God 100. We'll give Mother Teresa a 90, and an ax murderer 5. Ken, you're a decent sort and are trying to help others. I'll give you 75. Now the special thing about Christianity is that God sent Jesus to make up the difference between you and 100."

That appealed to me. I'd never heard Christianity explained that way.

"Now, a lot of people don't like the fact that the ax murderer gets the same shot at the ball as Mother Teresa," continued Bob, "but that's what grace is all about. It's not about deeds. If you accept Jesus as your Savior, no matter what your past has been, He rids you of your sins and brings you to 100."

At that point, Ken reached into his briefcase and pulled out a small tape recorder. He held it up between us and said, "Margie is over in the window seat and she can't hear what you're saying. I want her to hear this, so, if you don't mind, Bob, please repeat what you just said."

As we approached our destination, I said, "Ken, I want to introduce you to a friend of mine who can really tell you this story. His name is Bill Hybels and he's the pastor of a large church in Chicago, and he will be at the YPO meeting in Mexico City as a speaker." As it turned out, that was the only time Bill Hybels ever spoke at YPO, and I was able to make an introduction that would have a lasting impact on both their lives.

Bill Hybels met with Ken for lunch during the conference and they discussed and debated the claims of faith. When Ken eventually asked Bill how he could accept that offer of grace, Bill said, "It's easy for a One Minute Manager. All you have to do is bow your head and say, 'Lord, I can't save myself. I am a sinner. I accept Jesus Christ as my Savior and bridge between me and You. From this day forward I turn my life over to Him.'"[2]

Ken couldn't bring himself to "suit up" at that moment; he said he needed more time to process all that Bill and I had told him. But Bill's continued encouragement to "receive and trust" eventually led Ken to begin the relationship that is now the center of his life and work.

Today, Ken, Margie, and their adult children, Debbie and Scott, are engaged in helping large and small organizations manage people and projects more effectively. In the process, Ken helps those in the transitional phases of their lives and work learn the difference between being *driven* and being *called*. Driven people, he says, think it's all up to them; called people, on the other hand, understand that life and work are gifts of God's grace, and respond appropriately.

This idea, which Ken learned from author Gordon MacDonald, makes it possible to trust in the hand of providence, and for the knot in the stomach to go away. It makes it possible to believe that there's more to life than "fame and fortune," and that there is something more that we can be doing with our lives—something they can be doing through their leadership style in their everyday work.

A Middle Way

During a more recent conversation, while we took a long weekend to be together in the Napa Valley of California, Ken told me about talking with motivational speaker Zig Ziglar. "Zig is seventy-eight years old now," Ken said, "so I asked him, 'Zig, are you thinking about retiring?' He laughed and said, 'Retiring? No! I'm re-firing.' And then he said, 'Ken, there's no mention of retirement in the Bible, as far as I can tell. In fact, except for Jesus and David, nobody had much of an impact until they were at least sixty, and most of them were in their nineties before they did their best work.'"

Ken said, "I thought that was a wonderful approach. In fact, I think I'm going to be able to have a bigger impact in the next thirty years than I've had in the last thirty. I think my best years are ahead of me, which is really an interesting question to ask people. *Do you see your best years ahead of you or behind you?* If people see their best years behind them, then they're probably not going to finish very well, because you can't finish well when you're going backward."

When I asked Ken to describe his view of life after halftime, he described this lesson for someone who has just left a big company or some other enterprise that has been the primary focus for a number of years. Now that you're at a point in your life where you can do something truly important, you need to get under God's agenda and out from under your own.

"Success," he said, "is all about *getting;* significance is about *giving back.* But then if you look at the next step of finishing well, which is surrender to something greater than yourself, you need to ask, *To what am I surrendering?*" The answer is simple: You're surrendering to a vision that is bigger than your own. You're surrendering to the idea that you have been designed with a purpose and potential that you will never fulfill if you keep on trying to do it all your own way. "Ultimately," Ken says, "you're surrendering to God's plan for your life."

"The reason I'm so excited about the next thirty years," Ken told me, "is that I'm trying to stay on his plan."

If you've accumulated a lot of this world's goods during your journey, you may have to struggle with the idea of letting go of your own manifesto and signing onto that bigger plan. Henri Nouwen, the distinguished author and Catholic priest who did his last work at *L'Arche* communities in Canada, once told me that he didn't think you can go from success to surrender in one jump. "I'm afraid you'd be too angry about the things you have to give up," he said. "The pull of gravity of success is just too great."

But perhaps there's a middle way. What Ken Blanchard and I decided was that since wealth and accomplishment are so addictive, some of us may need to spend a little time at the "halfway house," which is significance; and that means using your resources and your skills to do good for others, right in the middle of your current work. It will make a world of difference in your life and theirs.

FINDING THE THING THAT WAS THERE ALL ALONG

Margie Blanchard, who is about my age, told me, "I was born at a fortunate time. There was a birth dearth in the early forties, so when I was ready for college, the colleges needed me. There were lots of slots because there wasn't a lot of competition. Then, when I graduated from college, I was about six years ahead of the *thundering herd* of baby boomers so I could be their teacher and guide, warning them about what they were about to get into."

I think that has been my good fortune as well, particularly dealing with topics like aging and retirement. There has been a "thundering herd" of baby boomers right behind me for years, and now that they're entering midlife, they know enough people my age to begin wondering what it's going to be like for them. Their kids are grown now, and it's getting quieter around the house. They've seen their friends getting divorced. They've been to the funerals of people in their forties and fifties, and they're wondering about the meaning of things.

They've reached the point where they know the right questions. Now they're looking for answers, and some of them are looking for company in their confusion. A large number of those who grew up in the sixties don't have any real spiritual reference points to rely on, so they're floating at sea. As a result, they've turned inward and are struggling to find the spiritual nourishment they need.

Margie told me that the chance to communicate with these people through their wide range of choices is what gets her motor humming. "I'm very excited about the kind of work we do," she said. "We help people's lives work better both at work and at home. Work is becoming an increasingly important place for people, as they're less connected to other organizations. Work is becoming a place where they have friends, where they find meaning. We help leaders—and that includes all of us—lead at a higher level and create the kind of work, home, and volunteer environments where people want to bring their full energies to the task at hand. It's a pretty exciting mission."

"I think you and Ken have done a great job of giving people models to examine," I said, "and I suspect that's what most people in a period of transition like this are looking for."

"I'm glad to hear you say that," she said. "With some guidance, I've seen people make some successful transitions. But I think we are also pathfinders. Good models are hard to find. I think it's a tremendous challenge to find the essence of what's going to be most important and fulfilling in these years ahead. In most cases, when I work with people who are ready and willing to focus on that essence, it comes down to 'discovery'—ferreting out the one or two recurring themes that have satisfied them in most of their life stages. Then we name them and figure out new ways to experience them in the future. For example, one woman I coached had a theme of showmanship in her life—starting from when she was a young girl. This showed up in several success stories she told me about her life, though she had never named them as such. As this woman considered options beyond her current job—which she was ready to leave for something less time-consuming in the future—we could see that her energy was greatest when she talked about volunteer or part-time projects that had her on stage or in the limelight, at least in part! Ultimately she chose to lead a community chorus—three productions a year—including supporting a successful scholarship for aspiring college music majors.

"Without models I think it's a tremendous challenge to find the essence of what's important: not to just keep doing over and over again the things you did in your forties and fifties," Margie concluded. "That's the temptation, and without new models, not everybody is going to find the path."

SECTION II
Building Life II

CHAPTER SEVEN

It's about Relationships and Priorities

IN THE MBA SCHOOLS, THEY DON'T TEACH ABOUT HUMAN BEINGS. ALL THE MAJOR COLLEGES THAT I'VE LOOKED AT ARE STILL TRAINING FINANCIAL ANALYSTS AND CONSULTANTS. . . . I THINK THERE WAS A TREMENDOUS DRIVE IN THIS COUNTRY TO SUGGEST THAT THE ONLY REASON TO BE IN BUSINESS WAS TO MAKE MONEY. . . .

YET, WHEN A TRAGEDY LIKE SEPTEMBER 11 HIT, WHAT WAS REALLY IMPORTANT WAS RELATIONSHIPS. WHERE ARE OUR PEOPLE? WHERE IS OUR FAMILY? WHERE ARE THE PEOPLE WE REALLY CARE ABOUT? I THINK IT WAS A WONDERFUL WAKE-UP CALL TO GETTING BACK TO VALUES. I THINK THE OTHER BIG WAKE-UP CALL WAS TO LET GOD BACK IN OUR LIVES.
— KEN BLANCHARD

There's a shift in midlife, and it's mainly about relationships—and priorities. To check your own priorities at this point in your life, take a sheet of paper and draw a target with a bull's-eye and three concentric outer circles. Like this:

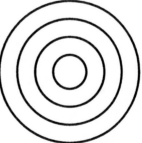

SYMBOLS TO PLACE:
$ = Making and Spending Money
A = Achievement
R = Relationships
✝ ✡ = Spiritual Life

Think about your life in four categories: (1) making and spending money, (2) achievement (which may or may not be acknowledged by money), (3) relationships, and (4) spiritual life. Be as honest as you can with yourself and put the element that's most central to your life in the center, then place the other three elements from next most important to the least in the outer circle. Try it. I often use this exercise as a technique to help people think about priorities and the allocation of their most precious resources—time and heart. Both are finite resources.

The first time I did this exercise, I was in my midthirties and intensely consumed with growing my television business. If I had been honest about it (and I wasn't at the time), I would have said that *money* and *achievement* were my two central values then, with *relationships* and *spiritual life* on the outer circles. Based on the conversations I've had with many people, I don't think this is extraordinary for first-halfers.

If you think not of what *ought to be* your priorities but what *are* your priorities as measured by allocation of time and mental energy, and if you are honest with yourself, the first half (particularly for men and increasingly for women) is about making your mark. A "crowding out" phenomenon pushes relationships and spiritual life toward the outer edges of the circles. They tend to get leftover energy. Now, well into the second half of my life, my priorities are exactly the reverse, with achievement and money on the outer circles. But that wasn't so when I was making an acquisition a year and growing my company at more than 20 percent each year.

Allocating Yourself among Competing Priorities

I talked about priorities with Armand Nicholi, editor of the *The Harvard Guide to Psychiatry*. Dr. Nicholi teaches at Harvard, writes for academic journals, is a gifted lecturer and speaker, and also maintains a vigorous

DR. ARMAND NICHOLI

clinical practice. He has many important things to say, but in the middle of our conversation he gave me the line that may well be the coffee-cup slogan for this book: "It's about relationships!"

Armand put the search for purpose in life into perspective. In leading up to that all-important line, he said, "You know, I teach people who are just starting out. As Harvard students, they're all bright to start with, and they often have talents or interests that they're actively pursuing. But early in the semester I ask them, 'What is your goal in life?' Invariably they answer, 'To be successful.' So I ask, 'What does that mean to you?' and their answer has some relationship to fame and fortune."

But then he offers the students another framework. "I tell them we all have a lifespan of about 30,000 days, and we spend about a third of that time sleeping. That means we have a waking lifespan of about 20,000 days. Then I say, 'If you had twenty days left, what would you do with them?' They universally answer that they would spend that time working on their relationships with family and friends, and if they're people of faith, with their God."

He lets that soak in for a few days, then in a subsequent lecture, he suggests to the students that "fame and fortune," which they claim to want more than anything, are actually in conflict with their highest stated priority of friends and family. They become so intensely focused on what they want to achieve through wealth and glory that they largely neglect the things they value most in life—their relationships. Most of his students have never really considered this perspective, and I suspect it may be an eye-opener for a lot of other people as well.

The trouble with fame and fortune as life goals is that they're so relative. Someone is always more famous than you, no matter how famous you may be, and someone always has a bigger fortune than you, no matter how wealthy you may be.

As I reflected on Armand's comments, I continued, "That's really interesting, but can you extend your analogy past your students to the person who is fifty-five years of age or older? There's your typical middle-aged patient sitting before you, unpacking whatever issues he or she has been dealing with. What do you see there?"

"Two words," he said, "*disordered priorities*. These people have spouses who are of secondary importance to them; they have children they're not close to anymore and who have turned to influences other than the family. And they've been so busy looking after their own interests that they've basically neglected God altogether."

So I asked him, "But don't they get it? Don't these people realize what they've done to themselves?"

"No, they don't, because it happens so gradually."

Unfortunately, or perhaps fortunately in some cases, what brings the problem out into the open isn't usually gradual—alcohol, drugs, suicide, or worse. And retirement for such people becomes a major problem, because after they leave the nine-to-five lifestyle they've been devoted to for most of their adult lives, they have nothing of comparable merit with which to replace it. "For the last thirty or forty years," Armand said, "they have been getting their sense of self-worth from what they do for a living, and when that's gone they don't know who they are. So, for the most part, they don't handle retirement very well."

Armand explained that we were made to work, and to maintain meaning in our lives we need to be engaged in work that has meaning and purpose. And the most meaningful work is that which involves helping other people. In other words, what matters most when we look back from the other end is just the opposite of what his bright young students pursue so eagerly— fame and fortune. Furthermore, the relentless search for wealth and influence actually interferes with happiness and joy, which most people equate with contentment.

"The people who feel best about themselves after retirement," he said, "are those who get involved in some kind of work or activity where they can make a contribution to others, such as volunteer work, mentoring, or teaching. Sharing your wealth through charitable giving and philanthropy is important, but sharing your knowledge is every bit as important. It's the opposite of 'fame and fortune,' but it has lasting significance. I've often said, 'The fruit of my work grows on other people's trees.'"

Losing Your Joy

Dr. Nicholi has spent a good part of his life studying the contrasts between C. S. Lewis and Sigmund Freud. He has given dozens of lectures on it, comparing one of the finest minds in Christendom with that of the "father of psychotherapy." He has written articles and a book on the subject, titled *The Question of God*, and he is currently working on a film about it. One of the issues he raises in that context is that of happiness or joy. Because of my own interest in the subject, I asked him why so many people in Life II feel a noticeable lack of joy.

"Joy," replied Armand, "is a deep-seated desire to have a relationship with the person who made us."

His response was precise but surprising—a definition of joy that I had never heard. As I thought about it, I wondered if some of our problems stem from a faulty definition of joy. We tend to think of joy as a state of utter ecstasy or delight, like playing tennis when we're "in the zone." It's supposed to be an emotional sensation, a kind of euphoria, like a runner's high or winning the lottery. But if Armand is right, joy may be radically different and much more important than what we'd thought.

As he explained it, joy has more to do with being in alignment with your task or assignment from God, and being in a right relationship with him and your significant others, than with your sense of personal gratification or happiness. Joy may be more like getting up in the morning and putting on your favorite shirt. It doesn't give you a rush or some great physical sensation, but it's something you do naturally and appreciatively. It's like breathing. It's also something you may take for granted until you're without it. This is certainly not the definition of happiness, but I suspect it has a lot to do with an authentic concept of joy.

People often lose their joy somewhere along the way. Sometimes they burn out, working themselves so far into energy deficit that they can never recover. Sometimes it's the polar opposite—too little work.

The bad thing that happens when people retire, Armand said, is that they don't replace their work with something else. By "something else" he means meaningful work that is helpful to other people. He said that people who don't find that sort of involvement will eventually come to feel totally useless, no matter what they were doing before. The fact that a short time ago they had "fame and fortune" doesn't mitigate their inner sense of worthlessness. They're used to doing things. They find it hard to stop. People who achieve have a habit of achievement that begs to be sustained.

So I asked, "What would you prescribe, doctor?" Here I was in the presence of an internationally recognized psychiatrist, so naturally I thought he would be a great source for a prescription. I visualized him with one of those white notepads that physicians use for writing prescriptions. His prescription involved three things: "First, life during the 'retirement years' needs to be free of the stresses we experienced during our working life. Second, the tasks we undertake during these years need to be meaningful work that benefits other people, or (and this is critical) another person. And, third, it needs to be fun."

I thought the last point was especially interesting. It was not what you might expect, but I could see the logic of it. Fun is like a green light on your control panel. It tells you that you're in the right zone. If the work you've chosen is painful and awful, you know something isn't right; but if you're having fun and loving every minute of it, that's a signal that you're going in the right direction. You're likely to continue doing what you have fun doing. If it's not fun, even if it's not difficult or painful, you will eventually stop doing it. In addition, I believe there's a problem with anyone's theology if it concludes that fun cannot be spiritual.

CASH, TOYS, AND TROPHY WIVES

A few years ago, Rogers Kirven, an entrepreneur from Florida, told me a story about retiring to a life without meaning that was utterly shocking to me at the time. But when I related the story to Dr. Nicholi, he wasn't shocked at all. Rogers was thinking of selling his business and enjoying the good life. He was in the final stages of a transaction that would put him into enough cash to guarantee financial security. Over dinner at a fancy Washington, D.C., restaurant with two friends who had already cashed out, he asked them how it was going. "Not so good," was the answer from both. With plenty of money, but without meaningful work, the basic structure of their lives, now centered on consumption of luxury goods and "toys," had imploded.

This news alarmed Rogers, and he stopped the sale of his company. Then, being of a researcher turn of mind, he set out to find other men who had cashed out, asking them about their experiences. He told me he'd found thirty-six men who had sold their businesses for $5 million or more, after taxes, before the age of fifty. Thirty-three of them had divorced within two years of the sale! And several had acquired new trophy wives.

I related this story to Armand and asked, "What do you make of that?"

He answered flatly, "It doesn't surprise me at all."

"Really?" I said. "Why not?

"They're struggling with feelings of self-worth. They tend to project these feelings onto others, and they're critical of them on the very things about which they're most critical of themselves."

"But what about all those trophy wives?"

He explained, "That's to help them feel better about themselves. It's a palliative."

He's right, of course. A friend of mine in Dallas, a superlawyer who has represented a lot of rich and famous people, told me the typical trophy-wife scenario needs two elements: a husband as a meal ticket and a wife as an armpiece. "For the woman," he said, "being a trophy wife is a professional role. She makes it possible for him to show up radiating success and achievement. The old guy she marries isn't exactly Prince Charming," he laughed, "but he's the meal ticket."

THE TOPLESS PYRAMID

When Armand spoke about "fame and fortune," which his students at Harvard claimed to be seeking, he described it as pathological in some ways. He stressed the fact that if his students really thought they only had a short time to live, they'd be spending it mending their relationships with friends, family, and God. Deep down, they know *it's about relationships.* But here they are, about to spend their next thirty years in a mad scramble for fame and fortune, which are antithetical to their declared values.

Consciously or unconsciously, most of the people who grew up in the late twentieth century have been raised with an idea developed by another psychiatrist, Abraham Maslow, which he called a "hierarchy of needs." Maslow speculated that all of us have basic needs and higher-order needs. He expressed his observations in what became known as Maslow's Pyramid, which I have drawn to look something like this:

TOPPING THE PYRAMID

As our needs for material things were satisfied, Maslow theorized, they no longer acted upon us as behavior motivators. We "graduated" to higher-order needs that had to do with achievement. Then came what he called "self-actualization." In Maslow's view, self-actualization needs (truth, justice, beauty, and the like) were the highest, most ultimate needs for human beings.

The word *self* is the key. It's a word we heard a lot in the '90s boom time.

You noticed, of course, that my rendering of Maslow's Pyramid above doesn't have a top, though his original rendition of it did. I drew it like this purposefully because I believe there's an even higher order of human need that I would call "self-transcendence," which completes the pyramid. It's what Dr. Nicholi spoke of when he said that true joy is being in full alignment with our Creator. It's what Jesus spoke of when he said in Matthew 10:39 that you must lose your life in order to gain your life.

Here's my completion of Maslow's Pyramid:

I asked Armand whether his patients, many of whom have experienced so much fame and fortune, felt that the dislocation in their relationships—what he had called disordered priorities—was a fair price to pay. Sadly, he said that in most cases they are so driven that they would probably do it again.

PAYING THE PRICE

Just as fame and fortune have a price, it's important to know that relationships have a price too. Authenticity and vulnerability are essential in building relationships. Authenticity and vulnerability are risky, antithetical to what most people consider success. Conversely, money and achievement don't seem to impress God as he's pictured in the biblical record. They fall in the outer two rings of the target we considered at the start of this chapter. And more often than not, money and achievement are cul-de-sacs or dead ends, and represent temptations and obstacles.[1]

Years ago, when my company was growing at more than 20 percent per year and I was burning with intensity and ambition, I had a conversation with a Bible teacher I greatly admired, Ray Steadman. We talked about money, and he told me that the word Jesus used most often when he spoke about money (which he did quite a lot) was "deceitful" (i.e., something that appears to promise one thing but delivers another).

"The deceit of money," Ray explained, "is that it gives you the idea that you're bulletproof." I understood the illusion of feeling bulletproof only too well. Having lost a twenty-four-year-old son,[2] I'll never again feel bulletproof. But I knew what he was saying: With money you may feel that you have no need of others. You can buy your way out of trouble. You feel you don't need God. You're independent, you think, until reality comes crashing down around your ears.

Stephen Covey, who wrote *The Seven Habits of Highly Effective People*, says we all start out dependent as children. The quest of adolescence and early adulthood is to achieve independence. But if we're wise, we eventually come to what Covey calls "*inter*-dependence." When asked, "Of all the commandments, which is the most important?" Jesus answered, "The most important one is this: 'Hear, O Israel, the Lord our God, the Lord is one. Love the Lord your God with all your heart and with all your soul and with all your mind and with all your strength.' The second is this: 'Love your neighbor as yourself.' There is no commandment greater than these."[3] I think that's what Armand was saying with his comments about "friends, family, and God."

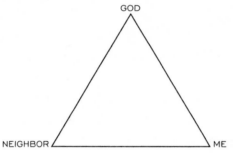

I think of this interdependence as a triangle involving three relationships, with God at the apex. Think of how this works in a marriage, which is the closest human relationship. When God is the commonly held value transcending the individual needs of the husband or the wife, there's always a higher court of appeal that the two can go to reconcile their differences. And as a husband and wife draw closer to God (as they progress up the sides of the triangle), they grow closer to one another as well. It's the same with any relationship. Common values and purpose draw people closer together.

WHEN THE TIME IS RIGHT

The movie *Shadowlands*, starring Anthony Hopkins and Debra Winger, is an excellent film about the marriage of the great writer C. S. Lewis. A scene in the film depicts Lewis after the death of his wife, sitting with his stepson Douglas in the attic of their house in England weeping together. It's a heartbreaking scene, but that movie taught me how to weep for the loss of my own son in a drowning accident in the Rio Grande River at age twenty-four. It taught me how to cry that hard, to let it all out, something I had never done before. That was a terrible time for Linda and me, but dealing with my emotions as we passed through that ordeal was necessary and pivotal to my letting go of other things later.

Ultimately, the grief that Linda and I experienced didn't take away our joy. I can now say that it was just the opposite—in fact, it revealed the other side of the paradox. After enduring the most terrible week of my life and trying to keep my wits about me while dealing with the tragic loss of my only son, I experienced God's grace as I've never felt it before or since.

For a solid week, our search for Ross was all over the news in Tyler, where we lived. People were around the house constantly. They had come to comfort us as people do when you've lost someone. I was feeling about as much agony as anyone could possibly feel, but simultaneously I felt as much joy as I'd ever felt. There was a remarkable sense of God's provision through that difficult time.

One of my friends, Art Ruff, a real estate developer from Dallas, drove over to show his concern. After observing my simultaneous joy/agony state, he said, "I know just what you are feeling. When I was a Marine in Vietnam with people under my command dying around me, I experienced the same sort of electric feeling of God's being with me in all that chaos and carnage. I've never felt that way since. You may not believe this," he said, "but you'll miss that feeling when it's gone."

Art was right. The night I came home after my futile search for Ross, or at least for his body, I sat with friends and prayed the most effective prayer of my life. "God," I prayed, "please give me the grace to receive any grace you would send to me from any source." Remarkable things began to happen. Before, I had usually been the provider rather than the receiver. This time, in my broken and vulnerable condition, I "got" most everything. Many of my comforting friends were inarticulate; they just held me and wept. Yet I felt like I knew just what they were "saying" to me. It was beyond words.

So many "graces" came to me that I began to record them in a journal. I identified 160 specific things that I took to be provisions from God to a hurting father. The feelings tapered off in about ninety days and, as Art Ruff said I would, I missed them. I'm no longer in that zone of intense dependence and self-transcendence. Now that things are back to normal, I have a hole in my life that I fill with other things. But having been there, I remember what it was like, and I feel that I can get back if I ever need to go there again.

The late, great devotional writer Oswald Chambers said, "Nothing is more difficult than to ask. We long, and desire, and crave, and suffer, but not until we are at the extreme limit will we ask. A sense of unreality makes us ask. . . . The first result of being brought up against reality is this realization of poverty."

WE TRUST REASON TOO MUCH

Relationships aren't reasonable. They come from a different place . . . like faith.

We tend to try to comprehend life from either end of two extremes: reason and faith. We've been taught by years of schooling and decades of television and op-ed punditry to reason our way through things—to trust our own personal calculus and that of experts—this despite the fact that, more often than not, the experts are wrong.[4] The modern tendency to depend solely on reason and dismiss faith as wishful thinking is our inheritance from Enlightenment philosophers.

But what happens when something occurs that can't be explained by reason? For me the death of my son was such an event. Just try reasoning your way through that! Then, and too often *only* then, do we resort to faith. Paul defines faith as "the hope of things unseen."[5] One might also call faith "the hope when things get unreasonable." Albert Einstein said famously, "What is incomprehensible to man is in the realm of God." We can't deny the power of reason, but our scientific age has refused to admit what Einstein clearly understood—that reason has its limits. We can peer into the realm of the incomprehensible only through the eyes of faith.

Is there a God? The annual Gallup Poll tells us consistently that 95 percent of Americans believe there is. But is he a God we can trust only when things are reasonable, when observation and evidence confirm that everything is in order? Or can we believe in the face of the incomprehensible, the inexplicable, the utterly unreasonable (the good dying young) that "all things work together for good to those who love God"[6]? Even in pain? Even in brokenness? Even in the shame of self-embarrassment? And even in agonizing grief?

Let's say that everything we need to understand life measures three feet long. I believe God has equipped us, in a time of instant Internet word-searched access to encyclopedic knowledge, to get 2 feet, 11-3/4 inches of the way through reason. That's fine. *But there's always a gap.* Stuff happens. Inexplicable stuff. Then what?

Faith is the spark that jumps the gap for me. Faith is what bridges the awful chasm of unreasonableness. It seems that God lets us take care of most things through common sense and reason. All of us trust something. It's okay to trust reason as far as reason will take you. But there's always going to be that gap—the incomprehensible factor that Einstein placed in the realm of God. And when something incomprehensible happens, we don't get to define what's right, what's fair. In that zone of unreasonableness, I'm not above God; God is above me. I'm out of control. I don't understand, and I won't understand. I *can't* understand. As I stood that day on the bluff overlooking the Rio Grande River, it slowly and grudgingly dawned on me that I would not see my son again during this lifetime. At that moment a verse came to me:

> Trust in the LORD with all your heart, and lean not on your own understanding.
> — Proverbs 3:5

I *did* trust then and I still do.

I know that I will see Ross again in due course. I can't prove it, but I know it. Loving someone deeply is not a thing you can understand through reason. Relationships aren't like that. Neither is faith.

CHAPTER EIGHT

It's about Family First

"HONOR YOUR FATHER AND YOUR MOTHER . . . SO THAT YOU MAY LIVE
LONG AND THAT IT MAY GO WELL WITH YOU."
— DEUTERONOMY 5:16,
THE FIFTH OF THE TEN COMMANDMENTS

The old expression "family first" has sometimes been an issue for people
called into work of greater significance in Life II. No one, regardless of how
strong-willed or independent-minded they may be, escapes the influence of
family. Sometimes it may be the lack of strong family bonds or a dysfunc-
tional environment that motivates our attitudes and behaviors. In other cases
the experience of a strong and loving family may shape the way we live for
years to come. In either case the role and expectations of family are central
concerns for halftimers considering their options for Life II.

For many people, the expectations of family involve family business.
Several that I interviewed felt a sense of obligation to be next in the line of
succession or to fill a leadership role created by their fathers. They felt obli-
gated to carry the baton as the next generation of a relay race before they
had the freedom to go on to other things.

I felt a special affinity for these people because I too had a "family destiny"
that shaped the first half of my life. My father died when I was in the fifth
grade. My mom found herself with three young children (I was the oldest)
and the need to make a living and a life. We moved to East Texas where she
bought a radio station, and in the early fifties, applied successfully for the
license of the only local television station in Tyler, midway between Dallas

and Shreveport. In the space on the FCC application form asking her reasons for seeking the license—a space usually filled in with high-sounding phrases prepared by a Washington lawyer—she wrote, "So that my children can take over the business someday." Only a mom would say that.

My mother was a strong woman who was always in business. First radio, then television. She was a genuine visionary in the early days of television. It's pretty normal to have strong women in business now, but when I was growing up in the 1950s, it was exceptional. In fact, before my mother could sign a contract without a male countersignature, she had to petition a Texas court to have her "disabilities removed." Her disabilities were that she was a female. Granting her petition, the court declared my mother a *femme sole*, a legal designation meaning a "woman alone" who was entitled to sign her own contracts.

While other moms were reading *Winnie the Pooh* to their kids, my mother sat at my bedside teaching me about balance sheets, depreciation, and ad-sales techniques. As a youth of fourteen, barely adjusted to the challenges of junior high school, I remember my mother taking me downtown to meet with bankers and lawyers, telling them (and me) that I was going to be their customer someday. She was determined that I be well-connected and respected in the business world. She even took me to the National Association of Broadcasters annual convention so I could learn my way around the television business and get "the feel of the industry."

To say I grew up with a sense of *family destiny* understates the matter. From the beginning I was expected to enter the family business. I loved the business, but I also had an obligation to fulfill before reaching halftime. And I wasn't the only one.

THE FAMILY BUSINESS

Dick DeVos is the son of Richard DeVos, cofounder of Amway and a legendary figure in the field of multilevel marketing. I'm sure Dick could identify with parts of my story, because the family business was also the central feature of his growing-up years. When I asked Dick to share some of that experience, he said, "My professional life actually started with the family business. After just one semester of college, I got bored with school and went to work for the company. I eventually did go back and finish my degree while I continued working full-time at Amway."

"Did you jump straight into a management role?" I asked.

"Oh, no," he replied. "I went through a good, long period of transition. I held a variety of positions, including some time in the executive training program. After I came out of that, I took over dif-ferent segments of the business and was eventually given the chance to lead the international division. That was an important time for me. During the early eighties that division went from around 5 percent of sales to more than 50 percent. I stayed there about six years before deciding it was time to go out on my own for a while.

DICK DEVOS

"I needed to stretch my wings, so I started my own company. When I was asked to come back to the family business in '92, following some early indications of my father's failing health, I'd expanded my management skills quite a bit. I took over as president in January '93, and over the next ten years we went through some dramatic increases, a pretty dramatic decline, and then a recovery that included a major restructuring of the company."

"Sounds like you were being tested by fire," I said.

"It was a kind of test. It was a particularly volatile time in the economy, and we had to rework the company's governing structures. We had to reset the management team, restaff the company, and reduce the workforce by 15 percent, which affected some 1,300 people. But I'm pleased to say that in the course of all that, we honored our obligations, both as business people to do what the business requires, and as Christians to treat our people with dignity and respect. Fortunately, the healing period after those traumatic changes was fairly short, and the organization grew much stronger and experienced exceptional growth in the years that followed."

"But you eventually realized that you wanted to try some other things. Is that right?"

"Exactly," he said. "I came to that point at about the time I reached the ten-year mark as president of the company. I'd taken the business up and down and back again, and we'd expanded internationally. We had dramatically impacted shareholder performance, and all of our numbers were moving in the right direction. I had a successor all ready to go, so I was ready to step aside."

Dick had fulfilled his obligations to the family business. He had been enormously successful, leading his company out of a serious decline into enormously revitalized performance. Now he was looking for something more—wanting to use his considerable talents for some significant achievement. I wanted to hear about his search for the right fit to match his abilities and interests. "Today you're active in several other organizations," I said. "Were you pursuing any of those interests prior to stepping down as CEO?"

"Yes, I was," he answered, "but on a fairly small scale. It's difficult to divide your focus and stay on task, especially when you're running a large organization that's going through changes. Now, however, I have more time. I can take an hour to explore a new idea or activity outside my core business. That's amazing! Previously I could spend maybe ten seconds on anything that wasn't business related."

"Meaning," I said, "that you felt responsible to be on the bridge of that big ship?"

"Absolutely," he replied. "I don't care what title they put on your door, when you're part of a large organization, it runs you a lot of the time."

I asked Dick, "Was it a difficult transition for you to step out of that role?"

"Well," he said, "I have a low threshold for boredom, and when the family asked me to take over the business, I told them I would only stay as long as the challenge was still there. Honestly, I figured I'd last six or eight years. In fact, I lasted ten, so I beat my own expectations! But I told folks that there was no way I was going to retire at sixty-five with a gold watch. So I tried to govern my heart, not to let myself get trapped emotionally or financially in the organization. But in spite of my resolve, I eventually found that I had invested more of my self-concept in that title than I realized at the time. I didn't see it until I stepped away. It was a big learning experience to discover that even when you're guarding against it, the power and the self-image you feel in that kind of leadership role can become almost addictive."

"And how's it going now?" I asked him.

"Pretty well," he said. "Where I'd had just one responsibility that dominated my life, suddenly a wide range of interests have grabbed hold of me, and I'm still exploring my options."

"A mutual friend of ours told me that you might even be a candidate for governor of Michigan one of these days," I said. "Is there any truth to that?"

"Well, we'll see," Dick said. "Politics has always been interesting to me, but the thing that's captured my heart right now is education reform. I'm deeply involved with an organization that I think will be an important player in the education reform movement. My own passion is to help low-income parents who often have the worst schools for their children and no economic means of escape. I find that inexcusable and morally wrong, and I believe that if parents are empowered to make better choices, then the system will improve."

TESTING NEW IDEAS

George Gallup is a wonderful man with a big heart, and I'm always more optimistic after being with him. He's also a highly gifted researcher, utterly rational, and very deliberate in his approach to most things. What strikes me about George is the vitality of his spiritual life, and his desire to do things that matter.

GEORGE GALLUP

If action follows faith, as George truly believes, then we as a culture will certainly benefit from his Life II decision. Pursuing survey data that reflect America's values and beliefs is George's passion, and it is still a big part of what he's doing today as chairman of the George H. Gallup International Institute, a nonprofit founded in 1988 by the Gallup family in memory of the late George H. Gallup Sr., and today sponsored by the Gallup Organization.

As we reflected on the changes in George's career, I asked him, "Did you have a halftime experience when you shifted your focus of interest in midlife?"

"Yes, I would say so," he told me. "I did have a halftime experience at age fifty-eight. This was during the time that the family sold the business, which had been founded in 1935, and formed the new institute."

"What did the halftime experience look like?" I asked.

"The *before* side of it was spending the first three and a half decades of my career with the Gallup Poll in all phases: developing questionnaires, interviewing, writing press releases—learning the ropes, basically. I had the great opportunity of working with my dad on almost a daily basis for most of this time. But in our late fifties, my brother, Alec, and I realized that we needed to be thinking about what would happen to the company after us. In 1988 we sold the family business to the late Don Clifton and his son, Jim, who is now CEO and president of Gallup. Under their leadership, I'm pleased to note, the company has grown rapidly in new and important ways."

"Sounds like a major change for you," I said, "especially since the family business had been pretty much your whole life up to that point."

"I didn't want to leave the exciting world of polling," he said, "and I wanted to do something in memory of my dad, who founded the Gallup Poll and had died in 1984. My father always viewed survey research as a vehicle for undergirding democracy and for promoting positive change in society, and so this became the focus of the George H. Gallup International Institute."

"Apparently you decided there was a mismatch between the work you were doing and the work you felt called to do," I said. "Is that a fair characterization?"

"I believe that's fair in the sense that I did not have any clear indication of the extent to which survey findings reported in the media were being studied at leadership levels, and whether or not they were affecting change." George did not want just to gather accurate data; he wanted to see that data applied in a way that made a difference.

"So that was part of my halftime awakening, if you will. The motto of the Institute, founded by the Gallup family, is 'Ideas from Progress' and its mission is 'to discover, test, and encourage application of new solutions to social problems.'"

"Do you have limits on what you study?"

"The institute examines new ideas and approaches in education, the environment, health, religion, and values. The institute seeks to become a clearinghouse for new societal ideas from around the world, inspired by the words of Dr. George Gallup: 'The progress of mankind depends in large measure upon new ideas, and the rate of this progress in turn depends largely upon the speed with which the ideas are disseminated.' One of our latest projects has been an index to measure the overall spiritual health of the nation, working with the Center for Research on Religion in Urban Civil Society at the University of Pennsylvania."

Support for the institute comes from the Gallup Institute Fellows, a core group of men and women in positions of leadership in many fields who, as agents of positive change in America, help carry out the mission of the institute. They provide ideas to be tested, respond creatively to institute surveys, fashion responses into policy statements, and through their own good offices, writings, and other initiatives, take these ideas to groups and policy makers who can put them into action.

George's father, George H. Gallup Sr., was one of the original pioneers of public opinion research in this country. While serving as research director at Young and Rubicam Advertising Agency in the 1930s, he launched the American Institute of Public Opinion. The Gallup Poll is still the most trusted survey organization of American thought, but George decided that, while he loved the business his father had founded, his own interests were somewhat different. Today he is pursuing his passion to probe beneath public attitudes to the bedrock of spirituality and religious beliefs that frequently undergirds and gives rise to these attitudes.

LONG-TERM INVESTING

Another man who grew up within the context of a family business is John Findley. The third of four children, John was raised in the Methodist church, but he wasn't much of a believer. After reaching halftime, however, things began to change, and he came to the conclusion that he could use his resources for better purposes. In our conversation, I asked him to tell me how he came to that point.

He said, "My father ran Findley Adhesives, the business my grandfather had started in Milwaukee back in 1911. I grew up in that environment. But when I graduated from college I decided it would be best to get some work experience somewhere else. So I worked for a company that made corrugated boxes using our adhesives. After two years I went into the Army Reserve, and when I came out I went to work for the family business."

"Did they put you straight into management?" I asked.

JOHN FINDLEY

"No, absolutely not. They shipped me off to western Michigan for a couple of years as a salesman. I hated being a salesman, but I especially hated being the president's son, because no one saw me as John Findley the person, but as the president's kid. It was as if I were only there because my father owned the company."

"You felt that was a sign of disrespect, I guess."

"It didn't do much for my self-esteem," he said, "and I didn't have a lot at the time. After two and a half years I quit and moved back to Wisconsin. I found a job, and my wife went to work teaching school. After another five or six years, I was ready for a change. One weekend my parents came for a visit, and I mentioned that I was looking for a job. My dad said, 'We're looking for someone with your skills, John. Would you consider coming back to the company?' I said I'd come for an interview."

"Were they ready for you to come back?" I asked.

"I'm not sure," he answered, "but when the president's kid goes to see the executive vice president for an interview, he's probably going to be hired. However, I had gained my self-confidence by that time, and I knew what I could do. I took the job, and they moved me about every two years to give me a perspective of the business. I worked in manufacturing, production, inventory control, administration, sales, marketing, and everywhere else."

"Did you discover who you were in the process?" I asked.

"Yes, I did. I know a lot of family businesses where the son, at age twenty-five or so, is made vice president, at thirty he's executive vice president, and he takes over the business at thirty-two. I was made a vice president at forty. In 1987 while a vice president, Dad and I bought the company, cashed the family out, and borrowed $59 million dollars to make it work. The day I bought the business, Dad announced that he wanted to retire. I asked him to stay around for a couple of years and he agreed. He did a terrific job working with me, and to this day we have a superb relationship."

John was especially proud of the fact that Findley was a Christian-based company with a warm heart for the community and the employees. "We gave away 5 percent of our gross profits," he told me. "That practice started with my grandfather, and I decided we ought to get the employees involved. So we gave a hundred dollars to every employee to give away each year. We did this through groups within the company. If a certain group had forty-five employees, we'd give them $4,500 and say, 'You guys can give this away anywhere you'd like.'

"We got involved in inner-city volunteer work and donated to families in the tough core of Milwaukee. We also had an annual Christmas party, and my wife and I would stand at the door and shake hands with all four hundred people that came in. We knew everyone and it was a friendly place to work."

"But you decided to sell the business," I said. "What led you to that decision?"

"I bought it when I was forty-two, ran it for eight years, doubled the business and sold it when I was fifty. Very tough decision. But God was calling me. I dreaded telling my dad what I wanted to do, and I thought of every question he would ask me. When I explained it, he just looked at me and said, 'John, it was never a question of whether you should sell it, but when.' That just floored me!"

It wasn't an easy decision, but John had no doubt it was the right thing to do. And rather than horde the profits, he put every penny from the sale into the Vine & Branches Foundation, which he created to invest in the needs of pastors and inner-city ministries. The writer of Hebrews says, "By faith Abraham obeyed when he was called. . . . And he went out, not knowing where he was going."[1] John Findley felt called to sell his family business and clear his agenda. Today he's using the resources he accumulated to serve others—an investment with enduring significance.

FINDING THE SWEET SPOT

Even people without the pressure to be loyal to a family business sometimes find that family expectations can conflict with one's true calling. Tom Wilson is president and CEO of the Leadership Network and my partner in reaching out to innovative church leaders and their congregations all across North

America. Tom's journey into kingdom work has been just as remarkable as any of the others in this chapter, but without a lot of the baggage.

Tom was the first person in his immediate family to finish college. "I raised the bar for our family just by going to college," he said. "And what you do after college, as all my family believed, is teach school. That was the top rung of the ladder. It's what my cousins and my uncle had done; so that's what I did.

TOM WILSON

"I got my degree in biology and education and was hired by Austin Middle School in Amarillo, Texas. I taught biology and life science, and I coached seventh-grade football, basketball, and track. That was my life, and I really loved it."

"What did your family think of that?" I said.

"They were proud as peacocks, because I'd reached the top of the ladder," he replied. "I taught for two years, but one day I was invited to come and observe a Young Life meeting. Young Life had a dynamic ministry to teens then, just as it does now, but it was new to me. When I saw what they did and how kids' lives were being changed, I knew it was something I wanted to be part of. So when I heard they were looking for a campus leader, I talked to the local board and they offered to fly me to Dallas to see how a Young Life club works.

"To be honest," Tom continued, "I'd never been on an airplane, and what really got me excited was the chance to fly to Dallas on a plane! So I put on a coat and tie and went up to Lake Highlands High School in Dallas. And on the way back I said to my wife, 'Linda, this is it! This is what I want to do.' I'm sure she thought I was nuts even to think about taking on a challenge like that when I already had more on my plate than I could handle. But she said okay, and that was it.

"Linda and I became volunteer leaders that year," Tom said, "and the program grew so quickly, from zero to five hundred kids in just a few months, that the local board decided they needed to hire a full-time staff person in

Amarillo. On the inside I was saying, *I want that job!* But there was just one problem: By that time I had a wife and a baby to take care of. Linda thought the idea was risky, and on top of that, I knew my parents would think I was crazy. They'd never heard of Young Life, and the thought of me giving up my teaching position for a volunteer job with a young people's ministry was a total shock to them. After all, I was doing what I was trained to do. This was not in the blueprints!"

"You felt the pressure of not fulfilling your family's expectations. So how did you deal with that?" I asked.

"I just kept praying and thinking about it, but all the while I was saying, *I really want that job!* Well, they flew me back to Dallas, and I met with a bunch of men who were already doing full-time staff work in other schools. The more I heard, the more I knew this was what I wanted to do. When my wife picked me up at the airport in Amarillo, I said, 'Linda, I'm going to quit my job at the school and go to work for Young Life full-time.' Fortunately, I've since learned that this isn't the best way to communicate plans to your wife! But Linda supported my decision because she could see that I was excited about this chance."

"You were making five hundred dollars a month teaching school and that was your security blanket!" I said.

"Yes, that's right," Tom responded with a laugh. "It seemed like a lot of money at the time, and Linda was basically in shock."

"Sounds like family expectations aren't just an issue for rich people," I said.

"No question," he said. "The last thing I wanted was to cause anxiety for my wife, my parents, or the rest of the family. But I just had this sense that I had found what I was supposed to do. Fortunately, Linda really got on board with it. My passion was touching lives. We led a club in Amarillo on Monday and Tuesday nights, then we drove to Borger for a meeting on Thursday night. We had a Thursday morning Bible study, and we went to the high school football games on Friday night. And I had to squeeze teaching and lesson plans in between all that."

"So you finally made the change," I said. "Did it turn out the way you expected?"

"When I walked into the administration building to turn in my resignation, I actually felt like I was betraying everything I had worked for and quitting something I loved. I thought, *What am I doing? This is what I was trained for!* I didn't even know how I was going to make a living. But I did make the change, and what finally won my family over was not the job, the money, or anything else, but the passion they saw in me."

"You'd found the place where God wanted you," I said.

"It was right in the sweet spot of my life," Tom said. "I had a consultant tell me one time that when you're not doing what you're supposed to be doing, it's like writing with the wrong hand. You can do it, and after awhile you can get pretty good at it, but it's always awkward. But when you find the sweet spot—what you were created to do—it's like putting the pen back in the hand where it belongs."

After a career of thirty years with Young Life, Tom's ministry through Leadership Network is bigger today, and the demands of his position are considerably greater than they were in those early days. But he's having a dynamic impact on American Christianity, and he'll never forget those experiences that opened the eyes of his family to a higher calling and changed his own life forever.

CHAPTER NINE

It's about Saying No

The Road Not Taken

Two roads diverged in a yellow wood,
And sorry I could not travel both
And be one traveler, long I stood
And looked down one as far as I could
To where it bent in the undergrowth;

Then took the other, as just as fair,
And having perhaps the better claim,
Because it was grassy and wanted wear;
Though as for that, the passing there
Had worn them really about the same,

And both that morning equally lay
In leaves no step had trodden black.
Oh, I kept the first for another day!
Yet knowing how way leads on to way,
I doubted if I should ever come back.

I shall be telling this with a sigh
Somewhere ages and ages hence:
Two roads diverged in a wood, and I—
I took the one less traveled by,
And that has made all the difference.

— Robert Frost

It's also the things we don't do.

One night in the cavernous entry gallery of the Dallas Museum of Art at a black-tie dinner, I found myself seated across from one of the original founders of Southwest Airlines. As always, I took it as a learning opportunity. At the time the major carriers were losing money hand over fist while Southwest was happily extending its string of quarterly profits. So I asked my dinner companion, "How do you stay in the black when everybody else is swimming in red ink?"

"It's because of what we don't do," he answered. "We don't do food. We don't do assigned seats. We don't do interline baggage. Our motto is, 'Low Fares.' That's what we do."

What keeps most of us from focusing on the things that matter is all the things that don't matter but add cost, particularly the cost of our most precious asset—time. We end up spending ourselves dry, adding small increments to our "money and status" accounts—which we already have plenty of—while depleting our "meaning" accounts, including our relationships with God, marriage partners, kids, lifelong friends, and the others we're called to serve.

Nobody I know has thought more clearly about the business of "yes and no" than Lloyd Reeb, a forty-two-year-old who is director of our Halftime work at Leadership Network. Lloyd has written about his own experience in a terrific new book titled *From Success to Significance: Halftime for the Not-so-Rich*. He is a case of "early arrival" in Halftime, having dramatically reallocated his time and energy to significance activities while still in his thirties. This meant saying no to a much larger income potential in order to say yes to a sense of calling and vocation.

I interviewed Lloyd, but I can do no better than quote from the opening paragraphs of his book. I've italicized a few words and phrases that are loaded with meaning, and I encourage you to make a few marginal notes about the things that resonate with your own life. Identify what Lloyd is saying no to. To what end?

> Ten years ago I made a midlife transition to *reorient my life* toward things that I consider to be significant. I no longer

have that sick feeling in my stomach of being *trapped in a life of busyness*, pursuing *things that will not last* at the expense of the things I value more. What seems strange to me is that I *work just as hard* as before but somehow I know *I am free* of the rat race. One difference is that I feel very little stress, at least compared with the gut-wrenching stress I experienced in my first half of life as a real estate developer.

I can remember those *sleepless nights* rolling around in bed wondering if the bank would fund my next real estate deal. Wondering if the consumer demand for my seniors' housing project was as strong as I predicted. I remember the sense that I might be *wasting my life chasing something that was an illusion?* Secretly asking myself if this *is what I was created to do?*

Sure, I still worry from time to time, like when stock markets fluctuate or unexpected family expenses emerge. But it's a very different kind of stress. I still enjoy working hard, reaching goals, I still take risks, but today *I do it out of a sense of calling rather than some unexplained inner drivenness.* I do it with a confidence that *I am in the sweet spot of what I was created to do.* And I am having the time of my life. I wake up every morning with a sense deep inside that I am so very lucky to *know what I am passionate about*, I know *what I am good at* (those few things) and I have been given the gift of being able to spend my life focused on those things.

In 1993 I made a halftime transition. That is, I pushed *the pause button* in the middle of the game of life to look back on the lessons and accomplishments of the first half, to *reflect on what will really matter in the long run* and then to *redirect my life* for the second half. Specifically I wanted to pursue the possibility of moving from *success to significance.* But without millions of dollars in the bank it would take creativity and intentionality to discover a way to pursue significance.[1] *(italics added)*

Virtually all the major lessons of Life II are stated with a wonderful economy of words in those four paragraphs. Lloyd is a model for those thinking about "finishing well," just as the success of Southwest Airlines is a model for the travel industry. His book is the halftimer's operating manual, a handbook for those who are doing it on a budget. Lloyd has downsized the economic side of his life to fit a lifestyle focused on family and contribution. He's decided on what he's not going to do in order to focus on those things he feels called to do.

TOM TIERNEY

TOM TIERNEY

There's a famous quote about a conversation between Steve Jobs, the founder of Apple Computers, and John Scully, the head of marketing at PepsiCo, whom Steve was eagerly recruiting to be president of his company. At one point in that conversation, when it appeared that John wasn't eager to leave his current position, Steve said, "John, do you really want to spend the rest of your life selling sugar water?"

John got the point and the job. But sooner or later most of us have to ask ourselves some similar bottom-line questions to make sure our lifestyle matches our stated objectives. That's where my friend Tom Tierney found himself. When I first met Tom as part of a group focused on philanthropy, convened by the Kennedy School at Harvard, I felt as if I'd known him forever. I liked him from the start, and we spent a lot of time together. Tom is former CEO of Bain & Company, and when he came to his own fork in the road, he founded a Bain-like consulting firm for nonprofits called Bridgespan.[2]

Tom once told me it was odd for a consultant to spend so much time with a nonclient like me. But we both sensed that we were on the same mission: to tap the energies, knowledge, and experience of this incredibly bright generation of boomers and help mobilize them toward the more significant work of helping others.

I wanted to get a little background on the mental and spiritual transformation that led to his change of direction. "Tom," I said, "ever since you graduated from Harvard, you've been on a fast track. You've had a pretty fantastic ride, but as you've told me before, you came to the point where you wanted to give something back. How did that happen?"

"While it was terrific to have a prominent position in a big organization like Bain," he told me, "and while it was terrific to have that kind of money, I knew for some time that I was going to make a transition. I asked myself, *Is this my life calling? Is this really my life's work?* And when I analyzed it, I knew the answer to those questions was no.

"I really wanted to make the world a better place," he continued. "And as much as I respected and appreciated the work Bain was doing, it wasn't obvious to me that a $2 billion Bain versus a $1 billion Bain would satisfy that need. So I started pursuing a *parallel career*."

"So you got involved in volunteer work?" I asked.

"Actually, I started doing some pro bono work for independents and nonprofits back in the eighties," he said. "I was experimenting with the nonprofit sector to find out how it works. I was curious to know if my experience at Bain & Company might be useful. Eventually I came up with a business plan, got it approved by the IRS, raised some capital, and started laying the groundwork for what would eventually become Bridgespan. I remember thinking, *I'm not qualified for this!* But something inside me just said, *I'm going to do it!* And it felt great."

"By most standards," I said, "it probably wasn't the most natural thing for you to do."

"No, it wasn't," he replied. "It didn't make sense for all sorts of reasons. I mean, why would a CEO go start up a little charity? But it felt exciting. It felt 'impactful,' if that's a word, using skills I already had. I knew how to grow personal service businesses."

"And best of all," I said, "it was building on your passion to make a difference in the world."

"Absolutely. But I *had to let go* to hold on to that passion," he said. "I had to let go of Bain. I had to let go of the CEO thing. I had to let go of the corner office. But once I released my grip on those things, I was no longer encumbered and I was free to say, *Now what do I really want to do? What excites me?* Not what *should* excite me, but what really excites me."

Tom learned that he had to say no to the good thing in order to say yes to the better thing.

BREAKING FREE

Letting go of all the emotional baggage that goes with reaching the top in a large company is not easy to do, regardless of the motivation behind it. "As long as you're preoccupied with all that first-half stuff," I said to Tom, "you really don't have the mental, psychological, or spiritual space to process that kind of change. So how did you cope with that?"

"Well, you're right," he said. "The first-half stuff can be pretty addicting. And besides, a kind of social reinforcement makes it hard to be truthful about your goals for the second half. When I told my colleagues that I'd decided to step down as CEO and focus on my new initiative, they were in shock."

"Because you were giving up the perks?"

"Yes," he said, "and because I was letting go of the trappings of success. One by one, many execs came around and asked if I'd gotten a bad medical report. I think they were worried that I'd gone off the edge! There were times when even *I* began to think I was a little goofy. But I had made up my mind, and I did follow through just as I'd said I would."

When Tom stepped down as CEO of Bain, he took a considerable cut in pay, visibility, and prestige. But over a period of several months he recruited some outstanding talent and opened an office for Bridgespan in Boston. Today the new venture has already become an important player in the non-profit world.

"What role did your wife play in all this?" I asked. "Leaving Bain after twenty years must have been hard for her."

"Not at all," he said. "Karen was incredibly supportive. Faith is very important to her, very central to her life."

"So the two of you worked your way through this change, and Karen was there backing you up?"

"Absolutely," he answered. "She brought to it the view that the title didn't matter. She said, *'Build a life, not a résumé.'* What matters is your life, what kind of a life you lead every single day, and the lives you touch. All the stuff that ostensibly matters in the world of big business—the title, the perks, the income—actually, it doesn't matter a bit, not even a little bit.

"Periodically," Tom said, "I would come home after a long day at the office and say, 'I got to meet so-and-so, the CEO of some big outfit,' and Karen would say, 'Yes, so what?' And I would think, *Oh, yeah, you're right.* Even before we made the big change, it was Karen who really kept me grounded in the basic values."

At one point, Tom told me, a headhunter called and said he could land him a top job in Silicon Valley, with a shot at making $200 million! "I went home that night and told Karen, and I'll never forget her answer. She said, 'Tom, you're pursuing a dream. I'd rather we do that and live in a trailer than do this other thing.'"

As I listened to Tom, I realized that to keep your focus on Life II, you sometimes have to say no over and over again.

FORREST GUMP FINDS THE WAY

Hamilton Jordan

I first met Hamilton Jordan at the home of Tom Luce. Tom had recruited Hamilton as one of two political consultants, one a Democrat and the other a Republican, when he was campaign chairman for Ross Perot's presidential campaign in 1992. When Tom and I talked to Hamilton, he told a colorful story about how he found his way in life.

"I grew up in a small town in South Georgia," he said. "It was a wonderful family; didn't want for anything. My father had grown up in the Depression, and he was the richest kid in Macon, Georgia. He had a car when he was twelve years old. His father was president of the bank, but then the Depression came along and they lost everything. The stock market crashed, my grandfather died of a heart attack, and my father went from being the richest kid in town to selling coffee door-to-door to put himself and his brother and sister through college.

"The reason I'm telling you this," Jordan said, "is that my father was a people person and a great salesman. When he got out of the service, he went into the life insurance business. I realized as I grew older that my father had been the number-one salesman in the country in terms of individual sales, but he never built an agency of his own. He never had teams of people working for him.

"I eventually came to understand that he had that old Depression mentality. *What happens,* he would think, *if I get a bunch of agents working for me, and the stock market crashes again?* My dad was the most risk-averse fellow I ever met, so he worked himself to death selling life insurance, one policy at a time. I saw him work nights and weekends. He was very good at it, but for all his hard work, his little agency was always down at the bottom.

"My mother, on the other hand, was much more driven," he said. "She was always pushing Dad to think bigger and to try more things. That was the only tension in their relationship. He didn't realize how important his work was to who he was, so he retired when he was in his early sixties and died of cancer two years later. He was just miserable from the time he stopped working, and I think that had an effect on him."

"That's very interesting," I said, "and sad at the same time. But where are you in that story? Are you more like your mom or your dad?"

"Well, to be honest," he said, "I'm not sure I'd say either one. I've had a sort of Forrest Gump kind of life. It seems like I've just happened onto so much stuff. In fact, I'm going to write a book about that one of these days, because it's so unusual.

"I wore braces on my legs for the first five years of my life," Hamilton continued. "I was pigeon-toed, so I looked like Forrest Gump with those big, clunky braces. Later I went into the service. Actually I volunteered, which was a crazy thing to do, and I was sent to Vietnam. That was a pretty seminal experience. But all my life I've met the most interesting people and ended up in the strangest places, and it was nothing I could have planned or predicted."

Hamilton said it sometimes seemed as if he was finding his way through life by trial and error—in some cases more error than anything else. "I've just happened onto a lot of stuff," he said. "And when I got into politics, it was certainly not the usual way that happens. After I got out of the Army I started working for Jimmy Carter. My job was to come up with campaign strategies that were practical and realistic. Along the way I became pretty good at visualizing and implementing strategies designed to put Carter in the governor's mansion.

"As the campaign manager, I had to worry about the money, the schedule, the media, and all of that. Somehow I managed to get Carter elected as governor of Georgia, and then when he was a long-shot underdog in the race for president, we won again.

"It wasn't because I was the best person; it was almost by default. When I served as Carter's top staff guy in Atlanta, I was just twenty-five. By the time I was named chief of staff in the White House, I was thirty-one. As you can see, those victories weren't based on a lot of political experience, but more on hard work and the right combination of circumstances in the country at the time."

"So there you were, thirty-one, a veteran, and at the top of your game," I said. "You must have been excited about all that."

"You know, people talk about how glamorous it is to work in the White House," he said, "but it isn't very glamorous. Everybody wants something. You get all these calls and letters, and people are always coming to visit you. But they're not coming to tell you that you're doing a good job; they all want something. And most of them want something they don't deserve. They want to be ambassador, or they want to be a federal judge, or they want some kind of benefit from the government.

"We got thrown out in 1980. Unlike most people in Washington, who see the president as a vehicle to get what they want, my commitment was to stand by Carter, and when that was over, it was over for me."

"What did you do after you left the White House?" I asked.

"I went home to Georgia and wrote a book about the hostage crisis. It was on the bestseller list, so I got all kinds of exposure, but it didn't make me a wealthy man. Then I just kept working out of my house and doing different kinds of gigs, pretty much a solo practitioner. And then I was diagnosed with cancer in 1985. Not too long after that, a search firm called and asked if I'd like to work with professional tennis. That sounded interesting, so I spent three years basically reorganizing the men's tennis tour. Unfortunately, all I really did was make a bunch of rich jerks richer, and nobody ever said, 'Thank you.' I was successful, but it didn't feel very good.

"After that," he said, "I took some time off, and then I met Tom Luce and got involved in the Perot campaign."

"That's right," Tom said. "And the first time I approached Hamilton to come and work with us, he said he would do it on one condition. He said, 'If lightning strikes and Ross Perot is elected president, I'll never step foot in the District of Columbia. Period, paragraph, under no circumstances. And I want you to know that up front, and agree to it.'"

In Hamilton's Forrest Gumpish bumping around from job to job, he learned enough about himself to know that he did not want to play the political game again. Though the prestige and money were great, he had found the boundary where he had to say no. The backroom deceptions and hidden agendas were no longer for him.

"You have had a pretty amazing ride," I said, "and I can understand why you wouldn't want to go back into the meat grinder in Washington. That was tough duty. But what occupies your time these days?"

"Since '92, I've just continued to pursue different kind of gigs—strategic planning and the like. I've invested in different start-up companies where I've helped them raise money or develop a strategic plan, and I've really learned a lot along the way."

"He's one of the most strategic thinkers I've ever dealt with," Tom said.

"Thanks, Tom," Hamilton said, "but I think my gift is knowing how to get people to do things. I'm a leader in that sense, and that's really what I enjoy doing. I've learned over time that the less I know about the subject matter, the more interesting it is to me. Somebody approaches me and says, 'We want you to help us figure out how to run a campaign for president or for governor of Oregon,' and that's not really interesting to me.

"But if somebody comes to me with a totally new subject that forces me to learn something fresh and different, that's exciting to me. For the last six or eight years, I've become involved in biotech companies. Some of them have a cancer focus, which is of personal interest to me, of course. What I do is sell the board on issues, get options on warrants, sometimes invest a little money, and help these guys make their companies function more effectively."

During our conversation, Jordan often referred to the way he always seemed just to stumble into things. He failed a lot, he said, but I couldn't help but notice that he always "failed forward," as my friend John Maxwell puts it. And he always got up and headed back into the fight to use the special abilities he had been given to work with. Along the way he's discovered who he is—a strategic thinker and a people motivator—and who he isn't—a politician. And he's learned how to say yes to the one and no to the other.

Focus, Focus, Focus

Several years ago, Jim Collins challenged me and a few others to create a "stop doing" list. He said that saying no was one of the pivotal variables his research team found in "Built to Last" companies. That was an incredibly difficult and painful exercise for me to complete because I am so opportunity focused. My instinctive response is always to build up a bigger and bigger bank of projects to work on.

Collins's subsequent best seller begins with the line, "Good is the enemy of great." For me that means my saying yes to a variety of "good" projects may be the greatest obstacle to allocating my (even for me) scarce resources to something greater.

Jesus said in the Sermon on the Mount, "Let your yes be yes and your no be no." He had just three years to accomplish his mission, and to do that he had to say no to a lot of things.

I began this chapter with Southwest Airlines. It's worth noting that since the time of Orville and Wilbur Wright, cumulatively, the airline industry has never made a profit. Only one carrier has beaten the odds, running a money-making operation year after year. Their secret? Most of it is having the discipline to say no.

Southwest Airlines's market capitalization is greater than all other major carriers combined. They're the only airline to be profitable since 9/11. They stick to their knitting, and they know how to keep their eye on what really matters, putting the interests of their people and their customers first, and saying no to everything else. It all comes back to executing their two word mission, "Low Fares." Their effectiveness is due in large measure to the things they *don't* do. The same is true for Lloyd Reeb and Tom Tierney.

Like the slogan says, "Just say *no!*""

It's about Giving and Receiving a Blessing

ASSURANCE OF FAITH IS NEVER GAINED BY RESERVE BUT ONLY BY ABANDON-
MENT. IN THE MATTER OF HUMAN LOVE IT IS A GREAT EMANCIPATION TO HAVE
IT EXPRESSED; THERE MAY BE INTUITIONS OF THE LOVE, BUT THE REALIZATION
OF IT IS NOT OURS UNTIL IT IS EXPRESSED. MORALLY AND SPIRITUALLY WE
LIVE, AS IT WERE, IN SECTIONS, AND THE DOOR FROM ONE SECTION TO
ANOTHER IS BY MEANS OF WORDS, AND UNTIL WE SAY THE RIGHT WORD THE
DOOR WILL NOT OPEN.
— OSWALD CHAMBERS

Sometimes just a few words can make all the difference. In the case of
Stephen L. Carter, just three words gave him the shove he needed to go
ahead. Listen to this description from a *New Yorker* magazine profile of the
well-known author:

> When Stephen Carter, who is the William Nelson Cromwell
> Professor at Yale Law School, was in eighth grade, . . . his his-
> tory teacher, Mrs. Ahlquist, made a comment that helped
> to change his life. "She said, 'You're pretty smart,'" Carter told
> me recently. "I had never thought of myself that way before.
> I had always been an ordinary student, and I had not stood
> out in class, academically."

A blessing can change a life. It changed mine. Looking back on my life
I find two people who gave me a blessing and believed in me. My mother
gave me the blessing I needed for Life I, and Peter Drucker gave me the

blessing I needed for Life II. My mother used to introduce me as "the world's greatest left end" when I was playing football in high school. I knew differently. I played behind an all-state left end through my junior year, which was the year Tyler High School played in the Texas state championship. I started only in my senior year. But the fact that somebody on earth believed in me, whether strictly rational or not, made all the difference in boosting my fledgling confidence. My mom told me over and over that I would succeed in business too.

Who has told you, "You can do that!" We naturally think of our parents, but for one reason or another, they may not be the ones who encouraged us most. My dad died unexpectedly when I was in the fifth grade, so I missed his blessing. But I got a blessing for my Life II from the person I most respect on earth: Peter Drucker.

Many people use the term *mentor* to indicate an ongoing relationship. But for me, the idea of receiving a blessing is richer and more powerful. It reminds me of Abraham giving his blessing to Isaac in the Old Testament, of Isaac giving his blessing to Jacob, and Jacob blessing his son, Joseph. Those blessings conveyed not only approval but legitimacy.

Peter Drucker's blessing was (and still is) the encouragement that allowed me to break free of the pull of gravity that came from living in a relatively small Texas town. I was always ambitious, at first for success, now even more for significance. But Peter was the one who said, "You can do it, Bob. You *can* realize that dream." His affirmation of my legitimacy has meant more to me than advanced academic degrees or election to public office.

With his acute powers of observing the futurity of present events, Peter "sees" a future which I in turn am able to see after he opens the portals. Then I embark on an experiment to see whether the idea proves to be real. I remember the words of one person who introduced me at an event, saying, "Bob Buford will bet on a blank piece of paper." It may have appeared that way to my introducer, but to me the confidence to go ahead without all the facts and analysis has often been based on the knowledge and perspective that were behind Peter's blessing and his authority in my life.

First you must "see" it. Then you can do it. Peter helps me to "see."

Karl Popper, the noted philosopher of science, said that science doesn't proceed through observation confirmed by verification; rather, it proceeds through wild, overarching conjectures that generalize "beyond the data" but are always sharpened by interaction with others.[1] Who sharpens your "wild conjectures"? Who has given your implausible idea a blessing? Who has said to your dream, "Go for it"? Who cheerleads for you? And even more important, for whom do *you* cheerlead?

First Ideas, Then a Blessing, Then Results

One of the great opportunities of Life II is to be a cheerleader for a younger person, or even a peer—to bless their plans, to give them legitimacy. I expect when I look back on my life one day, I'll find that encouraging others has been the most important thing I've done in Life II. Peter Drucker says his most important contribution will have been to help a few people realize their ideas.

Among the pathfinders I talked to during my interview odyssey are a number of men and women who have demonstrated by their lives and examples that they understand this concept. Wilson Goode gives a much-needed blessing to kids in Philadelphia whose fathers are in prison. Roger Staubach received a blessing in football from Tom Landry and in real estate from Henry Miller. Millard Fuller got a blessing from Clarence Jordan. Ali Hanna got a blessing from Nicky Gumbel, who in turn got a blessing from the fifteen-years-older Sandy Miller, who was his cofounder in the Alpha Course. Ken Blanchard got a blessing from a group of YPO members who heard him speak, encouraged him to leave his college professorship, and to turn his "One Minute Manager" ideas into a training company. These are blessings that just keep on giving.

At sixty-five, Merle Smith, who has been managing companies all his life, knows what he wants to accomplish in Life II. He says, "I want to help people get to a better place than where they were before." He's been doing that formally for nearly a decade now, but I suspect he's been doing it informally for much longer. When he began making halftime adjustments, he told me, he went from "running the business" to "guiding the business," which seemed consistent with his desire to mentor others, to help them become more self-sufficient and confident in their work.

"In 1994," Merle told me, "I went to a Promise Keepers event and took both of my sons with me. Howard Hendricks was speaking that day, and

MERLE SMITH

he used a phrase that hit me like a rock. He said, 'Every man needs a Paul, a Barnabas, and a Timothy in his life.' They need an older, wiser man like Paul, who doesn't have all the answers, but who has been on the planet longer and can help find them. Everybody needs a peer, like Barnabas, who can look them in the eye and say, 'You're screwing up! You know it; I know it; so get your act together!' And, finally, everybody needs a Timothy in their life, a younger man they can bring along and help to grow. That idea had a huge impact on me. Now, I don't think most men can mentor their own sons, because they're too close. They can teach and encourage their sons, but they can help other men in a more objective way."

"That's a great perspective," I said. "So how did you respond to Howard's challenge?"

He answered, "After I got home I ran into a couple of guys I knew, young guys, and I asked them to meet me for lunch one day. So we got together and just chatted about things. Then as we were getting up to go, I asked them, 'Would you like to do this again?' They both said yes, and that was the beginning. Since 1994 I guess I've met with a dozen or so young fellows on a regular basis—guys generally around thirty-five to forty-five—and I've tried to be an encourager for them."

"What do you do for them?" I asked.

"I just want to be there for them," Merle said.

"You mean, just let them talk?"

"Yes," he said. "Let them talk, and give advice when they ask for it. We talk about marriage, jobs, what they're going to do with the rest of their lives, and things like that."

"Do you enjoy that?" I asked.

"Oh, yes," he said, "I'm sixty-five going on thirty-three! The Lord could take me tomorrow, but that would be fine by me. But while I've still got this life, I want to use it, and this is something I really enjoy. It's not just sitting on boards, which I'm still doing with a few nonprofits, but being actively involved in things that are really satisfying."

"Why do you say that serving on boards is less satisfying?" I asked.

"Well, the people on these boards have hearts of gold," he said. "Nonprofits are great at ministering to people's needs, but the fact is, they're not always well-organized and they don't really like interference from board members. Boards spend all their time raising money and giving it to people who aren't good at business. It's important work, and I'll continue doing it, but it's not the same as being a blessing to another person."

"What do those personal relationships do for you?" I asked.

"Nothing except the pleasure I get from knowing individuals and seeing the little changes in their lives. It makes me feel as if I'm doing something worthwhile. I don't get paid for it, and I'm not looking for gratification, but I know I can hold them accountable. I also encourage them to get into accountability groups with other guys their own age."

Then I asked him, "Merle, what's your view of retirement?"

"I don't even think about that," he said. "It's not biblical. I have friends my age who play golf, volunteer for charities, or they just watch television and go out to dinner, and I don't understand it. You might as well get a gun and shoot yourself if that's all there is."

"What do you see in the lives of your friends who are retired?" I asked.

"I see very unhappy people," he said. "For the most part, they don't know what to do with themselves, and some of them are just too lazy to do anything about it. It's not my idea of success."

RETHINKING THE IDEA OF SUCCESS

Earl Palmer, seventy-one, who is a well-known Bible teacher from Microsoft country (Seattle), told me he's more interested in building relationships today than he ever was in his younger years. And he's especially excited about his relationships with young people who are on the cutting edge of the Internet world. "Many of the ways these young people found success," he told me, "have just evaporated before their eyes. When the tech bubble finally burst, some of the biggest companies in the business went through meltdown. On top of that, all kinds of insider trading and shoddy accounting magnified the nightmare for them.

EARL PALMER

"But I've found," Earl went on, "that this gives them a great opportunity for rethinking the whole idea of success. Three words are taking on new meaning for these guys: honesty, durability, and significance. Those are the things that really matter. You're the man who gave people a new way to look at halftime, Bob. I once told an audience that the point you were making in that first book was that *nobody remembers the halftime score;* where you stand at the end of the game is what really matters."

"I like that!" I said. "But I think you're the one who really originated that phrase."

"Okay, but I was speaking about your book. I said that you realized you wanted your life to count in terms of larger goals, and not just your financial success. You wanted to leave a durable legacy of integrity, an investment in hope. So you began searching for significance, which is not just about career choices but about using the talents and gifts you've been given for a greater purpose."

"That's right," I said. "Going through that process changed the way I keep score."

"That was exactly my point. Significance has caring written all over it. And significance happens when we enable those around us to discover their own significance."

"Well said. But what about these young entrepreneurs you've met?" I asked. "How are they dealing with the changes they've had to endure the past few years?"

"From the outside," he said, "it's not a pretty picture. Where is the hope for a better tomorrow that basically vanished when leaders in business, government, and religion stumbled into the dead-end streets of moral and ethical failure? That's what they need to know. The truth is, hope is given one day at a time. But we can only see it if we pause at halftime and decide to play for more important goals. And we find balance when we discover goals of honest and durable significance in the second half of the game."

"But do you think these young hotshots are ready for that message?"

"If you ask me to describe this young generation," he said, "I'd have to say they want to be instantly significant, which is the downside. In Seattle where I live, our churches are full of these young Microsoft types, and they're very impatient. They don't want to wait long for anything. But they're really on the cutting edge, and even as I fear for them, I really admire them."

"Sounds like you're talking to a lot of thirty- and forty-somethings," I said.

"Yes, a surprising number are showing up in church now, looking for something deeper and longer-lasting than what they found out there. They're restless. They want to make sure their lives are significant now, so I encourage them in finding that."

"And what about retirement?" I asked him. "Is that in the picture?"

"Not on your life!" he said. "Everybody around me is trying it, but I'm not. I'm in good health, the church wants me, and I'm doing what I like to do. My rule of thumb is, as long as I'm healthy, my mind is clear, I'm enjoying what I'm doing—and as long as my family is enjoying what I'm doing, I would add—I'll keep on going. And as long as I'm helping the young people around me to keep on growing, that's my reward."

Obviously, Earl Palmer is both giving and receiving a blessing.

Knowing Your Purpose

Howard Hendricks is a distinguished professor and lecturer who has influenced an entire generation of pastors and teachers. He is chairman of the Center for Christian Leadership at Dallas Theological Seminary and an in-demand conference speaker. In addition, he serves on several ministry boards and has written such books as *Living by the Book*, *As Iron Sharpens Iron*, and many others.

Because of his knowledge of Scripture, I asked Howard what the Bible teaches about finishing well. "I think it teaches a great deal," he said, "and I think it fleshes it out very well. But it's brutally honest also. A study conducted at Fuller Seminary asked the same question. They looked at one hundred people in the Bible about whom we have adequate data to evaluate how they finished. The conclusion? Only about a third of them finished well. Most of them failed in the last half of their life, which I think is rather significant."

"That is amazing," I said. "Why didn't they finish well?"

HOWARD HENDRICKS

"The thing that surfaced over and over," he said, "was a failure, not in their knowledge of Scripture but in failing to apply Scripture in their lives. It was the feeling that because they knew the Word, they were living it, which was as untrue for them as it is for us. Another reason was a failure to have an accountability group. Twice in Hebrews 13 we are told to obey those who have authority over us because they care for our soul. The point is that there has to be somebody to ask the significant questions, to hold us accountable. And that was the message that came back time and time again."

"What about those who did finish well?" I asked. "What traits would characterize them?"

"For one thing, they continued to learn. As long as you live, you learn. If you stop learning today, you'll stop growing tomorrow. I find that a lot of older people have thrown in the towel. They feel they've made their contribution, and they decide just to let the younger people carry on. That's really risky."

"So they think their learning is in their past?" I said.

"That's correct, and their achievements are in the past. They fail to realize that there's a difference between their *life* line and their *purpose* line. Because when the purpose line begins to drop off, it's just a matter of time before the life line drops off too."

"When you say life line," I asked, "do you mean your physical life line?"

"Yes, absolutely. The average person dies between two and seven years after retirement, and it's simply because they've lost their purpose in life. For most of them, their purpose was wrapped up in their work, and once they're no longer working they feel they have no meaning in their lives. They retire *from* something rather than *to* something. So the best way is to move to something with purpose that just keeps going right up to the end.

That way, as Paul says it, you cross the finish line running and not staggering."

"It sounds like this has a lot to do with calling, as well," I said.

"Yes, that's right," he said, "but with one important distinction. There's a difference between your calling and your career. *Your career is what you're paid to do; your calling is what you're made to do.* A person with a calling is a person who has purpose and meaning that will not end with the termination of a job. Those who are called will go and find new directions by virtue of how they're wired by God and what they're called to do."

"What about you, Howard?" I said. "What is it that gives you the most satisfaction?"

"I've done a lot of things in my life," he said, "but only one thing gives me ultimate satisfaction, and that's teaching. If I stop teaching I lose the reason for which I was put on the planet. Every now and then somebody introduces me and says, 'Howard has been teaching for fifty-three years,' and the audience either applauds or gasps. But this is what I was born to do. As long as I've got health, and particularly mental health, then I can perform at my level of expectation and I'm not going to stop. If the seminary decides it's time for me to move on, I'll just go teach in another venue. It may be mentoring or coaching or something else, but I'll spend the rest of my life teaching."

"If you think of the people who have blessed your life," I said, "who would stand out as an example of finishing well?"

"Well, I'd have to mention Billy Graham and my good friend Ted Engstrom, who headed World Vision. But Coach Tom Landry stands out too, as somebody who I think played and finished the game of life very well."

"Most of us know Tom Landry from the sidelines," I said. "But you knew him personally. What most impressed you about him?"

"He was a guy who never threw in the towel," Howard said. "He never quit."

"I wonder what was going through his mind when the Cowboys let him go after so much success."

"He came to the conclusion that it was a God thing," Howard answered. "It was God's way of saying, 'I'm through with you as far as football is concerned, Tom. But I've got a lot more for you to do.' So he spent an incredible amount of time and energy with the Fellowship of Christian Athletes, going around sharing his passion for reaching the next generation. It wasn't until he was struck down with cancer that he finally had to quit, but right up to the end he was forthright in his influence on these young men."

"So he just changed his venue," I said, "from coaching on the sidelines to touching people's lives in more personal ways."

"Right, and coaching coaches was his great passion. Somebody once calculated that a coach will impact, on average, something like 2,500 kids through their careers. Just imagine the kind of impact someone like Tom Landry must have had during his lifetime."

Howard was right. Tom Landry passed on tremendous blessings to an untold number of young people. His life was successful by every possible measure, not only on the football field but in terms of fulfillment as well.

"Is fulfillment connected to success?" I asked.

"I think it is," he answered. "I've done a lot of things, but I don't get the fulfillment from any of them that I get from teaching—from building value into the lives of other people, many of whom will go way beyond anything I've been able to do. That's my greatest joy; that's my greatest fulfillment."

"Sounds like you don't plan to change any of that either," I said.

"No," he said. "I'm 79 now, so I figure I've got another ten or so years to live, depending on God's plan for me."

"Some people have already given up by your age," I said, "but I'm glad to know that you're still going strong."

"Yes, I see people who give up too early," he said. "Even if they don't die physically, some of them seem to just die on the inside. That's not for me. My prayer is, 'Lord, help me not to die before I die.'"

CALM IN THE MIDST OF CHAOS

Some of the people I interviewed were just at the threshold of their Life II journey, looking down the road and planning their first steps. John Snyder is one of these men. He is venturing forward with plans not yet in sharp focus, but he's nevertheless in motion. John is a handsome sixty-one-year-old. Quiet, thoughtful, and deliberate, he's an island of calm in the midst of a turbulent business and family situation. I've known John for fifteen years through the World Presidents Organization, and I have come to admire his skill as a businessman in the always-tumultuous oil business. Despite pressures of all kinds and from all sides, he knows how to focus on his strengths and keep on going. He made a fortune during Life I by taking long shots; now, in Life II he's looking for a bigger challenge.

JOHN SNYDER

So I asked him, "What have you carried with you from your experience in the oil business in the first half of your life?"

"Well, the oil business is deal-oriented," he said. "It's about putting people, plans, and real estate together, and that's a process I've worked in most of my life. Maybe God put me in this business to show me how to do that. What I'm really looking for now is what Sir John Templeton calls a 'noble cause,' and I'm hopeful that it might be in the form of a shared dream that everybody in my family can participate in."

"Is this going to be another long shot," I asked, "like the ones you've tackled in the oil business?"

"Maybe so," he said. "That's characteristic of the things I tend to tackle. I'd like to find something big enough that it's not necessarily going to be done in my lifetime, though it conceivably could be done if I can get the process under way. You can see that's not a slam dunk. And I'm also working on establishing a family association in which my family will work together after I'm gone, perhaps for generations."

Part of the complication for John's new undertaking is a family that is divided in many ways. "I have three sons," he said, "and I'm proceeding on the assumption that they're all going to have children. But right now none of them actually has children, and there's a chance that only one may do so. One son is in prison, another has a homosexual relationship, and one did just get married and they'd like to have two kids."

"Your main goal, as you've told me before," I said, "is to have a family foundation where the whole family can make a difference in the lives of others. What's behind that?"

"I think it's driven by wanting my life to have mattered in some way," he said. "That's what's behind the 'noble cause.' If this family association succeeds, it has the potential to help every one of my heirs be more productive, have a happier life, and contribute more to society. Just the process of planning it has been wonderful. We have a family meeting every six months so we can communicate a little better, and we've had more closeness from those meetings than we've ever had before. Two of my sons have been participating, and that's been great.

"You know, Bob, the Lord's blessed me with more wealth than I really deserved, and a lot of other things I didn't deserve as well. I look at the money now as a tool to help the family be a productive part of society, to make the world a better place, which I think is a nice way to look at it."

In setting up his family foundation, John has found a way to say to his sons, "I am going to love you and I want us to work together. My love is not conditional on our sharing all the same values. It is a choice I have made."

"Finishing well for you," I said, "would have to include getting this family trust or foundation set up."

"Yes, it's getting the family association developed and seasoned to the point that it can go on without me. The financial side is already set up. We have established a mission and a vision, but it still needs development."

"Finishing well is really a joint project for you and your family," I said.

"Yes, family is still my main concern," he said. "My dad committed suicide when I was 20. He was 52 at the time; however, I kind of have a feeling that if I finish well, he'll sort of be finishing well vicariously through me. My mother is still living, and I would say she's finishing well. But when I say I want the family to be part of this, I mean getting the whole family involved in something that will mean something. It may be a long shot, but that's what I'm after."

CHAPTER ELEVEN

It's about the Power of New Purpose

THE QUALITY OF LIFE DOES NOT DEPEND ON HAPPINESS ALONE, BUT ALSO ON WHAT ONE DOES TO BE HAPPY. IF ONE FAILS TO DEVELOP GOALS THAT GIVE MEANING TO ONE'S EXISTENCE, IF ONE DOES NOT USE THE MIND TO ITS FULLEST, THEN GOOD FEELINGS FULFILL JUST A FRACTION OF THE POTENTIAL WE POSSESS. A PERSON WHO ACHIEVES CONTENTMENT BY WITH-DRAWING FROM THE WORLD TO "CULTIVATE HIS OWN GARDEN," LIKE VOLTAIRE'S "CANDIDE," CANNOT BE SAID TO LEAD AN EXCELLENT LIFE. WITHOUT DREAMS, WITHOUT RISKS, ONLY A TRIVIAL SEMBLANCE OF LIVING CAN BE ACHIEVED. . . .

WITHOUT A CONSISTENT SET OF GOALS, IT IS DIFFICULT TO DEVELOP A COHERENT SELF.

— MIHALY CSIKSZENTMIHALYI,
Finding Flow: The Psychology of Engagement with Everyday Life

WORK IS THE PSYCHOLOGICAL GLUE THAT BINDS A MAN TOGETHER.
— FRED SMITH SR.

Those who make the most of Life II are those who decide they are *not* going to live without purpose in the second half of their lives. The old model for those over 60 was pretty grim: forty years of hard work followed by a period of generally aimless retirement, and death soon after. For a large number of people who take this route, life expectancy after retirement is brief indeed, usually in the single digits.

Obviously, this is not what most of us want for our lives. But if we expect to change the scenario, we have to find a better way. That's what the journey of Life II is all about. The lesson I've learned from men and women who are making the most of "halftime and beyond" is that there is a better way, and it is to *repurpose* ourselves for a more fulfilling life before we come to the end of the curve.

In repurposing, you've found what's in the box—your core—and you employ your skills to express your core in action. But along the way you find that your Life I purpose is not adequate for finishing well, and you change it. You adopt a new purpose—one through which you can still express your core values and employ your native skills. That's repurposing.

A turning point in my own life was a conversation I had twenty years ago with Michael Kami, one of this country's top strategic planners. As I've related in my previous books, I made an appointment with Mike to explore my own halftime plans. I wanted to get his professional advice about some of the options I was examining. During the course of the conversation, Mike asked me to describe my basic interests and motivations, so I began telling him about all the things that interested me. But suddenly Mike stopped me in midsentence and asked a question that changed my life— "What's in the box?"

The question took me by surprise. I didn't get it at first. *In the box?* What does that mean? So I asked, "What do you mean by that, Mike?"

"What's central to your life at this point?" Mike said. "If there were only room for one thing in your life, what would it be?" He took a pencil and sketched out a small square on a sheet of paper and said, "From what you're telling me, Bob, there are two things at the top of your list of priorities, your religious faith and your career." Mike indicated that the shorthand for that was a dollar sign and a cross. And he pointed at the box and said, "Before I can help you decide how to focus your interests, you have to decide: What's in the box?"

Would it be the dollar sign or the cross? Suddenly I knew I had a choice to make.

Now and then, in the midst of life's complexities, we come to a point where the options are limited and clear. This was one of those moments. What would it be for me—more money, more success, or more energy transferred to the calling I sensed so strongly? I considered those two options for a minute or so—which seemed like an eternity—and then I said,

"Well, if you put it that way, it's the cross." And then I reached over to pencil a cross into Mike's box.

That one decision helped to frame everything I've done since that day. It wasn't that the small cross indicated that the work I felt called to do, to serve God, was my only loyalty in Life II. There were also family, customers, employees, recreation, and the like, but that little cross has designated the *primary loyalty* for my life between then and now. I also came to see that this same issue of "What now? What next?" confronts many others who come to this point in their lives, and that's what led to the writing of *Halftime*.

So my question now is: *What's in your box?* Those who have the most meaningful lives are those who have considered their options and gotten some clarity about their purpose in life. They have decided what they wanted to be at the heart and soul of their existence. A related question is *What do you want to be remembered for?* That's the question we really need to ask ourselves when we begin to focus on Life II.

LIFE-CHANGING CHOICES

Ali Hanna, who has clearly found his way in Life II, was born in Belfast, Northern Ireland, where he grew up in a middle-class home. His father ran his own electrical business, but as Ali told me, he was inattentive when it came to doing things around his own house. "It's funny," Ali said. "My father was an electrical engineer, but in our house the light switches never had cover plates on them because my father never got around to finishing the job."

"Sounds like the old saying, 'The shoemaker's children have no shoes,'" I said. "In this case, the electrician's children had no light-switch covers!"

"Yes, the old saying's true!" Ali said, with a laugh. "Many times as a little guy I reached for the switch in the hall and got an electric shock."

"But you were a good student," I said, "and one day you decided you were going to do things differently and become a scientist. What happened then?"

"Well, I graduated from Queen's University, Belfast, in 1968," Ali said. "I got my degree in physics, and then went on for a Ph.D. in nuclear physics at the Rutherford High Energy Laboratory in England. I spent four years doing that, but by the time I finished my education, I realized that as a physicist, I couldn't live in the style to which I wanted to become accus-

ALI HANNA

tomed. I wanted to make a lot of money, so I decided I'd better go into business."

"How do you go from nuclear physics to the world of business?" I asked.

"Business school," he said. "I was admitted to Harvard and finished an MBA there in 1974. After graduation I was hired by the consulting firm of McKinsey & Company in New York. I was planning to go back to McKinsey's London office, but by that time I was engaged to Nancy, who's a New Yorker. So I asked to stay in Manhattan for a couple months until we got married, and then we'd go to London."

McKinsey & Company is the kind of organization that can pay talented business-school grads top starting salaries, with the prospect of big bonuses down the line. And since Ali's main concern at that point was making money, he felt he was in the right job. If you had posed the question "What's in the box?" to Ali at that time, the answer would have been "Making a lot more money than a physicist could earn." Apparently his choices paid off, because Ali was soon a rising star in a group of managing partners.

"You never did make the move to London. Why not?" I asked.

"In the course of one project, someone said, 'You know, you could stay in New York if you wanted to.' And I thought, *Really? That might be good.* So I decided to stay in New York, much to Nancy's disappointment, by the way. I ended up staying in New York for twenty-three years, during which time I did studies for large corporations on strategy, marketing, operations, organization, and cost reduction, most of it in aerospace and telecommunications."

"So the work you were doing was next door to physics," I said.

"Yes," he said. "It was a great mixture of academia, which I'd originally set out to conquer, and the practical world of business. It was an amazing range, really, from the ultratheoretical to the reasonably practical. But by

1997 I felt that I'd done about as much as I could, so I announced to McKinsey that I was going to retire."

"What age were you then?" I asked.

"I was fifty-two," he said. "I really enjoyed consulting, but there are few consultants at McKinsey over fifty. We used to say it's not a dog-eat-dog organization; it's a dog-eat-old-dog organization. After a while the intensity, the travel, and the need to stay current with the latest in the field is just more than you want to do. And as you get older, the overhead involved in just keeping your basic life going keeps getting higher. You go from one house to two; some guys go from one wife to two; you go from one kid to three, and one day the kids are suddenly in college. And instead of coming home in tears, they come home in ambulances. So the complexity of life is just too wearing for most to go on much past fifty."

Ali was serious about his work, and his wife, Nancy, was equally serious about her religious life. She went to seminary and was ordained. She's currently a priest at St. Bartholomew's Church in Manhattan, at the corner of Park Avenue and 50th Street, which is right in the middle of some of the world's most expensive real estate.

Ali would drive Nancy to church, but he usually didn't go inside. "I would just sit outside in the car reading *The New York Times*," he said. "But one Sunday somebody came out and tapped on the glass and said, 'You know, Mr. Hanna, you can come inside; it will be okay.' So I went in, but I sat at the back. And as soon as services were over, I ran back to the car. I was desperately afraid that somebody would speak to me. Then one Sunday, they said, 'You know, you can take communion,' so I took communion."

Having grown up in Northern Ireland, Ali wasn't a stranger to the Anglican tradition. He was uncomfortable in the church at first, he told me, but while all this was going on, he happened to get a six-month assignment in London, which led to an instance of what I would call the "sliding doors" phenomenon. If you've seen the movie *Sliding Doors*, which starred Gwyneth Paltrow, you'll know what I mean.

The movie was about a young woman who went to take the subway, and missed her train home. The movie then went on to show not only her life as it was, but how it would have been if she had actually made the first train. If she got on the first train she would have met certain people and encountered one set of circumstances. By getting on a different train she met someone else, and in effect, her destiny was far different. The novelty of the film was that it actually showed both possibilities, one after the other, and you could see what would have or did happen in each case.

The sliding-doors event in Ali Hanna's life occurred during the several months that he and Nancy were staying in England on business. They attended Holy Trinity Brompton Church, a vibrant, nontraditional Anglican church in downtown London. There they encountered a Christian evangelism program called Alpha, which is an outreach to people with an interest in Christianity but who are held back by a lot of questions. On seeing Alpha for the first time, Ali experienced a life-changing epiphany. He discovered what belonged in the box. He said, "Whatever this is, Nancy, we've got to bottle it and take it back to America."

And that's just what they did. Ali and Nancy met with Nicky Gumbel, the developer of Alpha, and discussed taking Alpha back to New York. "If it worked out," Ali said, "I thought I might like to develop some networks and help expand Alpha all across the country."

TRANSFORMATION

Nicky Gumbel developed the Alpha program with another ex-barrister, Sandy Millar. Nicky is now the lead pastor of Holy Trinity Brompton, the Anglican church in London where Ali and Nancy attended while in England. Nicky had graduated from Cambridge and was well-embarked on a career as a lawyer when some sort of sliding-doors phenomenon happened to him. He had a spiritual awakening and was struck by the idea that many people, like him, rejected Christianity because they never truly understood the claims of Scripture. So, with Sandy's help, Nicky shaped the Alpha course to help people of all types examine the tenets of the Christian faith— to ask questions and get practical answers in a nonthreatening environment.

"I can understand your enthusiasm for the program," I said to Ali, "but what happened to your goal of making a lot of money? A ministry program like Alpha won't do that for you. Is this the same guy who gave up a career in nuclear physics because a life in academics didn't pay enough?"

"To be honest," Ali replied, "I didn't process the economics at all. I was so moved by what we had seen at Holy Trinity Brompton that I just went back to McKinsey and said, 'I'm going to leave.' I had an option to sell my stock, so I did that, and I agreed to work with a couple of my clients for a few years until I could transition out of it. And what happened next was that the Alpha work sort of increased and just squeezed out the client work. At the end of two years I just didn't have enough time for client work anymore."

"And you just allowed that transformation to take place?" I asked.

"I was a willing participant in it," he said. "God designed it all, and I never made any decisions. It just happened."

"And were you getting paid by Alpha?" I asked.

"No," he said. "Alpha doesn't pay me. I look at it in this way: I'm a pretty good consultant, and I had a good reputation at McKinsey. So if I ever needed to go back and earn a few dollars I could probably do it. But my problem is that with Alpha, I just don't have time to do consulting anymore."

"Would you say you were responding to a sense of calling," I asked, "or did the work just draw you into it?"

"It was all very organic," he said. "I didn't sit down and do a life plan. I just found myself being drawn into it more and more, until Alpha became my full-time focus."

The first time I visited with Ali in New York, we met at his office at 50th Street and Park Avenue, just around the corner from the Waldorf Astoria Hotel. I'm not sure what I expected. Seeing McKinsey's offices in an elegant high-rise in midtown Manhattan certainly didn't prepare me for what I found at the church. I came in the side door of St. Bartholomew's, around the corner and down a narrow hallway.

The hallway was covered in black-and-white checkerboard linoleum tiles, curling up around the edges. The receptionist sat behind a barrier, the purpose of which I decided was to restrain uninvited guests. This was certainly not the chrome-and-glass ambiance of Ali's former digs. Instead of a silent, smooth-flowing, carpeted-and-paneled elevator, I was loaded onto a rickety freight elevator that rattled up to the third floor, where I met Ali in a room that was obviously a classroom for kindergartners.

On my second trip a few months later, his office had been moved downstairs to the basement—a move downward in every sense of the word. Upstairs there was at least an ancient iron-frame window, but it felt more like the catacombs downstairs. One small air conditioner sat in the transom over the door, and it was leaking. Though not high style, that's how Alpha got started in America. Today Alpha serves more than 7,000 churches in the United States alone, and more than a million people have taken the course in the U.S. They say great things often come from humble beginnings!

Ali and Nancy are two of the happiest people I know. They are powered by purpose. Unlike people I meet in almost any other environment, these folks have a glow about them when they describe what they do. Their faces light up; there's almost an aura about them. They're filled with real enthusiasm.

I had to wonder how a man who abandoned a career in science because he wanted more money could leave a top consulting firm for a job that pays nothing. But, of course, I already knew the answer. The money wasn't what mattered anymore. Money and achievement had been the consuming passion of Ali Hanna's life for many years. He's still as driven a person as you'd ever want to see, but now seeing changed lives is more important to him than any of that.

A couple of years ago I spoke to a Chinese-Canadian pastor in Toronto who had been a successful executive in the corporate world. He'd been working (as he described it) for "stock options and pats on the back." But one day he realized the person giving him the pats on the back wouldn't even be there in six months, and he asked himself why he ever thought those things mattered. He gave up corporate life for ministry and never looked back. When I asked why he did it, he said, "Because it's about changed lives." I've heard that answer so many times in the course of these interviews, it has become a pattern.

THE GIFT OF LEARNING

Randy Best, who is a very young sixty years of age, is a natural-born entrepreneur and has been starting businesses of one kind or another since he was a teenager. He has a passion for testing himself against the limits, especially when it means challenging the status quo. "Almost every venture I've been in," he told me, "involved going against the status quo. I was always trying to fundamentally change the way industry operates. From the very first venture I ever attempted, there was always some significant paradigm shift in the approach I would take."

Over more than twenty years, Randy started dozens of companies. At one point he was involved in the management of twenty-one businesses at the same time. But one day he woke up and said, *Why am I doing this? Why do I have this need to start so many companies and take such risks?* "I suppose a psychiatrist would say that I was constantly testing myself, to compensate in some way," he said. "But I began to think how self-ish I was, always putting my family at risk, always pushing myself to see what my limits were."

RANDY BEST

But Randy told me about something else that impacted his thinking at the time—something that was personally gratifying for me to hear. "I remem-ber being together in Santa Fe where you spoke, Bob," Randy said, "and you described the concepts that you ultimately included in your book *Halftime*. That really started me thinking. That night I decided that what I was doing was foolish. It might have been an interesting test of nerves for a younger man, but over the rest of my life I needed to find some other way to express my need for a challenge.

"Whatever that would be," Randy continued, "I wanted it to be consistent with the ideas you talked about that night. I'm sure those ideas have impacted a lot of people's lives, but they had a profound intellectual impact on me. So I decided that I was going to test myself. I knew I wanted to do it in a social area. And I decided that the best way I could achieve something worthwhile and have a long-term positive impact would be to touch the lives of children."

What really mattered to Randy was touching people's lives where it counted. He had been active in church work and, over a period of time, had helped to organize, plan, build, and fund dozens of new church starts in Mexico. But as he explored other ideas, he thought of his own lifelong struggle with a learning disability.

Randy is dyslexic. To this day, he told me, he has never read an entire book for himself. He has listened to hundreds of tapes, and friends and family (including his mother and his wife) have read books, lessons, and reports to him. But suddenly he realized that his own struggles in that area could be the foundation for a new venture in the field of education. From this emerged the Voyager program that he now heads: an innovative learning initiative that has involved him in public education in a big way.

"My mother was a public school teacher for forty-three years," Randy said. "She started teaching at eighteen, became a principal at twenty-one, and gave her whole life to public education. So I was always around it. I went through public education myself, and it was excellent in my hometown. I realize, however, that this isn't true in most places. And ever since I read the report 'A Nation at Risk,' put together by a blue-ribbon panel of educators back in the early eighties, I knew that something had to be done."

The conclusion of that now-famous study was that American public education was a disaster, tragically flawed in curriculum, pedagogy, teacher preparation, and every other way. The researchers equated the decline in America's schools to an attack on this country by a foreign power. "When I read that," Randy said, "two things came to mind. First, I thought, *Somebody ought to do something about this.* And then I thought, *That person is me.*"

Ready for a new challenge, Randy knew that the goal wasn't making millions of dollars for himself but making a difference in the lives of millions of children. "Fortunately," he said, "this was something I knew I could do. I had a habit of sticking with things even when we were taking on water, and I could see that reforming public education wasn't going to be easy. But I knew that if I got started in this, I would never give up, and that maybe with that kind of determination, and coming at it from a slightly different angle, I could make a difference where others had failed."

The Voyager program, which is designed to prepare public school teachers for their classroom duties and to refocus the curriculum to make sure that kids learn how to read, has been controversial from the start. But it has also been effective, and it is now being adopted by some of the largest and most troubled school districts in the country, including New York City, Philadelphia, Washington, D.C., and others.

"In the beginning," Randy said, "my partner and I decided to limit ourselves to one or two of the biggest issues confronting the schools. If those things could be fundamentally changed, we would gain a foothold to change the whole system. I calculated that we could have as much as an 80 percent impact if we focused on just the top two issues, so that's what we did."

What are those issues? "The first was instructional quality," Randy said. "Poor education isn't the fault of children; it's the fault of adults." He believed that if instructional quality improved dramatically, then learning would improve in all areas. The second issue was to make sure that all children learn to read, and that was a personal matter because of his own experience.

RUNNING WITH ENDURANCE

Today the Voyager program has two affiliates, a higher education division focused on assisting the professional development of in-service teachers, and a reading program written and funded primarily by Randy. The investment of approximately $40 million to date, from his own resources and those of various other investors, has sponsored research exploring how the brain works and how young children learn. In their studies, researchers found that 95 percent of all children who attend public schools are "literacy capable."

"That discovery made a huge impression on me," Randy said. "When I heard that, I said, if 95 percent of our kids are literacy capable, then why in some districts are only about 20 percent actually reading? That's precisely the question Governor George W. Bush asked us at the time. Bush said, 'If 95 percent of our children *can* read, why do fewer than 50 percent of them read?' Well, that's the question Voyager is answering."

If all goes as planned, fully 95 percent of schoolkids will be able read in the next generation. Randy and his colleagues are creating materials to teach teachers how to implement these new programs. "So that's my challenge now," Randy told me. "And if I may say so, we're having a profound impact."

Randy is a great example of a life theme carried over from his business life into his second-half life of new purpose. His entrepreneurial skills were simply transformed from one venue to another, in this case to public education. His new challenge meant going up against trying to change the ingrained nature of an industry. But Randy wasn't looking for an easy job in the first place. He wanted to make a real and lasting difference. Clearly he is succeeding, and America and generations of young children will be the beneficiaries.

At the end of our conversation, I had one more question for Randy. "When I say the word *retirement*, what comes to your mind?"

He smiled and said, "Well, I know what the term means, but—and this is probably unfair—it says to me that you want to live your life completely selfishly. A retired person is just living for himself or herself; that's how I see it. They have put off doing the things they always wanted to do when they were younger, and now they're spending their remaining years satisfying their personal whims and desires. I can't even imagine that for myself. What do you do? You travel? You play golf? I can't even imagine not having a purpose beyond just living out my remaining years in such an aimless, self-indulgent sort of way."

"But," I challenged him, "surely for some people, retirement is a good thing—it's risk aversion, security, going someplace like the golf club where people are paid to cater to you."

"Not even a consideration in my mind," he said with a laugh. "The only way I think you should opt out where you're no longer trying to make a contribution is if you have some physical or mental problem. As long as you're able to do something meaningful, why would you want to go into some kind of holding pattern?"

"It's What Seems to Be at Hand"

As we have discovered in other interviews, a meaningful Life II does not always require an epiphany or a big change of direction. Sometimes people find significant purpose in their original calling and simply amplify and fulfill it throughout their lives by doing the job at hand. Such is the case with Vester Hughes, a nationally known tax lawyer who, along with Tom Luce, whom you've already met, founded the Texas law firm of Hughes & Luce.

Vester was thinking of his own mortality the day we spoke in the inner sanctum of his downtown office. I said, "Vester, you were telling me about a *Wall Street Journal* article this morning reporting that the average life expectancy for men in this country is . . ."

"Seventy-four point four years," he said, tapping his finger on the front page of the *Journal*, "and I will be seventy-five in May, so I've already beat the average. And that's all right by me. I may live another ten or twenty years. Or I may live ten minutes. We never know."

VESTER HUGHES

"In either case," I said, "you can now look back on an incredibly successful career as founder of a law firm and a prominent tax lawyer. Where would you say you've made the greatest contribution?"

"I know what I hope it would be," he said. "Helping other people realize who and what they can be. That ranges typically from helping them pay less taxes to helping them figure out how their financial situation fits in with whatever else they do in life. People tend to trust you when you're working on their taxes, and frequently that allows them to trust you with other things as well, including family problems, personal problems, or whatever. So I think that has been the most important aspect of my work."

"Do you have the sense of vocation or calling about that work?" I asked.

"It seems to me that whatever you do, if it's honorable and worthwhile, is a kind of calling. As you're well aware, Bob, my thought process is fairly short-term. I ask myself, *What am I supposed to do today? And what will contribute the most benefit from what I'm supposed to do today?*"

"You gave me a three-line prayer some time ago that I wrote down and have looked at every morning since. Do you remember that?" I said.

"Yes," he said. "It says, 'Lord, I can't do anything about yesterday, and tomorrow may not come. Let me be your man today.' And that's really the way I look at it. So many people try to live in the past or the future, but we can only live in the present. We'd have a lot less stress in our lives if we could just learn to live one day at a time."

"I imagine you run into a lot of people who don't always buy that logic," I said.

"That's right," he said. "I had been practicing law for several years before I noticed that people who come in to arrange their estate planning were always saying, 'If I die' instead of 'When I die,' as if there was any doubt about what drafting a will is all about."

"Do you ever mention that to your clients?"

"Yes, I do sometimes," he said. "I feel strongly that I don't have a right to decide all these issues for my clients unless they've given all of them some pretty serious thought. My father's theory was that there are three things that all people must decide for themselves. First, they can decide what they do for a living; second, they can decide if they want to marry and who they want to marry; and third, they can decide what their spiritual life is going to be like, or whether they will even have a spiritual life. There may be other things, of course, but I think he was right in seeing these three decisions as foundational to all others. The problem is that a lot of people never stop to think about these things in practical terms."

"You have a well-deserved reputation for being a good counselor," I said, "but it seems to me you have a strong desire to withhold judgment about people—a sense that you're not their judge but their helper."

"I think we're all at our best when we're a helper," he said. "As a lawyer, it's my job to recognize when someone doesn't have certain kinds of knowledge or experience. But my *purpose* is to help them accomplish whatever it is they want. If I make it more difficult for them, I'm not doing my job. In the end, I want to help them decide exactly what it is they want to do."

Vester's purpose has been to help people clarify their decisions on the most important goals in their lives. I said, "You're at a point in your own life where you have a lot of knowledge and experience, and you've used it to help other people. But what would you like to accomplish between now and the time you go to heaven?"

"Whatever the Almighty wants me to do," he said. "And I want to be whatever he wants me to be."

"How do you know what that is?" I said.

"Well, part of it is *what seems to be at hand*. Who needs my help? Who is within the scope of my experience at that time? *I discover what I'm supposed to do by seeing who comes through that door each morning.* I sometimes wonder if I'm doing what the Lord wants me to do each day, but I don't let that immobilize me. I just try to learn from my mistakes and keep on moving."

I concluded by asking, "What does finishing well mean to you?"

"I think finishing well is doing your best to conform to that which is better and giving that which the Creator would have wanted from you. In a way it goes back to what the philosophers called 'enlightened self-interest.' By that I mean doing those things that are in your own best interest but always moderated by a concern for how your interests and actions will affect the people around you."

"Enlightened self-interest, informed by faith in God, seems to be a smart idea," I said.

CHAPTER TWELVE

It's about Repositioning—
The Central Halftime Skill

To everything there is a season,

A time for every purpose under heaven:

A time to be born,

    And a time to die;

A time to plant,

    And a time to pluck what is planted;

A time to kill,

    And a time to heal;

A time to break down,

    And a time to build up;

A time to weep,

    And a time to laugh;

A time to mourn,

    And a time to dance;

A time to cast away stones,

    And a time to gather stones;

A time to embrace,

    And a time to refrain from embracing;

A time to gain,

    And a time to lose;

A time to keep,

    And a time to throw away;

A time to tear,

    And a time to sew;

A time to keep silence,

    And a time to speak;

A time to love,

    And a time to hate;

A time of war,

    And a time of peace.

      — Ecclesiastes 3:1–8 NKJV

Seasons are inevitable. We live our lives in seasons—phases of activity when preparation and inclination meet new opportunities and needs. No phase need be considered permanent. Opportunities change, needs change, and each season wanes as a new one begins. Some people move through life's seasons purposefully, anticipating the next and preparing for it much as we buy lighter clothes as spring approaches. Others choose to ignore the need for changes that seasons bring, much like one who continues to wear winter jackets into summer. Still others seem overwhelmed by seasons, and like bears, go into hibernation rather than face the next change.

How can you avoid getting trapped permanently in a choice that should have ended in a season? The key is to make use of those first seasons to gain knowledge of your core so that you can reposition yourself for full effectiveness and fulfillment in the second half. As Peter Drucker told me when we talked, "Early in their careers people tend to have a fairly limited time frame of four years or so. They can't visualize what comes after that." When they achieve a measure of success, the time frame expands. "Suddenly they begin to think about options that are twenty, thirty, or more years ahead of them." Imagine how the range of possibilities increases when you add twenty or thirty years to your frame of reference—a whole second adulthood!

The initial steps into a chosen career may be merely a phase, or a season in which you find out what's in the box. Or you may choose to enter a deliberately limited season in which you pursue an activity that you know will have an inevitable end. In either case, your experience creates a frame of reference that reveals a wider horizon, and the smart thing is to reposition yourself to enter the next season. In repositioning, your purpose, your skills, and your core remain the same. You've found what's in the box— your core—and you've found your purpose, and you employ your skills to put your core in action. Yet new opportunities present themselves with each season, meaning you must apply your skills to new projects and in new ways. That's repositioning.

Sometimes repositioning for the next season is a Life II decision. Or it may be a change to readjust your life to your core values. Seasons are variables that differ in each life, but just as surely as spring follows winter, your life will have seasons. The trick is to anticipate them and be ready.

Something That Will Last

I have enjoyed a long-term relationship with Dr. Larry Allums. He is my "personal trainer" in the classic texts of literature and history. Over the past four years, Larry has assigned me a book or play to read every two weeks. Then we discuss the work for a couple of hours. I get half of the work's insights through reading and half from the discussions. It's a wonderful, ongoing adventure.

LARRY ALLUMS

Since 1997, Larry has been director of the Dallas Institute of Humanities and Culture, an academic program now in its third decade in the city, founded by Drs. Donald and Louise Cowan and several former colleagues from the University of Dallas. Prior to this post, Larry was professor of English and a department chair and dean at the University of Mobile. He is a specialist in Southern literature, the classics, and the modern epic, but his intellectual appetite, as I can attest, is wide-ranging.

When I asked Larry for some background on how he came to such a career, he said, "I grew up with a real sense of having a calling. I got that in church from thundering sermons and my religious parents. My mother wanted me to be a preacher. We both prayed about that, but I discovered that my gift was really teaching, not preaching."

"How did you make that discovery?" I asked.

"As a pilot in the Air Force," he replied. "I found that I could teach people to fly with amazing success, and I enjoyed that a lot. I could have had a comfortable life in the Air Force. If security and comfort were what I had wanted, I would have been smarter to stay there. But I saw too many career pilots who flew their ten years and bottomed out. For the next ten or twenty years they'd end up in desk jobs, just waiting for their government pension."

So Larry repositioned himself and entered his next season. He left the Air Force, went to graduate school, got a Ph.D. in literature, and started his teaching career. "Was university life all you expected it to be?" I asked.

"Yes," he answered. "In general I think it was. My graduate career was one of the happiest times in my life. I was dog poor, working three jobs to stay in school. I was minister of education at a Baptist church, drove a taxi, and taught part-time during my grad studies. But I was absolutely delighted to be doing that. Eventually I graduated and was hired by the University of Mobile, and at each step I had a sense that I was headed in the right direction. I believe I was doing what God wanted me to do."

But Larry's call to teach was merely another season in his life. He had one more major change ahead of him before he found his ultimate Life II calling.

"The first half of my life was mostly about teaching," he said. "I knew I'd become a good teacher, but after some twenty years in the university environment, I began to think, *There's got to be something else.* That's ultimately what led me to the Dallas Institute."

Larry felt he'd bumped the ceiling in the Air Force and then again in the university classroom—he'd gone as far as he could go. Now his horizon is much bigger. The Dallas Institute is a one-of-a-kind organization that teaches current movers and shakers the lessons of the classics. It's not cloistered. The learnings, including mine, guide decisions and "Monday morning action" right now in real life. I chose not to sell my company for ten years after studying King Lear!

"You're still teaching," I said, "but now you're also administering a rigorous academic program in an urban environment. What changed?"

"I've been at this six years now," he said, "and what gets me up each morning is the whole prospect of building something that will last beyond my own life. When I was part of a university, I wasn't responsible for the university. I was a cog in a wheel. But today, I have hands-on responsibility for something worthwhile that will live long after I'm gone."

"After being a professor, department chairman, and dean," I said, "I assume you could have stayed on at the university and retired there. What made you change your mind?"

"Frankly," he said, "I saw what happened to too many of my friends when they settled into that life for keeps. You get tenure, which means you can't be fired without a horrendous fuss, and you settle into a routine. But after six or seven years you quit on the job. I could name twenty people that this happened to. They went to classes and showed up for meetings, but they quit publishing, quit exploring new ideas, and basically quit being intellectually alive. Job security, I decided, was not all it was cracked up to be."

"You saw people who would just spend the next forty years on autopilot?" I asked.

"Yes," he said, "and I don't know what happens to people like that. Something inside them just crumbles."

A Series of Overlapping S-Curves

When I think of the seasons that come and go in life, I often picture them as a series of overlapping S-curves. It's always clumsy when you start something new, so the initial direction is not up but down before you build new networks and acquire new habits. When things begin to work, the curve goes up, sometimes for a long while, but inevitably "stuff happens," as it did for Larry. Then it's time to begin going on to the next season. As you will read shortly, Roger Staubach began his parallel career in real estate seven years before he left pro football. It took me eight years 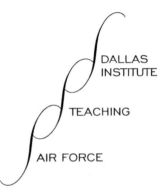 to transfer most of my weight from running a cable television business to the point where I could focus 80 percent of my time on the work of Leadership Network. Larry Allums began his next season while his career as a jet fighter pilot was nearing its end. He began teaching others to fly. Toward the end of his career as a literature professor, he began to function as a dean, and that role qualified him to lead the Dallas Institute.

"There's a natural progression in what you've done, Larry," I said. "But what makes you believe that your new assignment will be any different?"

"For one thing," he replied, "I can see the vitality and excitement in the people I work with. I want to be like Louise Cowan, the dynamic cofounder of the institute, who is as vibrant and intellectually alive at eighty-seven as when she was twenty-seven. I see in her what I suspect you see in Peter Drucker, someone who sets the standard for finishing well."

"Don't you think most people finish well?" I asked with a smile.

"No, not really," Larry said. "That sounds terribly judgmental, I suppose, but based on my experience, most people take the gold watch and just vegetate the last years of their lives. There's a small community on Mobile Bay called Fairhope, where I lived for eight years. It's made up largely of retirees. They've got eighty-eight boutiques down there where you can buy fresh-baked bread, French silks, arts and crafts of every description, and many beautiful things. But some of the most insular people I've ever seen live there. They took the gold watch and the Winnebago and the place on the beach, and now they're just putting in their time, completely cut off from the rest of the world. If that's retirement, I say you can keep it!"

A Practical Game Plan

When I sat down with Hall of Fame quarterback Roger Staubach, it was his ability to position himself for transition from one season to the next that got my attention. He had done a masterful job of developing a parallel

ROGER STAUBACH

career to step into while his first career wound toward its inevitable end. Roger was born in 1942. He was appointed to the U.S. Naval Academy where he was an All-American quarterback and winner of the Heisman Trophy in his junior year. Upon graduation he served as a naval officer for four years, and many people said he could never make it in the pros after that long service commitment.

But as all America knows, Roger proved them wrong. He was drafted as quarterback of the Dallas Cowboys football team and led the entire NFL in passing in 1973, 1978, and 1979. During his sensational career Roger led the Cowboys to seven division, five league, and two Super Bowl championships. In 1979 he had his best year, completing 267 out of 461 passes for 3,586 yards, with twenty-seven touchdown passes and only eleven interceptions. He was elected to the professional football Hall of Fame in 1985, his first year of eligibility.

Roger knew that sports wouldn't be his whole life, so he began preparing for life after football early on. He was being mentored by the legendary Dallas real estate developer Henry S. Miller who, along the way, helped him prepare for the career in commercial real estate that would become Roger's main focus after leaving the game. Rather than simply waiting for the inevitable career-ending injury or the threat of being put up on waivers by the team, as did so many of his fellow athletes, Roger began his second career seven years before he retired from the game in 1980.

"I had a personal vision," Roger told me, "of not being dependent on my old life the rest of my life." Football had made him a good living, and it made him famous, but he knew that playing pro sports was a young man's game. "I did some broadcasting," he said, "and I still do that from time to time, but I didn't want to do it as a profession, and I didn't want to coach. Those are all good things, but I wanted to do something different. I wanted to get my feet wet in business, and the more I learned at the Miller Company, the more I realized this was what I wanted to do."

Glancing around Roger's office I noticed no superstar pictures—pictures celebrating his glory as an athlete. I had been to his home in north Dallas, so I knew how he lived. They have a large, rambling house, but there too, the Staubachs prefer to live in a way that is functional and not pretentious. His Heisman Trophy is at home, not in the office. Roger leads his company through his skill in real estate and his gift for building relationships, and not merely on the basis of celebrity.

The one magazine cover I saw framed in his office was from a real estate journal. Pictures on the wall of his office were all of Roger with people like Michael Jordan, George W. Bush, and megacapitalist Warren Buffett, people whose celebrity is, if anything, greater than his own. There was just one picture of Roger with a group of his old teammates, and they weren't in football uniforms; they were just hanging out being friends.

During our conversation, Roger said that people are always asking him to use his celebrity for some cause or other. He does lend his name to a number of charities, but only when he truly supports their goals. My guess is that Roger could easily have become governor of Texas had he decided to run. He's been asked several times, but he knows what he wants to do and what he doesn't. He won't allow himself to be captured by the appeal of the political limelight. He's been a celebrity, and for many he still is. But leading 1,200 real estate professionals is his game now. "From my point of view," he told me, "politics is mostly about fund-raising. Going to parties every night and raising money for politicians isn't something I feel called to do."

"Financially," Roger told me, "I don't have to work anymore. But I still have work to do growing the business, encouraging the kinds of behavior that contribute to our success, and doing things that I have to do internally to make sure we maintain the kind of trust we need in this business. That's where I'm really trying to preach," he said, "doing our work in ways that help other people work better."

To illustrate his way of thinking, Roger said, "Somewhere I've got a copy of an old poem that says, basically, you don't die from the cold without; you die from the cold within. The poem describes five people sitting around a campfire on a cold night. They all have sticks of wood in their hands, but they have issues—racial, economic, personal. They disagree with each other on just about everything, so they hold back from putting their wood on the fire because they don't want to do anything that might help the other guys.

"The essence of it," he said, "is that they all eventually die, but not from the cold without; they die from the cold within. Their coldness for each other prevented them from putting the wood on the fire that could have saved their lives. I think that's a good object lesson, and in the time I have left, I want to make sure our people don't fall for that trap."

Roger Staubach has accomplished what Peter Drucker calls "repositioning yourself for effectiveness and enjoyment in the second half of life." Roger's life themes, it seems to me, are trust, integrity, and responsibility, the same traits that Roger admired most in his other mentor, Tom Landry. And they are the characteristics that Roger embodies today.

A REBALANCING ACT

Another person I interviewed, Bill Solomon, calls repositioning yourself for the next season "rebalancing your portfolio." Bill Solomon told me he's begun a new season of life, transitioning his companies to management by nonfamily members. "It's part of a transition from ballistic to organic," he says, "reducing the number of people who could make demands on my time." Bill told me he wanted to free himself of the demands of business so he could use his time more in line with the Life II season of his life, pursuing interests that have a longer-range dividend. For a time that meant putting everything else into neutral, so that's just what he did.

BILL SOLOMON

During a long and successful career as CEO of Austin Industries, a company that has built some of the largest structures in the country, Bill was aware that he was putting inordinate focus and energy into his job. "The job was so big," he said, "that everything else often took a backseat." But he was less fulfilled and happy than he wanted to be, so he made up his mind to do something about changing his lifestyle and adjusting his priorities.

"I decided I was going to *rebalance my portfolio*," he said. "I told myself I was going to do it; I acted like I was going to do it; but when I actually tried to do it, I found that *I didn't feel I had permission to do it.*" For a time Bill just went with the status quo, but all his impulses were telling him to get off the treadmill. "I was dealing with all these external issues like ownership transition and management transition," he said, "and feeling a lack of a sense of permission. It didn't take me long to realize *I've got a problem here. This is not an external issue: I need to deal with this problem.* And that," he told me, "is how one thing led to another."

Bill gave himself permission to get off the treadmill and begin the transition to his next season, Life II. "I realized I hadn't paid much attention to my health," he said, "so that became a priority. Peace of mind was something I lacked but really wanted, and attending to that was part of my portfolio rebalancing. I decided to get to a lifestyle where I wasn't always rushing, pushing, and stressing, and one that was more contemplative and peaceful. I knew that to do that I needed to carve out more time, so that was a major part of the portfolio as well."

Austin Industries still does big projects, like building a new terminal at DFW Airport. Bill is involved in a big project of his own, chairing a campaign to raise funds for major improvements in clinical care and several other initiatives at the University of Texas Southwestern Medical School in Dallas. He's also rebalanced his portfolio to enhance his spiritual life. He rises most mornings at 5:30 to spend a time of quiet reflection during which he has written a totally personal credo to think through and shape his beliefs. Faith has always been a factor in Bill's life, but as he told me, "Today my faith is richer than it ever was, but it's more personal and less institutional."

A Guiding Presence

Dr. Pat Thomas is a long-time friend and everybody's favorite doctor in Tyler, Texas. He has "repositioned" himself several times. Fresh out of surgery residency, he spent a difficult year as a combat surgeon in Vietnam. At the end of his tour of duty, he returned to Texas and launched his own surgical practice. After a highly successful practice, he moved into hospital administration, and from there to fundraising for a hospital foundation. At each stage of his journey, Pat told me, he witnessed the hand of providence guiding his steps.

Dr. Pat & Mary Dale Thomas

"Coming out of high school," he said, "I knew I wanted to be either an aeronautical engineer or a surgeon. As it turned out, I ended up studying medicine at SMU. When I look back over my career, I can see the Lord's hand making things happen that were way beyond my scope."

"So you give the Lord the credit for sending you to Vietnam?" I asked.

"Yes, I do. Of course, Lyndon Johnson had a little bit to do with that," he said. "I was working on my residency program at Bellevue Hospital in New York when they started drafting doctors for the Lebanese crisis in the Middle East. The chief of surgery at NYU got me a deferment, but I eventually had to serve, and by that time I was assigned to expand a field hospital in Vietnam that had once been the main hospital for the whole country. We took it from one-hundred- to four-hundred-bed capacity, and I served there for a year."

"That was in the early to midsixties," I said. "You must have seen a lot of action."

"If you've seen the movie *We Were Soldiers*, you'll have some idea just how intense it was. The movie's about the 1st Air Cavalry in the Iadrang Valley, in what turned out to be the first big firefight of the war. It was the first time U.S. forces suffered heavy losses. At one point we had to process seventy-six casualties all at once. My three surgical colleagues and I operated on multiple patients for fifty-four hours straight without leaving the operating room."

"What did you learn from that?" I asked.

"Regardless of the right or wrong of that war," he said, "I knew one thing for certain: I was needed there. I had a job to do, and it was my responsibility to take care of the soldiers that were injured. What I learned is that you go where you're called, when you're called, and you do the best job you can, willingly."

"I've known you long enough to know what going where you're called means to you," I said. "But I seem to recall that your wife, Mary Dale, has had a little to say about where you go too."

"You might say that!" Pat said with a smile. "While in Vietnam I had decided that when I came back I would go to Baylor Hospital and start a new practice in Dallas. In the meantime, Mary Dale had gone to Tyler to look at an opening for a surgeon to replace a physician who had died. I found out about it when she wrote me in Vietnam. She said, 'Pat, you can go to Dallas if you want to, but the kids and I are going to be in Tyler.' She made her point. Again, I think the Lord was working to get me to the right place with the right atmosphere in which to work and live."

"Has your wife had any other life-changing influences on your career?" I asked.

"She has, indeed!" he said. "Back when the U.S. first got involved in Operation Desert Shield and then Desert Storm, the evening news aired an announcement from the Defense Department asking for six hundred military-trained physicians to sign up for six months active duty. So one night I said, 'Mary Dale, I think I'll do that. Our kids are all grown now, and I'm an experienced combat surgeon.'"

"What did she say?" I asked.

"She said, 'They won't take you with your injury.'

'My injury?' I said. 'I don't have an injury.'

And Mary Dale replied, 'You will when I shoot you in the leg!'"

We had a good laugh, and then I said, "I can see that your wife has been looking out for your welfare, but do you also feel a sense of God's will for your life?"

"Very much so," he said. "If you look at all that has happened in my career, you can't help but see it. Had I not gone into the military, I'd probably still be in New York, and if I hadn't gone to Vietnam, I might be practicing in Dallas. But for some reason, the Lord wanted me in Tyler."

Then the season changed for Pat, and he repositioned himself for a much greater responsibility. "You moved from private practice to become chief of surgery for two different hospitals simultaneously," I said. "How did you find the time to do all you did?"

"It's a matter of priorities," he said. "You make time for the things that matter. Even when I was the busiest as an operating surgeon, I taught Sunday school every Sunday for eight years. Then in 1993 I became copresident of an integrated healthcare system. My career goal was not to be a hospital administrator. In fact, back when I left Vietnam the Army had asked me to stay in, saying they'd keep me in teaching hospitals for the rest of my career. But I turned it down because I didn't want to be an administrator. Then there I was, years later, a hospital administrator. Then when I retired from regular practice in July 2002, I became part of the hospital foundation for major gifts."

Obviously Pat's illustrious career has been through several seasons, and he has successfully repositioned himself each time. "So what's in the future for Pat Thomas?" I asked. "You're sixty-eight now; what do you foresee as you look ahead?"

"I'm so thankful for everything I've been given," he said. "It occurs to me that if I die today, I couldn't be happier than I am. I'll be eternally grateful for all the opportunities I've had. I still have abilities and I've found a new usefulness. When I retired from regular practice in July 2002, I became part of the hospital's foundation for major gifts. I can't just sit around and do nothing, so I'll be busy right up until the end. If I were looking back from age eighty, I'd want to say the Lord has given me yet another opportunity to serve him. Now I spend much of my time in finding physicians for friends, visiting hospitalized friends, working in charitable organizations and in major gifts acquisitions for our faith-based health system. I also have the benefit of spending time with my grandchildren. One of my favorite sayings is, 'Service to others is the rent we pay for the room we have on earth.'"

"That makes a great motto," I said.

"Yes, but it's not just a motto," Pat said. "It's what I truly believe. I want to be totally used up when I die."

CHAPTER THIRTEEN

It's about Finding (or Creating) the Right Context

IT ALWAYS SEEMS TO COME BACK TO CONTEXT.
BY THAT I MEAN APPROPRIATENESS OF FIT.
— JIM COLLINS

You can choose the game, but not the rules of the game.

Every game has its rules. The NFL and NBA require big, strong, fast guys who can play long seasons with lots of pain. Working for a Wall Street investment bank requires longer working hours and a much more aggressive pace than being an Allstate agent in a small town in Iowa. If you don't own your own jet (and few of us do!), you have to show up at the airport an hour early and put your shoes through the metal detector, just like everybody else.

Every game has its own rules and you don't get to make them up. You choose your game and adapt to its rules. But if you find that the rules chafe, restrict, and don't allow expression of your potential, you either change games or create your own. The game you choose is your context. Once you know your core, you need to find the context that brings forth the best from your unique gifts and abilities.

Jim Collins, at age forty-five, is the author of two best-selling books about business. He has worked in the labyrinths of big business (Hewlett Packard), has consulted for businesses (McKinsey & Company), and has taught at a leading business school (Stanford). But he told me that business has never been his primary interest. The *context* of business as a giant social experiment is what really captures Jim Collins's imagination.

We began our interview talking about context in an utterly different sector, that of politics, and in particular some of the lessons Jim had observed in the acclaimed three-volume series by Robert Caro on the political career of former president Lyndon Johnson.[1] "The real lesson I take from those books," he told me, "is that it always seems to come back to context. By that I mean the *appropriateness of fit.*"

JIM COLLINS

"Johnson was often described as the consummate politician," I said. "He really knew how to wheel and deal behind the scenes, so hammering out a compromise bill in the Senate cloakroom was right down his alley. The problem, as I understand it, was that those street-fighter instincts didn't serve him well in the Oval Office."

"Absolutely," Jim said, "and I think that's what Caro's books show. His whole life Johnson wanted to be president, and he saw the Senate as a stepping-stone to his ultimate goal. The irony is that he didn't have the wisdom to realize that the Senate was where he really belonged. When he finally got his wish to become president, the context of executive leadership was wrong for him. It wasn't his fit, and ultimately, I believe, it was his failure in that role that killed him."

"Sounds like he was trapped between Parkinson's Law and the Peter Principle," I said. "He had a strong desire for the top spot, but when he got it he had risen beyond the level of his competence. Johnson didn't realize he already had a good thing. His down-home manners and his old back-room deal making didn't work for him as chief executive, where diplomacy and subtle persuasion are called for."

"I think there's great wisdom there," Jim responded. "It's a warning lesson in life. If your ambition is X and along the way you discover that where you really belong is Y or Z, then it's not smart to keep bucking for X. Johnson would have been much wiser to stay where he was, which is why I think Caro titled his third volume *Master of the Senate.* That's what Johnson was really suited for."

FINDING YOUR THEME

"At a Young President's Organization meeting several years ago," I said, "I was asked to squire Bill Donaldson around. Bill is now the head of the Securities and Exchange Commission. He went to Harvard Business School, was cofounder of Donaldson, Lufkin, and Jenrette on Wall Street, and then went to work for Governor Hugh Carey of New York. After that he worked for Henry Kissinger in the State Department and was dean of the Yale School of Management when I met him.

"What he told me," I told Jim, "was that each of those jobs had completely different contexts, and each context had an utterly different set of rules. He said that in business, it's all about the bottom line; in politics, it's all about power and who's in charge; and in academia, it's all about process and organization. Whenever business people came to Washington, he told me, a lot of them failed because they were playing by the wrong rules. They didn't realize that changing the context meant changing the rules, and consequently a lot of people who moved from one context to another didn't do well."

"The question I hear all the time," Jim said, "is 'Can a leader be effective in any context?' In other words, is leadership a sort of generic skill that works in any environment? I believe the answer is no. Some remarkable individuals are able to cross over into other areas, but they're more the exception than the rule. Anyone who changes fields ought to stop and consider how the rules of the game will change before sticking his or her neck out too far."

"Your own career has spanned some pretty diverse contexts," I commented. "How did you make the transition from the business world to academics, and then to the world of research and book writing where you are today?"

"When I look back over my experiences," he said, "I see a thread that's been there all along. When I finished high school and came to Stanford, I didn't get a job like most of my friends; I started a rock-climbing school. It was a tremendous growth experience, and fortunately I didn't kill any students along the way. After graduation I went to McKinsey & Company and stayed for a little over a year. The work was intellectually stimulating but didn't guide my passion. Then one weekend I stumbled across some orange binders in a storage room. Tom Peters had an office right across from me, and those binders, as it turned out, were background materials for the research he eventually included in his book *In Search of Excellence*. I pored over those binders and was absolutely fascinated. That's where the seed was planted."

Years ago those orange binders stimulated in Jim Collins an interest in human organizations—to discover what makes some of them "great" when others remain only "good." He has worked from that time till now on that research theme.

"From McKinsey," he said, "I went to Hewlett-Packard, and the whole time I was there I was thinking, *I wonder what makes this place tick?* Looking back now I realize I didn't go to HP because I wanted to know about computers but because I wanted to learn how a great company operates at ground level."

"So at a fairly early age," I said, "you found your theme."

"Actually it was three themes," he responded. "The first was teaching, the second was learning, and the third was trying to find out how social systems—companies and large organizations—really work at their deepest and best levels. But in all those themes I was clearly interested in research and intellectual inquiry. When I made that discovery, I decided to go back to teach at Stanford. And an interesting thing happened. All my life, until that moment, I had a nasty habit of chewing my fingernails. But from the first day I taught in a Stanford Business School classroom, I never chewed them again."

"Because?" I said.

"It was as if all my life up to that point I'd had some underlying anxiety," he said. "I was off track and hadn't found my niche. But when I got into teaching and research, everything clicked into place. I thought, *I'm a professor figuring out how great things work, and that's the essence of what I am.* From that point on, I locked in on the field I'm interested in."

"But you didn't stay with teaching very long. What changed?"

"The problem," he said, "is that I'm constitutionally unemployable. I've always had an entrepreneurial streak. When I needed a job in college, I didn't go to work for a climbing school; I started a climbing school. When I got into teaching, I became a professor of entrepreneurship. But I eventually realized I needed to go from being professor of entrepreneurship to an entrepreneurial professor, and for that I didn't need to be in the confines of a traditional university."

"So you had to deinstitutionalize yourself," I said, "to find a context where you could be creative and work within your niche."

"That's right," he said. "And that meant I had to create my own organization."

"I understand that," I said. "I'm as unemployable as you are. Something about an institutional context brings out the worst in me."

"Yes," he said, "and there are ways to wrestle with that, of course. I eventually realized I had to find a context that would fit me like a glove. At a gut level, I think, there's a need for a self-created context where you're not wasting energy battling the fact that you're in somebody else's context."

"So when I say the word *retirement*," I said, "what comes to mind?"

"I understand that change is refreshing," he said, "but I don't understand retirement as a concept. In terms of economics, I could retire right now. I've achieved enough that I could go off and become a full-time rock climber. But the biggest reward for me is not to cash out but to have the opportunity to continue my work."

As I listened to Jim, the biblical parable of the talents flashed into my mind. In that story, the reward for being a "good and faithful servant" was more work. But I left the thought unspoken and pressed on.

"So you prefer to work, but not in an institutional setting, I take it," I said.

"Precisely," he answered. "Today I describe myself as a self-tenured, self-endowed researcher. I have the freedoms of a fully tenured Harvard professor, but I can wander around on the playing field of my own interests and do pretty much whatever I want. I have the resources and a platform from which I can move to the next stage in my work. It's the perfect context for me, and it's highly productive and rewarding."

In one of his recent research projects, documented in the book *Good to Great*, Jim set out to discover how average performers become stellar performers. With his research associates, whom he calls "the chimps," Jim found eleven companies that fit the model of going from good to great. The most striking sentence in his assessment of why most companies don't become great ones is "Good is the enemy of great." Today he's focusing on what he calls "Level 5 Leadership," and his most surprising discovery is that the top performers are (1) genuinely humble and (2) fully devoted to the mission.[2]

Jim is also a friend of Peter Drucker's, and told me during our interview that he's taking Peter's advice and repositioning himself again. He's taking the knowledge he acquired from the new research and applying it to other situations—particularly in the nonprofit sector where it may have an even greater impact.

LIFE IN THE MIDDLE

Every context brings with it a set of rules, some written but mostly unwritten. These rules are the cultural norms of that particular context. Even professional sports stars who are gifted with extraordinary athletic abilities have to function as part of a team. Michael Jordan can't win by himself. Tiger Woods can, but that's the exception that proves the rule. Tiger's team includes his father, who is his coach, and a wide variety of sponsors and friends who have "rules" of their own. Some people require a large corporate environment where their abilities are complemented on every side by the abilities of others, and where a sort of instant prestige is written on their business card. Others, however, function better in a less-structured environment.

In most cases, the rules and regulations allow the context to function. Large companies like P&G depend on such rules, as do sports organizations such as the NFL. Even the mafia has rules. Nonprofits have all kinds of rules. Churches do, and there are even different "rules" for house churches in China, megachurches in Orange County, and Roman Catholic cathedrals in Europe. Ultimately, each of us must find a context that fits our own skills and temperaments.

Fortunately, by the time we come to Life II, we've already discovered much about what works through a lot of trial and error. But one thing is certain: Unless you create your own context, as Jim Collins has done, or as I have done, you have to find an organizational form that brings forth the best in you. A symphony orchestra conductor can't function without a symphony, and a great salesman needs a great sales organization. Yet there are limits on how expansive and original one can be in such organizations. It's a trade-off either way.

I was involved in an entrepreneurial organizational setting for the first thirty years of my career. I was first a subordinate and then CEO, growing a family business in television and cable television. Then, in the next season of my life, when the "rules" of that context didn't allow me to follow the dream God had breathed into my heart, I created Leadership Network and wrote the book *Halftime*, which allowed my horizons to expand in many new directions. I didn't ask permission. I just followed the vision I was given, formed a team, and began to serve.

LEARNING NEW RULES

Rudy Rasmus was raised as an only child in an enterprising family. "My dad was a believer," he told me, "but not a churchgoer. Basically he raised me not to trust preachers and church folk." Moving through life, Rudy said, he eventually took over management of "the family business"—a brothel. "The girls were self-employed," he said. "They didn't work for me directly, but I provided the facilities for the activity."

RUDY RASMUS

"So you were the landlord of a brothel?" I asked.

"Actually, it was a motel in the inner city. I also had a liquor store right down the street, but that was my countercultural activity. My productive activity was as a real estate broker: I sold real estate by day and by night I ran this other operation. I did this for most of my adult life, but in 1984 I met the woman who would ultimately become my wife.

"When I met Juanita," Rudy said, "something about her just knocked me out, and I eventually realized it was her faith. She led me to Christ, and when we got married in 1985 I followed her to church. I was still running the business and still involved in counterproductive activities around the city of Houston, but something began to happen.

"When I first went to the church, Windsor United Methodist, I just sat there as a lot of nonbelievers do, looking for fraud—for something wrong. I ended up meeting the pastor, Kirbyjon Caldwell, and he became the first preacher I ever trusted. We eventually struck up a friendship, and I was shocked that this guy was willing to accept me, knowing all that I did for a living. His acceptance really helped break through to me. He embraced me and I became his real estate broker. Shortly afterward, he asked me to serve on the administrative council of the church.

"I still had a lot of questions about the Bible," Rudy told me, "and I still wasn't a true believer. But by the end of 1990 I had accepted Christ, and that was a monumental time for me. My father wasn't happy about that, and he used some pretty colorful language to let me know just what he thought. But I began to change, and everybody could see it. One of my employees, who's in the church now, said he knew the day it happened. He said from that day on everything was different about me. I discovered a conscience, and that conscience really began to convict me about the business I was in."

"How did you deal with that?" I asked.

"Well, one day I went to my dad and told him I couldn't accept the proceeds of that business anymore. He said he knew something was wrong with me, because he had raised me as a good materialistic capitalist. After that I started changing my lifestyle and trying to make a living by other means. It was hard at first. But by the end of 1991, I went to see Kirbyjon and told him I was accepting a call to the ministry. Now, to be honest, Bob, I had no idea what that meant. But Kirbyjon just leaned back in his chair and looked at me, and he said, 'Why?'"

At first, Rudy told me he couldn't really answer Rev. Caldwell's question. But as God worked in his heart, he realized he had a passion to pass on the message that had transformed his own life. Rev. Caldwell encouraged him to study and grow in his knowledge of Scripture, and in 1992 he told Rudy about a large downtown church whose membership had dwindled to nearly nothing. Rudy decided to go check it out. He explained that this church might provide a possible expansion site for the huge and growing Windsor congregation.

"I drove downtown," he said, "and stopped the car in front of the church. Before I even got out of the car I called my wife, Juanita, and I said, 'Baby, this is it! This is the place!' I was so excited, and at that moment I knew that not only had I made it to the place where God had been leading me, I had also found my purpose in life. At that point I had never preached even one sermon, and I hadn't even walked into the building. But sitting there at the curb, I knew that church was the place where I was supposed to be."

"Was your hunch correct?" I said. "Did you go ahead with your plans?"

"When I got out of the car," he continued, "I saw homeless people all around the building. That stuck in my mind, but it didn't slow us down. We moved into the building in July 1992, and by October we had our first service. As things were set up, Kirbyjon was appointed as pastor of two churches in Houston, and my wife and I became ministry leaders on that campus. We weren't called to be ministers in the Methodist church at that point, but we were responsible for creating a ministry opportunity in that building."

Rudy told me that to help the new church plant get started, Rev. Caldwell sent a choir from Windsor to sing at the 10:00 A.M. service. "I was getting instruction and coaching at the time," Rudy said, "and with that wonderful, big-budget choir there every Sunday morning, the church began to grow. Along the way we realized that our mission would have to include those we had to step over to get inside the church—the homeless. So we decided to provide one meal a week to these folks.

"We didn't know it at the time, but God was setting up something even larger," Rudy continued. "As a result of that one meal, we caught the attention of a religion writer for the *Houston Chronicle*, and in March 1993, in our first year, just before Easter, they ran a front-page story: 'Downtown Church Serves the Homeless.' That created a boom. Folks read the article about a church that was doing what they felt a church should be doing, and suddenly people began showing up. Within a year we went from nothing to over five hundred members. Today we have 8,100 members with three worship services, and the facility is basically maxed out. The congregation is very diverse, about 48 percent male and 52 percent female, and they come from 150 zip codes in the Houston vicinity."

With Methodist churches all over America bleeding members, Rudy's church in inner-city Houston, once a hangout for the homeless, is now alive and thriving. What changed? Rudy found the context where he truly belonged. He'd found God, and God gave him a task that fit his passion.

Sometimes you have to change games to find what Jim Collins called an "appropriateness of fit." Jim Collins made that change, and so did Rudy Rasmus, as well as a number of people who work with me in bringing half-time to others through workshops in churches and cities around the country. Mike Shields ran a $4 billion Wall Street money management firm; John Leffin was a partner at Accenture; Lloyd Reeb was a senior housing real estate developer; Greg Murtha was a banker; and Tom McGehee worked in a sophisticated collaborative idea-sharing system for Ernst & Young/Cap Gemini, with collaborative centers in fifteen cities around the world. These men are all in their forties, and they've all discovered that their calling is to help churches become more effective, and to help half-timers make the transition from success to significance.

Like me, in order to do the work they felt God was calling them to do in Life II, they needed a change of context. And, like me, they are each creating their roles within the "rules" of that context.

SECTION III
Making It Happen

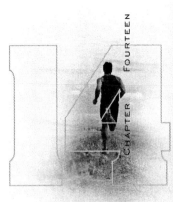

CHAPTER FOURTEEN

It's about Putting Yourself at Risk

IT IS NOT THE CRITIC WHO COUNTS, NOT THE MAN WHO POINTS OUT HOW THE STRONG MAN STUMBLES, OR WHERE THE DOER OF DEEDS COULD HAVE DONE THEM BETTER. THE CREDIT BELONGS TO THE MAN IN THE ARENA, WHOSE FACE IS MARRED BY DUST AND SWEAT AND BLOOD, WHO STRIVES VALIANTLY . . . WHO KNOWS THE GREAT ENTHUSIASMS, THE GREAT DEVOTIONS, WHO SPENDS HIMSELF IN A WORTHY CAUSE, WHO AT THE BEST KNOWS IN THE END THE TRIUMPH OF HIGH ACHIEVEMENT, AND WHO AT THE WORST, IF HE FAILS, AT LEAST FAILS WHILE DARING GREATLY, SO THAT HIS PLACE SHALL NEVER BE WITH THOSE COLD AND TIMID SOULS WHO HAVE NEVER KNOWN NEITHER VICTORY NOR DEFEAT.
— TEDDY ROOSEVELT

No guts. No glory.

I'm convinced that when I get to heaven and come face-to-face with my Creator, there's going to be a final exam, and as I visualize it, two questions will sum up the part of my life lived on earth: (1) "What did you do about Jesus?" and (2) "What did you do with what I gave you to work with?" One question about belief and one question about action—not action in lieu of belief (the old word is "works") but action that grows out of belief. It's both/and not either/or.

I quarrel with a timid form of Christianity made up exclusively of piety and attendance at ritual events. Fifteen years ago, I spent the entire Christmas holidays studying the parables, those powerful stories Jesus told to illustrate the nature of his kingdom. Peter Drucker told me once, "There are two ways of teaching: the Greek way and the rabbinic way." The Greek way, he explained, is based on analysis and breaking down a subject into its logical outline sequence (I A, B, C; II A, B, C). The rabbinic way always begins, "Let me tell you a story."

Jesus was, after all, a Jew who taught as a rabbi. His parables and his life were his teaching form. What I learned from the parables has deeply influenced Life II for me. Reflecting on them is as close as I can get to interviewing Jesus. So for the next couple of pages, I'd like to digress from the interviews to tell you what I personally learned during those critical few days.

Five Lessons I Learned from the Parables

1. *The marketplace*, which I define as the normal life, not the life of the cloister, *is the field where most of life is to take place.* How we use what we've been given in everyday life in contact with others and meeting their needs shows our commitment to God. And our demonstration of this commitment in the arena gives him the data for the separation of the wheat from the tares, the fruitful servants from the timid and unproductive, the righteous from the wicked, the sheep from the goats.

2. *We are all tested for fruitfulness and stewardship.* The time when we will be held accountable is a "surprise audit" (the Master's return), not announced in advance.

3. *God rewards the risk takers.* He entrusts to them more responsibility. The reward for a duty performed is more duty to perform. ("Because you were faithful in a very little, have authority over ten cities."[1]) The man who attempts to "build greater barns" and who says, "Soul, you have many goods laid up for many years to come; take your ease," is condemned as a fool.[2]

4. *There is a downside to timidity as well as an upside to taking risk.* Possessions are a trust to be invested for a return. The timid and fearful who bury their talents are cast "into outer darkness" where there is "weeping and gnashing of teeth."[3] The talents of the fearful (fear is the opposite of faith) are taken away and given to the most productive. The fig tree is given many chances to produce, but in the end, when proven barren, it is cut down and burned.

5. *God demands primary loyalty.* ("You shall have no other gods before Me.")[4] God uses whatever is most valuable to us as a test of our primary

loyalty. His test is to ask us to go further than we can go with our own logic and reason—into areas of faith. David goes against Goliath. Abraham is asked to sacrifice Isaac, for whom he has waited a lifetime. The rich young ruler is asked to sell his possessions to follow after Jesus. We are asked to be at risk, beyond the zone of our comfort, control, and comprehension.

We are called to risk all to gain that one thing that has real value. It's the "pearl of great price," worth giving up all else to attain. It is "like a treasure hidden in a field," yet to use the title of Thomas Merton's book, it is actually "hidden in plain sight." It is the "surpassing value" for which Paul suffers the loss of all things and counts them as rubbish in order to gain eternity.

"In My Father's House"

Perhaps nobody practices and embodies these lessons of the parables better than sixty-eight-year-old Millard Fuller. We met in Dallas during his whirl-wind tour of the U.S. for Habitat for Humanity, the organization he founded and still leads. Millard would be in seven states and eight cities that week stirring up the troops to build housing for the poor. "No more shacks!" is the personal mission state-ment on Millard's T-shirt.

MILLARD FULLER

Millard, as much as any man I know, exemplifies putting one's self at risk. His business expertise and entrepreneurial drive made him a millionaire at twenty-nine. But as his business prospered, his health, integrity, and mar-riage suffered, prompting him to reevaluate his priorities and direction. The Fullers decided to sell everything they owned, give the money to the poor, and find a new focus for their lives. In 1976 they founded Habitat for Humanity. They put everything at risk to find that one pearl of great price.

Knowing very well that the word *retirement* is not in Millard's vocabulary, I asked him, "Millard, have you ever heard about this thing called retirement?"

"Sure I have," he said with a laugh. "I remember the words of Jesus, who said, 'Take up your cross until you're sixty-five, then lay it down, then take up your fishing pole and move to Florida!'"

"That's great!" I said, laughing with him. "But seriously, what do you think about when you hear that word?"

"Bob," he said, "I haven't found the concept of retirement in the Bible. There was, however, one guy who found his barns full, and he tore them down in order to build bigger barns. But something bad happened to him. What happened to all his stuff then? Well, my understanding of Scripture is that all of us are on this earth by the grace of God. We had nothing to do with it; one day we just looked in the mirror and there we were! That's God's gift, but what we do with that gift is up to us.

"I remember a boy in my high school," he continued, "who was one of the most naturally gifted athletes I've ever known. But he drank alcohol, smoked cigarettes, and didn't exercise, and his God-given ability was squandered. It was sad. I still remember thinking, *How can you just waste your God-given abilities that way?* God has given me certain talents, and I think it's incumbent on me to use them to the best of my ability, for as long as I'm able."

I said, "You'd think retirement would be in the Bible if God had thought it was important, wouldn't you?"

"Yes, I agree," he responded. "It's pretty clear that when God calls somebody, it's for the duration: You're called to be faithful in that calling for as long as you're able. Now I do think there's justification for changing course at various times in your life. If I live a full life, into my seventies or eighties, there will come a time when I'm not able to travel to seven states and eight cities in a week. But I can fulfill God's call in other ways, and I hope that when the time comes I will have the wisdom to know how to make that shift to serve in other ways."

"Do you have any idea how many volunteers you mobilize to work with Habitat each year?" I asked.

"Hundreds of thousands," he said, "if not millions."

"Do you think they're better off for having volunteered? And if so, how?"

"Anyone who has ever been involved in this work will tell you that they've been blessed," Millard replied. "Our most famous volunteers are former president Jimmy Carter and his wife Rosalyn, and I've heard them say many times that they have been blessed by their twenty years of work in this ministry. I think *blessing* means making a difference in someone else's life. It's seeing the tears in the eyes of those you've helped, feeling the hug of a new homeowner, or seeing the joy in the eyes of a child who will have his or her own room for the very first time."

"A lot of regular church attenders would tell you that they're doing all they need to do for the kingdom," I said. "Are you suggesting that they're missing something?"

"Well, going to church is important. The Bible says we're not to forsake 'the assembling of ourselves together.'[1] But that's not the end of it. It doesn't say that the first and greatest commandment is to *go to church and get other people to go to church*. We go to church to be inspired and motivated, and equipped to be the light of Christ in the world. The first part of that passage says, 'Let us consider one another in order to stir up love and good works.' We are supposed to go out and be the salt and leaven in society—to be agents of change. To use that old metaphor, salt is good for nothing as long as it remains in the box. Only when the salt is poured out is it valuable—when it flavors the food.

"Many Christians don't get out of the box," he said. "So we have a bunch of salty Christians just salting each other, week after week, and they don't get outside and do what they're supposed to do as the body of Christ in kingdom work, being salt in society."

"I thought we were the most Christian nation on earth," I said. "What's wrong with this picture?"

"Well, there are a lot of professing Christians in this country," he said, "but it's one thing to profess something, and a very different proposition to be serious about it. Just standing up and saying that you're a Christian doesn't mean much. A true Christian seriously wants to know what Christ's claims are on his or her life. The popular phrase that was such a trend for a while really asks the right question: 'What would Jesus do?'"

"Millard," I said, "I would be interested to know what the idea of finishing well means to you."

"Henry David Thoreau said the mass of men lead lives of quiet desperation," he replied. "Well, I don't lead a life of quiet desperation. I feel blessed.

I've had forty-four years with a wonderful woman, and I've got four kids and seven grandkids. I wake up every morning excited about what's going to happen that day. I have problems and frustrations and challenges, like anyone else, but overall it's a joyous kind of life, and exciting. So I just feel privileged to do what I do. And I think the organization I'm privileged to head is in good shape. If I dropped dead this afternoon, Habitat for Humanity would be on solid ground, and I'm thrilled to know it would go full speed ahead without me. It's not dependent on my leadership."

"And your feelings about the life to come?" I asked.

"In my Father's house there are many Habitat houses," Millard said. "That's the Fuller translation! But the truth is, Jesus is the construction foreman, so I know my house in heaven is in good hands, and I don't have to worry about that. I spend my time thinking about where I am today, which is here on earth. That's where I feel that God has placed me to be his faithful servant for as long as I have the privilege of having life."

LIVING ON THE EDGE

Bob Roberts is a classic entrepreneur, but he's not a dot.comer or a real estate tycoon. Like Millard Fuller, he's an entrepreneur for the Lord. Bob is

BOB ROBERTS

part of a new breed of Christian leaders who build big churches and then build leaders to multiply them so that they serve not hundreds but thousands. He's square-jawed, muscular, and hyperenergetic, the kind of guy you would want to follow into war or up a mountain face. His passion is building the teams that build churches, and expanding the kingdom.

When I asked Bob to fill me in on the work he's done, he told me, "The best thing I've done is to start a church and stay. That may not sound like much of an accomplishment but for a hyperactive type-A like me, it is! Since that first church, we've now started over fifty churches, with twice that many daughter churches across the country. Many of those are now grouped in clusters, and these clusters are starting other churches in their cities and even adopting nations around the world as part of their mission field."

Bob is a risk taker who attracts other risk takers. Ever since I met him, I've noticed that people are attracted to the adventure of what he's doing, and they're encouraged by the impact of it. Changed lives versus more money? Bob would say, "No contest!"

"When Christians get involved in the kind of work we do," he said, "it changes them. If you go to a Third World country, as we do, and start touching the world in places and ways that make a real difference, you come away with a whole new kind of love for the world. It takes more than just hard-working people; it takes smart people, intentional people. When you say you want to build an aqueduct around Afghanistan, or to build seven new schools in the villages surrounding the city so that the Madrassas aren't the only source of education for the children, then you'll need engineers, builders, educators, financiers, and others to come alongside and lend a helping hand. That's part of what we do; we connect people so that God's work can go forward."

"Do you have a problem finding people to do these things?" I asked.

"My biggest challenge," he said, "is keeping businessmen in the business world and keeping doctors in the medical world. Once they get out there and see the results of this work, they think, 'Oh, man, this is really exciting! I'm going to quit my day job and go to seminary!' And I say, 'For God's sake, don't do that! God has already given you an education, a network, and a way to make a wonderful contribution. Why would you want to forsake that?' So I tell them to stay with what they're doing, but to use that knowledge and expertise as a platform to *make a difference in the world.*"

"However they get involved," I said, "whether it's through their church or their professional calling, it sounds like there's a certain amount of risk for the men and women who are doing this kind of work."

"There's always risk," he said, "but it's not unreasonable risk. Mike Reed was a vice president at Salem Communications in charge of their national sales program. You talk about growth! Salem probably expanded a hundredfold while Mike was there. Mike was a big part of that, and he just left it all behind to come alongside this ministry and basically run the church.

"Mike's risk," he said, "was leaving behind a world where he was successful and comfortable for a world that would be a new challenge. He took that risk. Another guy who did that is Ross Paterson, who was one of GE's emerging young execs. He left it all. Now he's doing consulting on the side three days a week to make enough to get by so he can spend a day and a half each week managing all our operations in Afghanistan.

"And there are others," he said. "Ken Gravenor was one of the key execs at Nokia, responsible for their financial operations in North America. Ken left it all behind, and today he's doing consulting on the side and developing our community development center in a suburb not far away. That's the kind of dedication and enthusiasm you find when people catch the vision for what God is doing in the world."

"You are forty-five now," I said. "I would think longevity might be a concern for you, with some of the places your ministry takes you. I'm sure there's risk involved."

"Well, I think about that sometimes," he said. "I have a lot of life insurance, but working in Afghanistan I've learned how to work with governments and how to get things done. I'm looking at doing the same right now in Iraq with one of our clusters. I look at those places in the news where all hell is breaking loose, and I believe that if Jesus were here, that's where he'd go. We've looked at traditional missionary approaches to going into those countries. I'm not saying they're all bad, but I believe we have to take not just the Billy Graham evangelistic approach but the Mother Teresa approach as well."

Bob knows that though we hear little of it in the United States, persecution of Christians throughout the world is rampant today. Yet it doesn't deter him in the least.

"We take our young churches to some of the tough places in the world, and there is inherent risk in that. More people will lose their lives for the gospel in this century than in any century in history, I believe. But if it means God will get more glory and mileage out of me if I sacrifice my life this way, then that's okay with me."

"I don't know a lot about Afghanistan," I said, "but I'm inclined to believe it's a fairly dangerous place for Christians at the moment. Doesn't that ever worry you?"

"I would rather live a shorter but fuller life of vital ministry than rust out waiting for a challenge," he said. "I'm a mountain climber and I like to be out there on the edge. Last summer I was in the middle of the desert in Afghanistan with ten young Muslim imams. I was the first Christian pastor they'd ever met. I wound up there under unusual circumstances and I was nervous—they could easily have shot me. One was the local warlord. We had become friends, and they wanted me to tell them about Christianity. I thought, *This is incredible! We may have a friendship but there will be no middle ground on this issue!*

"But, to make a long story short, the warlord started bragging about how I was going to build a school in his village, and pretty soon the others said they'd like us to build one in their village too. I said I couldn't do it, but I knew some other pastors who would be willing to help."

"Obviously you made it out alive!" I said.

"Believe it or not, I agreed to read the Koran if they would agree to read the Bible: we're going to do it together with them. Common wisdom would tell you, *Don't go out in the desert and meet with Taliban imams!* It's out on that edge, and there's the potential of losing everything. But you also have the potential for the greatest gains. That's why I say that the people who turn the world upside down, who really make a difference for Christ, are those who live on the edge and take the risks because they know the payback is so much greater."

At the end of our discussion, I asked Bob, "When you look back on this work in years to come, what do you hope to see here?"

"At one time," he said, "I would have told you my goal was to plant two thousand churches in the next twenty years. In fact, at the rate we're going we'll have several thousand churches. We're starting churches all over the world, from Australia to Singapore to Kenya in Africa, and beyond. So there will be cluster churches all over the world, and one day we may see some of them planting churches in America. "Building churches and the supporting humanitarian infrastructure," he said, "is what keeps me going."

THE RISK YOU CAN'T AFFORD NOT TO TAKE

There are other, subtler kinds of risk—less dramatic, less showy—but I wonder if these closer-to-home risks may not be the most frightening for those of us who aren't going to find ourselves anywhere near Kandahar. A man who came to grips with this more personal level of risk was Tom

TOM MCGEHEE

McGehee, a dynamic young executive making his way in the corporate world.

Tom had become a Christian in college through Campus Crusade, and his conversion had a big impact on his post-graduation plans. "Suddenly it wasn't what do *I* want to do," he told me, "but 'God, what do you want me to do?'" Throughout his career, Tom has always asked this question before making his next move.

Tom was planning to be a teacher, but a friend who had recently graduated from Marine Officer Candidate School convinced him to give the military a try.

After twelve years as an officer in the Marines, Tom decided to leave the service. He looked around for a while and eventually landed at EDS, where he went into their sales program. He was trained to call on Fortune 100 CEOs, and he wound up working on $100 million outsourcing deals. After five years he went into consulting and once again enjoyed great success. "I was meeting a lot of powerful people and having high-powered dinners, but I was just a guy in a suit," he said. "I felt pretty lost about who I was."

Eventually, in 1997, Tom became partner at Ernst & Young, where he remained until 2002.

"Unfortunately," he told me, "the landscape kept changing. Ernst & Young was bought by Cap Gemini, and I sensed that bigger changes were just down the road. Their approach to doing things had changed, and I had to deal with the emotions of all that. I had to decide whether or not to stay with the organization. I realized, *There's the risk you can't afford to take, but there's also the risk that you can't afford* not *to take.* It appeared just as risky for me to stay there, spending my time fighting the corporate bureaucracy, as it was to take something I loved and start doing it on my own."

Tom's risk was significant, because he felt that in order to bring his collaborative process abilities to both corporate and kingdom organizations meant he would have to start his own business. Still, he relied on that faith-affirming question he had learned to ask in college: 'God, what do you want me to do?' So he left Cap Gemini and waited for God to show him the way. As it often happens, the door opened quickly for Tom. He established WildWorks, an organization focused on unleashing the power of collaboration both for companies and for churches. WildWorks quickly gained corporate and church clients.

"What I found," Tom said, "was that until you take that first step, you can't see the other steps that are out there. I had a business plan, a process, and I knew what I wanted to do, but once I actually stepped out and made the change, God suddenly opened up more opportunities than I could ever have imagined.

"I wanted to serve the kingdom just as much as I wanted to serve businesses, and I came to the conclusion that I could do both right away. I've got two kids in college and I had to feed my family, so there were practical concerns, but I wanted to take these ideas to the church, and that's what led me to where I am today."

Tom's risk paid off in huge dividends, not only in business income but also in terms of his own fulfillment of God's purpose for him, not to mention the many churches who enjoy the benefits of the world-class knowledge he possesses. "When I left the Marine Corps," he continued, "I had a friend who said, 'You know, Tom, I'd really like to leave, but I've got a family and I just don't know what I'd do.' To me, it's not about what you'd like to do, but what you feel called to do. That's the risk you can't afford *not* to take. There's a lot more to life than just your temporary security. You can hold onto something so long that you lose the chance to make a change, and that's what I didn't want to do.

"My biggest challenge now," he said, "is deciding what opportunity I want to chase next. It can be risky at times, but it puts a whole new perspective on your day!"

TRIAL BY FIRE

Mike Shields, who is now part of the Leadership Network team, has an amazing story to tell, as I've mentioned briefly in passing. He was part of an investment team that was running up the score in the tech boom on Wall Street. When I spoke to him, I asked him to tell me about the events that changed his life. "The quick story," he said, "is that I moved to New York in May 1992, after ten years with a large financial institution in Charlotte.

MIKE SHIELDS

"After five years with Scudder, Stephens, & Clark, managing money for large institutions, I went to an investment boutique owned by a well-regarded New York financial institution, U.S. Trust. In my first two years, that fund grew at an astronomical rate, from $800 million to almost $8 billion—an almost tenfold increase."

"You were on some kind of roll!" I exclaimed.

"Right," he said. "Practically everything we did paid off—the right stocks, the right moves, and a ton of tech stocks in the mix. And those stocks were screaming. In 1998, we were up 92 percent. So a lot of people were looking at us, wide-eyed. It was like the old Gordon Gekko line, 'Greed is good!' Then came March 1999, when the head of our division resigned and invited the whole team to join him in a new venture."

"You mean, right in the middle of that incredible roll, the boss just walked away? How did you react to that?" I asked him.

"I was dazed," he said. I suspected he might be up to something, but nobody had any idea what he was about to pull off. With $8 billion onboard, if he left and took the team with him, most of the big clients would look at all those numbers, look at the team that made it happen, and before you know it the entire $8 billion would follow."

"So what happened?" I asked. "Did this risky gambit pay off?"

"Well, he was counting on the domino effect," Mike said. "If one or two members of the group resigned to go with him, he figured everybody would follow. And by the end of the day, twenty-four of the twenty-six members of the staff had resigned and joined him in the new company."

"And what about you?" I said.

"I was one of the two who didn't make the switch."

"Why did you stay?" I asked.

"Ultimately," he said, "it was because I thought it was the right thing to do. As a Christian, I thought, *We have to take the risk. We have to go against the grain, and sometimes we have to do it in fairly dramatic fashion.* Well, this was one of those times."

There were many other twists and turns in Mike's story as he related those tumultuous events to me, but the biggest change was yet to come. "Take me to 9/11," I said, "and tell me where you were when that happened."

"As it turned out, I was in the conference room that morning with a staff member, on a conference call with a stock analyst. The call started at 8:15, and at 8:45 someone in the analyst's office shot her a message saying that something was happening downtown—a plane had run into a building—but she just ignored it. She didn't want to be interrupted. A few minutes later she got another note, and this time she said, 'Something's up. I've got to go,' and she hung up.

"My colleague and I had been sitting in an interior conference room with no windows," Mike said, "and we didn't know what was up either. So we turned on CNN and CNBC to find out, and that's when we saw the news. And as we stood there in an office watching these terrible things unfolding on television, a woman who worked for me suddenly realized that her husband was there, in the middle of all that.

"She was hoping he'd be able to get out of there," Mike said, "but before long she realized that he was gone. It was a helpless feeling—I ached for her. It was a long, hard day. Nobody knew what was happening for several hours—you know, Bob; you were in New York that day too."

"Indeed, I was," I said. "It was unforgettable. But what a tragic set of circumstances for you. I know there were a lot of tears and emotions that day, but I'd be curious to know what difference all that made in your view of your life and your job."

"I was just entering the halftime phase of my life," he said, "and I'd have to say that experience was a real accelerator. Suddenly I had a new sense of urgency, combined with the knowledge that life is very uncertain. We tend to take for granted that the next breath will be there and the next day will be there. And it also gave me an enhanced view of the lack of eternal significance of what I was doing.

"I was living the dream, but I wasn't doing much about the things that really matter. I was spending all my time working on dollar signs and career achievements but spending almost no time on my spiritual side or relationships that should have been at the center of my life. And I thought, *Why am I doing this? That other stuff just ends.* So that's when I decided I needed to do something about how I invest my resources."

"So you left the firm," I said. "You went through a couple of major transitions, and then what happened next?"

"The last straw was something that happened at a party in Greenwich, Connecticut, where we lived. It was just a run-of-the-mill party at a club. I'd been spending practically no time at home because of the job, and my daughter, Meredith, who was three at the time, was running around playing. And at one point she ran right by me and went up to another man and called him *Daddy.* That was huge. It was a major impact—maybe even more than 9/11. I knew it was going to be hard, but I knew I had to make some changes. During that time I read your book *Halftime,* and I felt as if you had written it just for Mike Shields."

"So, step by step," I said, "you made the switch from your busy New York lifestyle, moved back to North Carolina, and got into faith-based work full-time."

"That's right," he said, "but it didn't happen overnight. A lot of good friends helped me along the way. It was a lot to work through—a sort of polynomial equation!"

"Good way to put it," I said. "And what are you thinking now?"

"I'm as confident as I can be that God put me through that halftime experience so I could, at a minimum, relate to other guys in similar situations who are wrestling with midlife issues. And when I began going deeper, carving out time for reflection and prayer, what emerged was a passion for people in midlife. I didn't know how that would play out at first, but for the first time in my life I knew I was right where God wanted me to be, and I'm thrilled to know that."

Like Tom McGehee, Mike had found the risk you can't afford *not* to take. And he decided to invest his life in something with a truly long-term payback.

CHAPTER FIFTEEN

It's about Finding the Right Fit

PEOPLE DECISIONS ARE THE ULTIMATE—PERHAPS THE ONLY—CONTROL OF AN ORGANIZATION. PEOPLE DETERMINE THE PERFORMANCE CAPACITY OF AN ORGANIZATION. NO ORGANIZATION CAN DO BETTER THAN THE PEOPLE IT HAS. . . . IF YOU WANT PEOPLE TO PERFORM IN AN ORGANIZATION, YOU HAVE TO USE THEIR STRENGTHS—NOT EMPHASIZE THEIR WEAKNESSES. . . . THE PURPOSE OF A TEAM IS TO MAKE THE STRENGTHS OF EACH PERSON EFFECTIVE, AND HIS OR HER WEAKNESSES IRRELEVANT.
— PETER F. DRUCKER

One reason people stick with their "success life" right on through Life II is that the shift into a "significance context" is often hard to make. The difficulty is in finding the right context to fit one's skills. Just as it's hard to find the right match in marriage or career, it's often hard to find the right context for doing work of significance after the Life II decision is made. It's doable, all right, and certainly worth the effort, but it's sometimes hard.

People quickly discover that the rhythms are different between the business world and the nonprofit world. The measures are different too. It is easy to know if you win or lose in a profit-and-loss world; you've got the balance sheet to tell you. But success is not so apparent when the measure is changed lives, as in a church or university environment. And most times, lives don't change instantly. So much for instant gratification! And, usually, so much for awards, recognition, and financial bonuses as well! Shockingly, when a highly qualified, highly paid professional offers to work for free in the area of his or her skills, they may hear, "Uh, thanks, but we don't know quite what to do with you." The big issue of finding one's fit emerges in the conversations that follow.

REACHING ACROSS THE GAP

Joe Miraglia was senior vice president of human resources for Motorola's ninety thousand employees and the creator of Motorola University, with

JOE MIRAGLIA

branches around the globe. He left that world behind ten years ago in order to invest himself in helping accomplished people find their place in kingdom work. As a "life planning coach," Joe spends most of his time now helping people match their skills and interests with organizations in need of savvy half-timers. He's been on the board of two huge mega-churches. From his experience in both the corporate and church worlds, he told me halftimers often have serious difficulties with "fit" as they attempt to make the change from one world to another.

I asked Joe to describe the common characteristics of the people who come to him for advice. "They all want to make changes," I said, "but what are the hurdles they have to overcome?"

"The first question," he said, "is always how they're situated financially. Sometimes money is a problem." In other words, sometimes the heart is willing but the bank account is weak. Joe went on to explain the second hurdle. "Sometimes the man or woman who comes to me may be ready for the change but the spouse is not. So that's a crucial issue we deal with. But after that, most of these people have a pretty good idea of what they want to do. They just don't know how to connect or how to do it.

"I only work with Christians," Joe told me, "so whenever we do life planning a lot of them want to find a way to work with churches or parachurch organizations. But getting connected is difficult for them. In the first place, the entrepreneur won't find many entrepreneurial situations in churches. Someone who is used to managing large, complex organizations will find it difficult to utilize those skills in the church environment. The easier thing to do is to identify people's passions and what they want to do. The more difficult thing is to find a place for them to connect so they actually can do those things."

"Obviously, there's always a period of adjustment in any change," I went on, "but why is it hard for these executives to make the transition?"

"Part of the problem," he answered, "is that they're not used to selling themselves to others. They've been in an organization where everyone knows who they are and what they do. Leaving that safe environment and selling themselves again is new and uncomfortable for them. They don't like the feel of that, so the tendency is just to give up.

"Sometimes I tell them my own experience. I got a Ph.D. and became a college professor by age twenty-five. I had won some teaching awards and had good credentials when I came to a point where I wanted to help a small Christian college in teaching business. So I called and made an offer to help—for free. The dean said, 'Send me your vita.' I said, 'I haven't prepared one in years, but I'll do that and send it to you.'

"I decided I'd be humble," Joe continued, "so I sent the vita and I waited, and waited, and waited. Finally I called him and said, 'You know, there's no charge here. I'd just like to help.' But the guy was totally unimpressed and never called me back. I don't know what his problem was, but that's not an uncommon experience. So I tell people, 'Don't be hurt when people don't immediately see how they can use your very impressive skills. The fact is, most of them don't know what to do with someone like you.'"

"Part of the problem," I remarked, "is the gap between nonprofits and the business world."

"More like a chasm, I'd say!" Joe responded. "And people who are at that point can't understand why it's so hard to make the connection. For one thing, people who've come from large organizations are used to solving complex problems, and the nonprofit world usually doesn't have that level of complexity. Executives are also used to working with bright people, and they don't always find the crispness of thinking, the argumentation, the openness of debate, or the willingness to try new things in the nonprofit and ministry environment."

"I also think a lot of people who are looking for ways to get involved expect that the ministry world is a more perfect world," I said. "It can come as a shock to find that churches, parachurch organizations, ministries, and nonprofits are made up of regular people too, with all the same problems and foibles as anyone else."

"You're so right," he said. "And this sometimes upsets volunteers. They think the human values of the organization should be better than they are. But what really matters, in the long run, is the good that's being accomplished by the organization. What I tell people who come to me is to keep trying to make the mental and emotional adjustments as comfortably as possible, but to focus on the results. Because it's worth it."

Essentially Joe was saying, "You've got to kiss a lot of frogs to find a prince!" Encountering a lot of options by trial and error is the best way to find your fit. It's a new world you're entering. It's a lot like watching kids at a junior high dance. The boys are on one side of the room and the girls are on the other side, checking them out. They both want to dance, but getting together is awkward and uncomfortable, so there's anxiety in the air. But the potential for success is there if they'll just persist and reach across that gap of discomfort.

LIVING PROOF

I know a great example of someone who went through the grueling frustrations of finding his fit but hung in there and found his niche—Lloyd Reeb, who works closely with us in the Leadership Network. Lloyd now occupies a position of service in a large community church where he's making a world of difference.[1]

LLOYD REEB

When I asked him how his transition came about, Lloyd explained, "In the early nineties I realized I was going to be able to spend a significant amount of my time doing something other than business. I had no idea what I would do or how my skills would be useful, so I started looking around and came across a book called the *Operation World Handbook*. In the back of that book I found a list of thirty-five or forty leading ministries. So I decided I'd send a résumé and cover letter to every one of those ministries, giving them an idea of what I'd done, what my skills were, and what I'd like to do. Then I waited to see what they'd have to say."

"So before long you had a flood of letters at your door," I said.

"Actually, no," he said. "I sat back and waited, expecting that out of all those ministries I would get some idea of where I might fit, but that didn't happen. To my great surprise, not one of them had any idea how to use a real estate developer like me. And instead of asking questions or trying to explore what I might be able to contribute, they sent generic literature geared more to a kid coming out of seminary. And in some cases they thought that because I was in real estate, I'd know how to do construction work. One suggested I might want to be a carpenter in Brazil. Clearly they didn't understand how to use a skill set like mine, and I certainly didn't understand the world of ministry well enough to know how I might fit in."

Lloyd eventually found a fit serving as director of communications for an international mission agency on a part-time basis. He was using his skills, but he was frustrated by the slow pace of the work. So he kept looking for ways to contribute. When Lloyd and his family found Mecklenburg Community Church in North Carolina, which was meeting in a gymnasium at the time, he was captivated by what he saw and experienced—a safe place where people could explore Christianity.

He began by volunteering to help in simple ways. But when he shared his heart with the senior pastor about his desire to serve, that conversation led to his taking the position of pastor of outreach, helping organize and grow the church. Six years later, Mecklenburg is a booming community of faith operating dozens of ministries inside and outside the church. And Lloyd is constantly exploring new ways to employ the skills of high-capacity marketplace leaders like himself.

"Now you're the guy on the other side of the desk," I said, "finding ways to plug people like you into ministry. So how do you deal with the high-capacity men and women who come to you looking for ways to contribute?"

"Almost every time I speak to congregations, I cast a vision for how high-capacity marketplace leaders can impact their world through Mecklenburg. Invariably someone will approach me afterward, tap me on the shoulder, and say, 'If you've got some time, I'd really like to talk to you.' So we'll have lunch. Unlike what I experienced back in the nineties when I tried to enter halftime, when people come to me I spend the first half hour just listening, to find out what made them successful and what turns their crank.

"In some cases," Lloyd continued, "we may spend the next few months helping them to understand the halftime experience, to think at a deep level about what their gifts are and how they might be applied. Only then do I begin to craft what might be a 'made-to-fit opportunity' for them."

Lloyd told me about one high-powered guy, "a turnaround artist," he called him, who had come to him looking for a place to get plugged in. They talked at length, and after Lloyd learned more about the work this man had been doing in business—fixing problems in high-volume, high-ticket package goods operations—Lloyd put him to work as a "turnaround artist" for underperforming ministries. "The challenge I'd like to give you," he said, "is to bring you alongside one of our ministries that's performing in the lowest quartile. You take that on for the next year and get it performing in the top quartile, and that's all you have to do. Then if that works out, next year I'll give you another one to fix."

When I asked Lloyd how the assignment was going, he told me, "He's having the time of his life. He's blown away that we'd cut him loose to use his unique marketplace skills to make a leveraged kingdom impact."

"I Don't Know What to Do with You"

John Leffin went to work for Accenture, a leading international consulting firm, right out of business school. He thought he'd stay three or four years,

JOHN LEFFIN

but ended up staying for twenty-one. He's a mid-westerner of German descent, solid and reliable, the kind of guy you would want running your project or coaching your son's football team. He gets things done. He was named a partner and eventually moved into human performance and change management. But the need for a move from success to significance was building steadily inside him.

"For a period of time I was basically on autopilot," he told me. "Life was good, we traveled a lot, and I was able to be there for most of my kids' major events. But things were changing, and I encountered some defining moments along the way. One of the biggest was when my dad died of cancer. He'd battled it for two years and managed to walk my sister down the aisle at her wedding. But I think he just ran out of gas after that, and he died a month later. I was thirty-seven at the time, and that was a tough year for me.

"About a year before he died," John said, "we had gone hunting together. I remember sitting in a deer stand with him when he said, 'Don't get me wrong, I'm not delighted with this thing I'm battling, but I have no regrets. I've had a good ride. When I look back on my life, I don't think I'd change much.'

"Dad had a strong faith, and to see him going out with that level of peace was tremendously reassuring for me. If there's any consolation in that disease, it's that you have a little time. I had a chance to write him a letter and tell him how I felt about the impact he had on my life. I was able to put on paper some things I hadn't been able to say before.

"When I was made partner in the firm about a year before my dad died, I thought, *Okay, I'm a partner. I achieved it. Now what?* I felt a sort of letdown and began to wonder where my career was going. Also, I never really had a chance to grieve my dad's death, so I had to get past that. I just went back on autopilot for the next six or seven years.

"During this time my wife was quite active in the church heading part of the music ministry. While all this was going on, I read your book *Halftime*, and it really resonated with me. The 'thrill of the hunt' and 'the next big deal' didn't get me excited anymore. When a big position opened up in our practice, somebody asked me, 'John, do you think you have a shot at that?' I didn't really care. The thrill had gone out of it, and I was having to work a little harder to get my motor running."

After reading *Halftime*, John looked for opportunities to get out of the grind and put more energy into work with significance. He thought he saw his chance when the company announced a new "flex-leave" program in which employees could take off six months, retain benefits, and receive 20 percent of their salary. But management wouldn't hear of it because they trusted no one else to manage his major clients. So he resigned himself to staying on.

Then as John put it, "About that time a friend put me onto a Christian financial adviser who took a whole different approach from anything we'd ever seen before. Previous advisers told us how we could make more money, but this guy asked us, 'How much is enough?' He showed us that I could walk away from work that day and we'd be fine, financially."

Two months later John's company came out with a one-time offer, waiving restrictions on sales of company stock for partners who wanted to leave the firm. John said, "That was a no-brainer for us, and we said, *How much more of a sign do we need to tell us that this is the time to move on and do something dramatically different?*

"Through my wife's church activities," John told me, "I had gotten to know the pastors quite well. So I made an appointment with the senior pastor and said, 'Here I am. I'm ready to go to work, so use me.' But to my surprise, *he didn't know what to do with me.* He told me later, 'I was threatened by you, John. Here was this type-A, hard-charging guy, and I didn't know what to do with you.' That created a certain level of tension between us. It was frustrating because I was offering to do whatever he wanted for free, and I couldn't understand why he didn't jump on that. I was beginning to think I'd made a pretty stupid decision."

John eventually realized that if God was really behind his decision, then God would work it out and he could just wait and relax. "It took me a year to stop watching the stock ticker on the Financial News Network while I worked out," he said. "But when I realized I had no control over this thing, I let it go. And that was liberating.

"The thing that sealed the deal," he said, "was something my seventeen-year-old daughter said to me. One day I called a family meeting to tell them what was going on with me and explain some of the options. My daughter Melissa responded, 'Well, Dad, you can do whatever you want; I'm cool with that.' Then she looked me in the eye and said, 'I just want to say it's been really nice having you home lately.'

"I know enough people who can't wait for their teenagers to get out of the house, so when you have one who says 'I like having you around more,' it's pretty hard to turn away from that.

"I decided to stop second-guessing my decision to leave the company.

Something told me to stay the course, so I started spending my quiet time thinking and praying about what to do next. Then along came an e-mail one Saturday morning from Leadership Network, signed by Bob Buford, talking about the opportunity to work in developing partnerships with dynamic churches. I responded to that message, and that was the beginning of the change for me."

John had to yield to God's timing to find the right fit. But when he found it, the change was dramatic. "How's it feeling now, John?" I asked.

"I realize now that a lot of my identity was tied up with the job, the title, and the perks. It takes awhile to explain," he answered. "My wife teases me about it: I used to hate breakfast meetings, but now I'm having breakfast meetings to talk about kingdom work, and I just can't wait to get there! Colleagues who knew me at Accenture tell me, 'I haven't seen you this pumped in years!' I feel like I'm on top of my game."

THE LONG ROAD TO RIGHT FIT

Byron Davis grew up in Monroe, Louisiana, and came to grips with the harsh realities of life after joining the Marine Corps at the height of the

Vietnam War. At the end of his hitch, he earned his business degree and went to work in the toy business. He spent nearly two decades on the fast track and was named CEO of Fisher-Price in 1993. But somewhere along the way, Byron decided he didn't want his legacy to be a tombstone, so he took early retirement, moved south, and today is using his knowledge and resources to make a difference at Seacoast Community Church in Charleston, South Carolina.

BYRON DAVIS

When I asked Byron where he got his motivation, he said he owed his awakening to the Marines. "I ended up in Vietnam, and it was eye-opening. I was a grunt corporal, and one day I had this epiphany that there's a whole lot more to life than people realize—more to your soul, more to life and death—and that's when I just turned it over to God. I said, 'Okay, God. You're in control here, and I'm going to trust you.' I made the promise you always hear about: 'Just get me out of here, God, and I promise I'll pay it all back.'

"Well, after the military I went back to school. When I graduated, I worked for a manufacturer's rep in Dallas, where I got into the toy business. Two years later I got a call that Fisher-Price was hiring, so I interviewed and they hired me. I figured I'd be there a couple of years, but they promoted me to sales manager. I moved to Buffalo, got married, and spent the next six years learning how to manage a large sales organization.

"It was a good time," Byron said, "but we hated the snow up there. About that time the sales manager for Dallas died, and they were moving people down there to start a regional office. I put my name in the hat. It would be a demotion, but I wanted to go south. They said, 'Okay. If you want it, you can have it.' So I spent three years in Dallas. But when they fired the national sales manager, they called me back to Buffalo." So we moved back to New York. That decision led to other promotions, and after twenty years I found myself at the top of the company."

"What did you learn from that?" I asked him.

"Ever since the Marine Corps I'd known that focus has a payoff, but I had become too focused and didn't see a lot of things that were happening around the edges. My prize back then was my own success, but I discovered I was losing perspective on what God had in mind for me and my family."

"It had been a long time since the Marine Corps," I said, "but it sounds like you were coming under fire again."

"That's right," he said. "Work was the center of my life and I didn't see that my family was really struggling. I sensed there were problems, but I was always busy, out of town, getting up early, coming home late. When I got home I'd knock back a Scotch and just sit on the couch watching TV, doing whatever I could to relax."

"You were paying a price at home for your success," I said.

"Absolutely. There was no balance there," he replied. "Of course, it was my own doing. I began some recalculating. I decided I'd been paying too high a price for success. I had climbed to the top of the ladder, but I'd leaned my ladder against the wrong building. Money, status—none of that was worth losing my family over. I knew I'd neglected the most important things in my life—my health, my happiness, my family."

"What led you to that conclusion?" I asked.

"You see it when your son fails to get up in the morning to go to school. He wouldn't come out of his room. My daughter was having problems too, and even attempted suicide at one point. That was the wake-up call. It was like, *Whoa! Wait a minute! What's this all about?* My wife and I had lost touch with each other. Our family was on the verge of collapse, and obviously something had to change. So I decided it was time to get off the bus. I was CEO, but I went to the people who owned Fisher-Price and said, 'I'm retiring.'"

"How old were you?" I asked.

"Forty-nine," he said. "Over the years we'd gone on several vacations along the Carolina coast, and we really enjoyed that area. So when I retired in April, we moved to Charleston. We bought some property, put the kids in school, and by that time my daughter was ready to enroll at the University of South Carolina, about a hundred miles away."

MAKING THE RIGHT CONNECTIONS

"Before we left Buffalo," Byron told me, "I asked our pastor if he could recommend a church in Charleston. He said, 'Oh yeah! I know just the place: Seacoast Community Church.' I had to look around to find it when we got there, because they were holding church in a Shriners building at the time. But when I walked in, there were a thousand people in one room. There was this guy blowing a saxophone, playing *Amazing Grace*, and I looked around and saw all these people worshiping. Everyone was smiling, and I was utterly captured by that.

"When Greg Surratt got up to give his message, he talked about the Bible in your life, and it was so real and practical. I said to myself, *You know, this is something special, and I want to be a part of it.* God was tugging at me, but my wife hated it. She said, 'This is just too weird, Byron! Contemporary music? I don't get it. And some of the people were raising their hands!'

"Well," he said, "after two or three more visits, she was on board. It was like, *Wow, this is really something!* So we got involved. Six months later I introduced myself to the pastor and said I wanted to help. We made a lunch appointment, we talked and prayed, and Greg said, 'Byron, I've got a book for you to read. It's called *Halftime*, by a guy named Bob Buford.' I read that book, had my quiet time, and I just sort of meditated on what God had for me. I worked through what was in my box, and I decided the best thing I could do was to help this pastor build a church. So one day I called Greg and said, 'I'd like to be a volunteer. You just tell me what you need and I'll do it.'"

"And what did he say?" I asked.

"He said, 'I don't know what to do with you, but we'll find something!' He used me as a sounding board for about a year. We had a good give-and-take relationship. Then one day the city started making a big stink about the church. It was getting too big, they said. They didn't want any more growth. We had proposed a new 3,000-seat auditorium, but the city put the brakes on that. Then one day Greg and I got into a conversation about how Wal-Mart manages growth, and the upshot was that we launched our first off-site campus, in a shopping center about a mile down the road.

"About that time we went to one of your Leadership Network conferences and heard about what was happening with churches in California, Illinois, and other places. So we made a thirty-six-hour trip and went to all those churches. We saw three services in three venues, and we knew that was the way to solve our expansion problems. We put together the financial model, and today we have a dynamic, growing ministry program."

"Sounds like you were able to use all your business knowledge in a powerful way," I said.

"For twenty-four years God had me in training for that moment: finance, marketing, advertising, sales, people management, leadership. It's really amazing how it all came together."

"And the community's not worried about those venues because they have adequate parking, and there are no zoning problems," I said. "No more political football."

"Right," he said. "It's a God thing."

"Your family problems are better too. But your income isn't quite what it used to be!"

"No," he said, "but fortunately I had a good employment contract, and I'm doing okay. My daughter went off to college, and now she's working at Barnes & Noble. Our son is in the Army and really liking it. The Army's a disciplined environment, and that's just what he needed. Both of them gave their lives to Christ, and that's made a huge difference. My wife is very much into the church now; her gift is hospitality and she's always involved."

Thinking about Byron's active involvement in that booming ministry, I recalled Pastor Greg Surratt's comment on another occasion when I asked what sort of deal he had made with Byron to get him so fired up. Greg told me Byron had come to him saying he wanted to pour his life into something. He'd received teaching opportunities at the colleges, and several companies had called him about coming in as CEO. "Byron asked me what I thought about all that," Greg said, "so I sat down with him over coffee at Barnes & Noble one day and I said, 'Well, Byron, you can do all that, or you could just come and work for me for free, and we can change the world together.' I guess that must have done it."

At the end of my conversation with Byron, I said, "It looks like God took those tough times, along with Greg's challenge, and turned your life around. Was it worth it?"

"Oh, Bob," Byron said. "I can't tell you how grateful I am. God took the evil and used it for good. Then he brought me to a place where my skills could make a real difference. And along the way, he made a new man of me."

Byron Davis found his fit.

CHAPTER SIXTEEN

The Way Out Is Through

IT IS THE LAW OF PROGRESS TO ADVANCE BY MISFORTUNE.
— NAMATIAN

SOULS ARE LIKE ATHLETES, THAT NEED OPPONENTS WORTHY OF THEM, IF
THEY ARE TO BE TRIED AND EXTENDED AND PUSHED TO THE FULL USE OF
THEIR POWERS, AND REWARDED ACCORDING TO THEIR CAPACITY.
— THOMAS MERTON, *The Seven Story Mountain*

"Life is not easy." Millions of people resonated with that opening line of Scott Peck's best-selling book *The Road Less Traveled* in the 1960s. I don't know anyone over the age of fifty who hasn't taken a hit below the waterline at some point—the death of a child (my experience) or a spouse, the betrayal of a friend, a bright shining bubble of a business deal that burst right before your eyes (also my experience). Stuff happens, and plenty of stuff has happened to the people I interviewed in this chapter.

Several years ago, a philanthropist funded a longitudinal study of a cohort of healthy men—graduates of an undisclosed top college—most of whom went on to distinguished careers for the next three decades of their lives. The results were released in a book titled *Adaptation to Life* by George Vaillant. In the introduction Vaillant referred to an earlier research project that had furnished the dominant motif for his study:

> A major conclusion of this investigation was that "no especially blessed individual turned up in this assessment; the luckiest of the lives here studied had its full share of diffi-

culty and private despair. . . . The conclusion to which the
assessment study has come is that psychopathology is always
with us and soundness is a way of reacting to problems, not
an absence of them.[1]

Vaillant went on to report his own research conclusions: "Three decades
later, as they pass their fiftieth birthdays, most are still alive and without
disabling physical illness. Over ninety percent have founded stable families.
Virtually all have achieved occupational distinction. *Yet there is not one of
the men who has had only clear sailing* [emphasis added]. Thus, over the
years the focus of the Grant Study became how men adapt to life."[2]

The same proved true for the people I interviewed in this chapter. All were
successful, yet none sailed through life without encountering major storms.

THE DRAGON TAMER

You can't be much more of a superstar than Mike Ullman. Mike was a former
White House Fellow and a major player in the international retail world.

MIKE ULLMAN

Mike has always been able to do what Andy Grove
calls "separating the signal from the noise." Mike
thrives in the sort of chaotic everything's-coming-
apart environment that reduces lesser men to tears.
He's done it in Asia (the Wharf Company) and the
United States (bringing Macy's through and out of
bankruptcy).

While he was CEO for Macy's, fending off aggressive Wall Street lawyers on one side and Seventh
Avenue garment district people on the other, being diagnosed with multiple sclerosis wasn't part of his game plan. In spite of this diagnosis, Mike
went on to run DFS Group (the world's largest duty-free retailer). After
that, he ran a Paris-based company with a portfolio of sixty luxury brand
companies (Louis Vuitton, Fendi, Tag Heuer, Moët Chandon, and more).

Mike was able to turn those organizations around, but when the majority
equity of DFS Group was sold to the world's largest luxury-goods maker
based in Paris, he fully expected to step down as president so the new owners

could name their own hand-picked leader. He was more than comfortable with that. Not only was he ready for a change of scenery after spending so much of his career in Asia, the doctors were telling him to keep his travel to a minimum—the stress just made his MS symptoms worse.

But to Mike's surprise, the new owners practically demanded that he stay on as president. They wanted someone with experience in Asia, and they especially wanted someone who had handled a major turnaround. So after praying about the decision with his wife, Mike accepted the job and took on the most demanding role of his career.

"When I got into it," he told me, "it was a successful company making five hundred million dollars a year in profits, exactly the opposite of Macy's. But immediately I had a huge crisis; the owners started disagreeing with each other about how to sell the company, and it turned into a big turmoil."

"What caused the crisis?" I asked him. "Too many owners?"

"There were four owners," he said. "Three wanted to go one way and the fourth wanted to go another, so there was a big public fight. I would like to have distanced myself from all that, but I couldn't walk away from it. We were in the process of a major restructuring, moving from seven regional businesses to a coherent global business with new merchandising and information systems, as well as recruiting a new team.

"I had decided that once they sold the company, it was time for me to do halftime!" he continued. "But when I met with the chairman of the French company that bought us, he suggested a ten-year contract. I told him I was thinking about leaving, and he said, 'No, no! I bought the company because of the management, the team, and the reputation.' I said, 'Well, I've got a disease, I don't speak French, I don't want to be in a big company, and I don't want to be in a public company because of my health.' His response was, 'Look, Mike, I paid four billion dollars for this thing, and I'm counting on you.'"

They debated back and forth until, finally, the owner told Mike, "Why don't you just stay on long enough to find somebody to run the company. You get things straightened out, and when you hire your successor, you can leave." Mike agreed. Almost immediately he began flying back and forth between San Francisco and the corporate headquarters in Paris. He told me that one year he made some forty trans-Atlantic flights to Paris, which did nothing for his family life or his health.

He didn't speak the language, he was working in a radically different culture, and he was dealing with crucial financial issues, all of which must have been utterly dizzying. But through all that he was convinced that if the Lord had put him into that situation, the Lord would give him the strength to get through it.

Career as Calling

"If I go back and review the decisions I've made in my career," Mike said, "such as why did I leave IBM, why did I go into retail, why did I go to Hong Kong, the logic isn't all that clear. But once I became a believer, those decisions were much easier to make. It was so obvious when I prayed about it that it wasn't really a risk. It was something I felt rather than thought out. It was as if I knew, *This is what God wants me to do, and if it's not the right thing, God will help me figure it out.*"

"I guess that made you a little different from most of the people you were working with at the time," I said.

"Oh yes," he replied. "But Cathy and I decided that maybe that's what my ministry was supposed to be. I wasn't supposed to go and preach about what I did but to model a behavior that made people wonder why the things I did always seemed to work. I hope it had an impact on some of them, so they could see another way of doing business. I'm not sure I can measure that."

"Any examples of that?" I asked.

"I made a friend when I moved to Hong Kong," Mike said. "We were attending the same church, but he wasn't all that serious about it. Actually his wife was the committed Christian in the family. He agreed when they got married that he would go to church with her. We were having breakfast together one morning when he said to me, 'Mike, you always seem so concerned about things being done honestly.' And I said, 'Yeah, you know that's important to me.' He replied, 'Well, I'm not sure I could do much business, if I was honest in everything I am selling.'

"I asked him, 'Well, have you ever tried the honest approach?' And he responded, 'Not really.' So I said, 'You might try it. Who knows, you might actually do better.' He just laughed. But when I saw him a few weeks later he said, 'You know, Mike, I started trying to do things honestly, and it works! People trust me! It changed my life!' Well, that really inspired me," Mike said. "You never know who's going to be watching what you do, which is obviously more important than what you say."

Today Mike serves on the boards of Starbucks, Kendall Jackson, Taubman, and UCSF Medical Center and is chairman of Mercy Ships, which retrofits oceanliners into floating hospitals that travel the globe bringing hope and healing to some of the world's most needy. And he sees his work now not only as his calling but as a ministry. Despite his illness, he continues to pursue these interests, often feeling that the more he pours himself into his ministry activities the stronger he becomes, spiritually and physically.

"It seems like you've always played through your illness," I remarked to Mike.

"Maybe it's just a form of denial," he observed, "but I've always felt that it was better for me psychologically to focus on something productive. It's unusual for me to say it this way, but I really do feel that I was called to do all these things, which means I've been given not just a desire to do them but the strength to see them through."

Mike could easily have given in to his illness and called it a disability that forced him into retirement. But the thought never seems to have occurred to him. At one point he was looking for a halftime, but he wasn't looking for a way out of the arena of usefulness—quite the opposite. As it turned out, he didn't enter halftime on his own terms. He didn't quit his career and enter a separate ministry as did many of the people in this book. Instead he found himself called to a significant ministry within the work he was already doing. He worked through his illness to become an inspiring beacon for God in a rough-and-tumble business environment where such beacons are rare.

I asked him if all those companies came to him or if he sought them out, and he replied, "It just kind of happened. That's what I mean when I say I felt it was a sort of calling. It's almost like God gave me those challenges, but he also gave me the strength to meet them. Sometimes they were illogical, like when I was running a division of LVMH and was asked to move to Paris to become the *directeur general* to lead the entire company. I was the least likely person for that job. I didn't speak French; I wasn't interested in moving to Paris; I had a serious illness; I wasn't even in the luxury-goods part of the business, which was two-thirds of the company. But I was picked by the chairman who owned half of the company.

"The only thing I could conclude," he said, "was that it was a God thing. So it was my duty to go do that job in a way that served the owners and ministered to God. It was easier for me to say yes, because I thought, *This doesn't make any sense to me on a human level. It has to be a God thing.*"

And if that were not enough, Mike is doing another "good thing"—the kind of thing he calls "practicing my faith." After rearing four sons, he and Cathy have adopted two physically challenged daughters from Hong Kong.

FINDING PURPOSE IN THE MIDST OF CHAOS

Cathey Brown discovered her purpose in life through her personal tragedy. She had alcoholic parents. She was a perfectionist child who refused to ever be out of control. She was determined to never end up like her mother and father. So she became a high achiever in school. She made top grades, was on the drill team, and served in student government. From the beginning, Cathey set her sights sky-high.

CATHEY BROWN

Today, at age fifty-four, she's an attractive, accomplished woman who describes her journey in the most compelling way, recounting how she let herself slip for a time into the very habits she had worked so hard to avoid. Hard work, a divorce, and various business struggles eventually led her to seek relaxation first in alcohol, then in prescription drugs, until one day she realized she couldn't control her cravings. She was an alcoholic.

"This all came about after my daughter was born," Cathey told me. "I began drinking and abusing prescription drugs, and I struggled with my addiction for a long time. When I got into my own recovery, I learned about the problems that adult children of alcoholics have to deal with. I had grown up in that environment, and finally I had a label for it. But I suddenly realized that my daughter was at extremely high risk for repeating the same thing.

"I really wanted to do something to stop that pattern," she said. "I looked around for whatever was available, but I didn't find anything. I discovered a lot of kids like my daughter, kids who needed some type of support group, some type of education, some type of outlet for talking about what was going on in their families, but there was nothing for them. They needed a different way to cope with their background than I had. Somebody needed to teach them that their feelings were okay, and rather than act out or push themselves to the limit as I had done, they could learn how to cope with it.

"I found out that there were some healthy things kids could do," she said. "So when I saw that nobody else had a program to give them the skills and information they needed, I decided I'd have to get involved and do it myself. I had learned it and I wanted to pass it on."

Today, Rainbow Days is a recognized agency serving children of alcoholics and others who are at risk of becoming involved with drugs. It's an exciting program with solid results that was born from genuine need and Cathey's deep desire to serve. During our conversation I mentioned another interviewee's comment: "You can either surrender to Christ or you can fight against the problem and turn to things like overwork, drugs, alcohol, or whatever, as a crutch."

"I would agree with that," she said. "I can think of two times in my life where I have vivid memories of surrender. The first was with my alcoholism, which gains complete control over you physically, mentally, and emotionally. You eventually lose the power of choice. For me the only way to deal with that was to completely surrender my addiction to God and let him take control, because I couldn't do it. And through my addiction was probably the only way he could get my attention, because in everything else, I thought I was self-sufficient. Yet I found I couldn't work my way out of that one.

"I tried to study my way out of it," she told me. "I tried to rationalize my way out of it. I tried to bargain my way out of it. But finally, one day when I was in my office by myself, I just got down on my knees and cried my heart out: 'God, I can't do this! You have to do it, and I don't know what else to do except turn it over to you.' The next morning I woke up—I'll never forget the date, April 17, 1981—and I just had this feeling in my heart that I wasn't going to drink anymore.

"They teach you in twelve-step programs to take it one day at a time," Cathey said. "So I asked God to get me through that one day. He did, and the next morning I asked for the same thing. The first few months it certainly wasn't easy, but the compulsion and the urge to drink were no longer a dominating force in my life. If I asked God in the morning to help me not drink, I wouldn't drink that day. It didn't mean I didn't want to, but if I was faithful to ask for his help, that made all the difference."

There was another threshold, she told me, that required a second surrender. "When I first started Rainbow Days, I put in a lot of long hours, and at one point I realized I was letting this new thing take over my life. It was the same old fear—I had to be perfect; I couldn't show any sign of weakness. But I was killing myself in the process and that led to another turning point, both for the organization and for me personally.

"It was a painful time," she continued, "and God had to bring me down once again to the point of physical, mental, and emotional helplessness before I was willing to surrender. It was a dark, gut-wrenching time. But I went through it and came out on the other side, and as a result I have more internal gauges today. I can check myself better. I don't have a problem admitting my mistakes like I used to, and I have balance in my life."

Not only did Cathey Brown work through her debilitating obstacle but her calling emerged directly from it. Out of the dark chaos of her addiction emerged her purpose—a work of true significance in helping others.

Dealing with Consequences

Denis Beausejour was a highly talented and hard-driving businessman who regularly put in hundred-hour weeks. He was one of the senior executives responsible for expanding the enormous global reach of Procter & Gamble, and he was definitely on the fastest of fast tracks.

"As global vice president of marketing," he told me, "I was responsible for our advertising operations worldwide, along with our ad agencies, the R&D we did for the training of our marketing leadership, and selection of the marketing leadership."

"P&G at that time," Denis said, "was the leading producer of brands that have more than a billion dollars in net sales. The pressure for results was intense, and I was constantly traveling."

DENIS BEAUSEJOUR

From Hong Kong to Jakarta, Singapore, Bangkok, and many other Asian capitals, Denis was always on the road. For relaxation, he said, he developed the habit of watching movies on TV in his hotel room— movies he shouldn't have been watching at all—and then one day on a business trip to Thailand he discovered that, for just a few dollars more, he could have the same thing in real time, live, in his room.

Denis finally realized this addiction was taking control of an otherwise disciplined life. Then one day he decided he just couldn't live this way anymore. He confessed the whole thing to his wife and made a dramatic turnaround. In our interview it was clear that everything in his life had changed since winning this battle. In the first half he was utterly driven by his passion for success; but in the second half, he is now driven by the need for spiritual surrender.

"What was missing from that part of your life that caused you to go into halftime?" I asked him.

"The biggest thing that was missing," he said, "was the discovery I made in Hong Kong—that there is a God, and that he actually loves me. That called for a more personal relationship with Christ, something I had to discover from scratch. That was the real missing piece in my life, and the consequences of not having that relationship were very nearly disastrous. But you know, Bob, when at age thirty-eight you finally get it, you appreciate the relationship in ways you never could if you'd grown up your entire life with it. I could never take it for granted—certainly not now."

"That was a pretty big turnaround for you," I said.

"Yes, and when I went about systematically rebuilding my worldview and reassessing my priorities," Denis said, "I came to the conclusion that what I could do, and wanted to do, was turn my attention to things that would have an eternal impact. I don't mean just philanthropic or spiritual activities; I wanted to refocus my own thinking and reorder my priorities. This all led me to make a radical audit and redesign of my life that happened over a period of six or seven years. I was still at P&G while this was going on, and for the first couple years I was attending seminary as well."

Denis cleared his calendar and began to study the Bible. One character that he really resonated with was Solomon, in whom he found many similarities with his own experience. "What I'm most intrigued by," he told me, "is the degree to which, step by step, Solomon accommodated himself to the culture around him, to the point that he ended up walking away from God. And I ask myself, *How much can we accommodate ourselves to the culture and the people we love and are trying to influence?* Solomon not only turned away from the true God but worshiped the pagan gods of the surrounding tribes. He indulged in the same excesses they did, and he became little different from those outside the covenant." The price he paid, Denis says, was despair, heartbreak, loss, and deep sorrow.

I've read the book of Ecclesiastes at least once a year for many years. It's the world's greatest work of existential literature. Existential—a big word that to me means making choices in the face of multiple options, which is a *very* twenty-first century problem. By the time he reached the end of his life and looked back on what he'd done, Solomon was deeply ashamed of himself. I think that's the real source of the anguish in the book of Ecclesiastes.

What price did Denis pay for his hard-driving, self-indulgent lifestyle? Despair, disappointment, debauchery, distrust, and self-destruction. Once he came face-to-face with his failure, God reshaped his life in precisely the opposite direction. He's no longer addicted to his prurient interests, and he's focused on making a difference in his new life.

"When you go through a change like the one I've experienced," he said, "you lose confidence in the old things you trusted, whether they're your abilities, projects, or whatever. Then you begin to gain confidence in new things, so you have a confidence exchange going on. But it's destabilizing at first, because some of your old pathways and instincts either don't work or become repulsive to you. With the new ways, you're like a baby deer, all wobbly and unbalanced at first, but it's fun as all get out."

"And what does the term *finishing well* mean to you now?" I asked.

"Finishing well to me primarily means that I want, more than anything, to be found obedient and faithful. I would rather have that twenty-five years from now than any success at all. Finishing well means I'm not trying to write my own plans; I just want to be available for whatever God assigns me to do."

I kept thinking about how much courage was required to overcome the "pull of gravity" for someone as driven and self-reliant as Denis had been in the first half. His gain—the same gain I've heard over and over in these interviews—has been the gain of *changed lives*. Denis has used his world-class marketing skills to help psychologist/author Henry Cloud and other Christian leaders, and he feels that he's working now for eternal impact, for things that don't end, and for things that are rich and eternally rewarding.

"I guess I'm through the first three years of my formal halftime," he told me, "and I got into halftime largely through the calling of the Spirit of God, reading books like *Halftime*, and the sense that I wanted to do something different with my life that would have more lasting value. I wanted something that had more highly leveraged consequences than what I could contribute at P&G."

"What now?" I asked. "You've continued to expand your interests, and you're doing a lot of public speaking. What's next for you?"

"As I think about the next twenty-five years," he said, "I'm thinking about how will I influence people and multiply myself. In 2 Timothy 2:2, Paul talks to Timothy about teaching what he has learned to others, who can then teach it to even more. He says, 'The things that you have heard from me among many witnesses, commit these to faithful men who will be able to teach others.' Basically, there's four generations of multiplying going on in that verse, and that's what I'm thinking about.[3]

"I don't know if I've found the sweet spot on the other side of halftime yet," he told me. "It's like the cylinders of a combination lock haven't clicked yet. I'm confident it will come in God's good time. In the meantime," he said, "my goal is to live in a way that's consistent with God's will, building his kingdom."

Living with Purpose

Someone who really understands the sacrifices involved in kingdom living is a young man I interviewed in Chicago. Jeff Small had an outstanding back-

JEFF SMALL

ground in business. He was all corporate, all success, and at age thirty-eight, he was a key executive with Ameritech, the telecommunications giant. But one day Jeff came to realize he wanted more out of life. He wanted to make a difference in the world and not just get rich. So he left all the corporate perks behind and joined the staff at Willow Creek Community Church, where he is known today as "the $100 million man." He earned that title by spear-

heading a fund-raising drive that eventually culminated in pledges to the combined Willow Creek ministries of more than $100 million.

What makes Jeff's story even more remarkable is that he's been diagnosed with an extremely rare form of cancer, and in the course of his various treatments and surgeries, he's had twelve pounds of cancer removed from his body. As I talked to Jeff, it became clear that finishing well would mean something different for him than for most of us.

When I asked Jeff to tell me how this ordeal had affected his thinking about life and death, he said, "The strange reality of having your mortality with you on a regular basis is that it makes you very deliberate about what you embrace. You become intensely focused on trying to find the things that are life-giving, and you embrace them and don't let them go." The reality is that Jeff lives, as it were, with two time frames. He is very much in the present—living, loving his family, working at the tasks he's been gifted to do. But he has one eye on the life to come as well. The cancer is still there, and the prognosis is still uncertain.

"I keep trying different things to see if we can knock it down," he told me. "But I have more sense of purpose, more thirst for life than I ever did prior to this last year and a half." And in the midst of his personal battle, Jeff had the conviction that he was, in his words, "being asked to just give my life in a complete and total way." That awareness gave his work a new level of excitement. "I'm excited about the future. Sometimes I say the experience of having cancer has been an exciting, wild ride. I can't embrace that statement completely," he said, "because it's also a white-knuckle ride for your life. But I even embrace that a lot more than I used to."

I said to Jeff, "Finishing well—that could be a clear and present reality for you, and you're saying it could even be near term."

"That's right," Jeff said. "For me finishing well is not about doing things in the future; it's about becoming somebody, and just being deliberate about being the man that God made me to be."

Jeff Small's courage in the face of his uncertain future is nothing short of inspiring. It certainly helps explain why the hope of heaven is such a clear and present reality for followers of Jesus. What we do here is certainly important, and what recognition we may receive for our efforts here and now is gratifying. But the next life is what really matters, when our accomplishments will be recognized and accounted for by our Maker.

Eternity matters. As Jeff Small sees so clearly now, there's more to life than the here and now. If we truly believe that eternal life exists, we have to know that the biggest part of life is yet to come. Look at what Paul says:

> That's why I don't think there's any comparison between the present hard times and the coming good times. The created world itself can hardly wait for what's coming next. . . .
>
> Meanwhile, the moment we get tired in the waiting, God's Spirit is right alongside helping us along. If we don't know how or what to pray, it doesn't matter. He does our praying in and for us, making prayer out of our wordless sighs, our aching groans. . . .
>
> God knew what he was doing from the very beginning. He decided from the outset to shape the lives of those who love him. . . . After he called them by name, he set them on a solid basis with himself. And then, after getting them established, he stayed with them to the end, gloriously completing what he had begun.[4]

THE WAY OUT IS THROUGH

Uncertain. Unpredictable. Destabilizing. Scary. Trying things you've never tried before. These are the words that describe Denis Beausejour's halftime experience, still very much a work in progress. The same words could describe Mike Ullman's experience in working huge enterprises out of deep financial trouble. And the same words describe Cathey Brown's one-day-at-a-time battles with addiction, as well as the dual time frame experience of Jeff Small.

What's the lesson here? Robert Frost captures it for me in one of his memorable lines: "The way out is always through."[5] Nobody said making transitions or accomplishing significance would be easy. The opening paragraph of the George Vaillant book quoted at the beginning of this chapter contains these lines: "What is mental health? I submit that health is adaptation . . . good psychological health becomes apparent only when the going gets tough."[6]

But it was also equally apparent listening to Mike, Cathey, Denis, and Jeff that they didn't feel at all alone in their trials and challenges. We are all works in progress. Admittedly those were not particularly appealing words I used above to describe the journey: Uncertain. Unpredictable. Destabilizing. Scary. But other words describe it just as surely: Fun. Exhilarating. Exciting. Rewarding. They show the other side of a balanced equation. Just as resistance generates muscle, working through our worst experiences generates joy. The challenges we encounter are no reason to quit the journey. They provide occasions to seek wisdom and strength to continue. If the thing before you is what God wants you to do, he will provide that strength. If it's not, he will show you another way.

A poem sits across from my desk, and I read it every day:

When I walk to the edge
of all the light I have
and take that step into
the darkness of the unknown

I believe one of two things will happen.

There will be something
solid for me to stand on
Or I will be taught to fly.
— S. Marlin Edges

It's about Staying the Course

THE DEFEAT OF DESPAIR IS NOT MAINLY AN INTELLECTUAL PROBLEM FOR AN
ACTIVE ORGANISM, BUT A PROBLEM OF SELF-STIMULATION VIA MOVEMENT.
BEYOND A GIVEN POINT MAN IS NOT HELPED BY MORE "KNOWING," BUT
ONLY BY LIVING AND DOING IN A PARTLY SELF-FORGETFUL WAY. AS GOETHE
PUT IT, WE MUST PLUNGE INTO EXPERIENCE AND THEN REFLECT ON THE
MEANING OF IT. ALL REFLECTION AND NO PLUNGING DRIVES US MAD; ALL
PLUNGING AND NO REFLECTION, AND WE ARE BRUTES.

— ERNEST BECKER, *The Denial of Death*

Some occupations last.

Perhaps you've noticed that not everyone who comes to terms with
their second-half objectives in these pages has chosen to change careers, or
even change directions. The reason is some occupations have context and
significance in themselves, and the only change necessary is to recognize
that the perspective just gets bigger in Life II. And the payback is for a
longer term.

If you've pursued a young person's career in which stamina, high energy,
self-sacrifice, and daring are essential requirements, chances are you'll
experience some dramatic changes as you grow older. Roger Staubach saw
the change coming seven years out and began his transition to a field where
he could make a difference without all the physical and professional risks
of the gridiron. But others have found themselves in professions that only
grow richer and more rewarding as they grow older.

The question is, *What context brings out the best in me?* Let me introduce you to some people who've asked that question and found the answer in the careers they already had.

I interviewed Dr. Donald Seldin at the Univ-ersity of Texas Health Science Center in Dallas. The center is a landmark medical facility and one of the

DR. DONALD SELDIN

top-rated research labs in the world. Dr. Seldin, at eighty-two years of age, works every day in his office with files, research reports, and books spilling out of every shelf, and he's been there from the beginning. He was the only full-time member of the Department of Internal Medicine on the Dallas campus in 1951.

Although he's well past retirement age, Seldin is constantly busy with new projects and adventures. He's writing a new book, though his bibliography is already 202 books and articles long. When he showed me a picture of the shack he worked in back in 1951, I was stunned by the contrast with the sprawling billion-dollar, high-tech campus where he works today! He was chair of the department of medicine that produced two Nobel Prize winners and recruited two others —more than any other medical school in the country—and he has since become a commanding figure in the medical world.

I was also amazed by his capacity, and I asked him, "Dr. Seldin, you resigned from full-time teaching when you were sixty-eight years old. How long did you do that job?"

He said, "When I resigned, I'd been chairman almost thirty-eight years— I think that's a world record for a department of medicine. I remained a member of the faculty, but at that time I decided to go on halftime status."

"How long do you plan to keep working?" I asked.

"Well, first of all," he said, "that's not only dependent on me. But from my point of view, I'll be here as long as I can contribute and get satisfaction from my work. I still have lots of opportunities to read, study, and work, inside and outside of medicine, both nationally and internationally. So I find this life rich and fulfilling."

"Sounds like you've sifted the things that work best for you in this season of life, and that's what keeps you going," I said. "But I'd be curious to know what's keeping you away from someplace like Palm Springs or Boca Raton?"

"What appeals to me is the life of the mind not just a life of leisure," he answered. "Medicine is still my passion, but I get excited about archaeology, painting, literature, and poetry too. We just came back from seeing two fabulous plays in London, *The Three Sisters* by Chekhov and *The Dance of Death* by Strindberg. I'm also very interested in music; I also just obtained a remarkable recording of the *Diabelli Variations* by Beethoven, with Maurizio Pullini."

Apparently, beach life and a retirement village aren't in his plans. Dr. Seldin doesn't intend to stop doing what he loves—conducting research, writing books and articles, and speaking about medicine to people at all levels. However, he did come to a point where he decided to discard the things that were burdensome and refocus his energies on the things he loves. For him, his profession is still not work at all, because he does it on his own terms, and he's having a wonderful time. While I was there, he took a quick call from a European colleague he was planning to meet at the Yale Club in New York the next day. As he closed the phone conversation he said, "All we need to settle is the table of contents, then I'll do my part." Entry number 203 on his bibliography!

No Final Curtain

Stephen Clapp is dean of the Juilliard School of Music, Drama and Dance in New York. As the Juilliard reputation would suggest, the school has some of the most rigorous entrance requirements and demanding standards in the country. "From the many thousands of applications we receive each year," Stephen told me, "about 2,800 are actually invited to audition for admittance. From those, about three hundred are ultimately selected."

"But I understand that once the students are admitted," I said, "they have a say in who their instructor will be. Is that right?"

"Yes," he said. "When students apply, they indicate their teacher preferences, and I'd say most of these students know exactly who they want to work with. They know who's best in strings, piano, dance, or whatever, and we try to honor those requests as often as possible."

"Some of your instructors are legendary," I said, "and I understand that many have been teaching forty or fifty years. How does that work?"

STEPHEN CLAPP

"There's no tenure here," he said, "but no one is fired unless there's a gross dereliction of duty, or unless demand for their classes drops off dramatically. That happens every couple of years or so, but as long as students keep asking for them, and as long as the caliber of their work remains high, they can keep teaching at Juilliard."

"So there's no mandatory retirement age?" I asked.

"No, not at all," he said. "For these people, music and teaching has been their whole life. And as they reach their eighties and nineties, most of them figure they have more to contribute than ever."

"Eighties and nineties?" I said. "Do you have instructors that age currently on the staff?"

"Absolutely," he said. "One of the classic stories around here is Mischa Elman, who was one of the great violinists of the twentieth century. All through his life, he practiced with his pianist every morning for three hours, and he continued playing until the day he died, in 1967, at the age of seventy-six. There was a point when he realized he couldn't play the notes as fast as he used to, so he just played them slower. He's a model of the way many of our faculty members have lived their lives. If you were to ask any of them, 'Why don't you retire?' it would be a slap in the face. One of our best teachers was still meeting with students until two months before he died, at ninety-six."

"That's amazing!" I exclaimed. "And inspiring too. I heard you mention one of your teachers who comes to Juilliard each week from some distance, and had some help getting here. What's the story there?"

"Yes, she's one of our best instructors," he said. "Eighty-nine years of age and still popular with students. Her pupils say she doesn't always remember their names or what they played last week. But when she listens to their performance, she knows exactly what's going on, how to fix a problem or make it better, and how to make it flow. She needs help getting to the train station at home, and someone meets her here to make sure she gets to

Lincoln Center all right. But other than that, she's going strong and has some good years ahead of her."

The majority of the faculty is much younger, of course, but Stephen told me that he has three professors in their eighties, and all are teaching performance classes. "These people don't have any question about the purpose of their lives," he said. "Their whole focus is to teach and play beautiful music." And they don't consider that work at all.

While Stephen and I were seated in the Juilliard cafeteria, he directed my attention to an eight-year-old Asian girl in a little pink sweater sitting at a table nearby. She had just played a recital the day before and was having breakfast with her father. She seemed so young and small, with her feet dangling several inches above the floor. But Stephen said she's a marvel when she gets a violin in her hands. She was the very picture of what Stephen had told me earlier about his own Life II aims.

Stephen said he doesn't plan on retiring; instead, he wants to teach precollege kids who are highly gifted and still moldable. He doesn't plan to be an administrator forever, but it's obvious that, for him, retirement is simply not an option. Getting back to full-time teaching, especially with prodigies like that young Asian girl, is where his interests lie.

THE MUSIC PLAYS ON

The role of the performance teacher at Juilliard is to listen to students play and perceive what's missing in their technique, whether it's passion, control, rhythm, or the style needed to capture the spirit of the composer. Clearly age is not a factor in doing that, and each of those incredible people in their eighties can see and hear these things today as well as they ever could. In my interview with Dr. Seldin, I mentioned my conversation with Stephen Clapp and asked, "Do you think there are parts of the brain that remain vibrant and engaged as we grow older?"

"Yes," he said, "I believe there is. Long-term memory and imprinting may be sustained in the setting where there has been intellectual and emotional commitment. In other words," he explained, "if there's a strong cognitive commitment for many years, reinforced by an emotional commitment, then those activities may be sustained well beyond other activities that do decay."

The parts of the brain that are focused on the things we love remain resilient and vibrant into late old age, he told me. I had never thought about that before, but the subjects you imprint most deeply and emotionally will stay with you long after the memories of television programs, traffic jams, airport lines, and all the other trivial things we encounter in our lives are gone. I really like the sound of that!

RALPH KIRSHBAUM

When I was a young man I often went to performances by the East Texas Symphony Orchestra, which was founded and conducted by an imposing figure named Joseph Kirshbaum. Recently I had the privilege of meeting, for the first time since high school, his son Ralph, a performing cello soloist who is now fifty-seven and touring the world with leading symphony orchestras. As we talked in the Aspen airport, I asked Ralph how long he expected to keep up his vigorous concert schedule. "I think I can keep playing into my midseventies," he told me, "perhaps longer. Music is my life. I can always continue to teach after I stop playing concerts. So why would I want to give up such a life?"

That's an excellent question which further illustrates that some careers, like those in the arts, are not just jobs but a way of life. Another musician I met in Aspen is Lawrence Dutton, the violist of the six-time Grammy award–winning Emerson String Quartet, which performs over a hundred concerts each season. In addition, Lawrence performs as soloist and guest artist around the world and makes time to teach at two music schools. Larry is a gifted performer, but from the start, he told me, he was driven by his need to succeed.

"In the beginning," he said, "the drive had a lot to do with building the career of the quartet and trying to get a recording contract. When I joined the Emerson Quartet, we were fortunate to win an important chamber music competition, the Naumberg Award. And we eventually landed a contract with Deutsche Grammophon, the world's biggest label for classical music. Our recording of the six Bartok string quartets was nominated for two Grammy awards in 1990, so we went to the award ceremony in L.A., and we won."

"You must have been on top of the world," I said.

"At first it seemed like everything in my whole life had led to that moment," he replied. "It was an exhilarating experience for all of us. But before long, this incredible depression came over me. It was like there was nothing left to shoot for, no more hurdles, nothing to achieve. If you're an athlete, you just keep going from one game to the next, and winning is everything. But it's not quite the same for musicians.

LAWRENCE DUTTON

When you're successful, you just stay there and try to get better. Winning that Grammy was an Everest-type moment, and an eye-opener for me."

"Were you a person of faith at the time?" I asked.

"No. It's important to me now," Larry responded, "but it was not so much then. In fact winning that first Grammy was part of the change. After the euphoria faded, I felt such emptiness inside; I'd been riding the success train for thirteen straight years, ever since I left school in 1977 and joined the quartet. But then it hit home that there was a lot more I still needed in my life. I had thought about spiritual things earlier in my life—the pop-culture type, at least, Zen Buddhism or whatever the flavor of the month was—but nothing came of it. After I got married we started going to church in New York, at Fifth Avenue Presbyterian, and I thought that was interesting."

"But apparently something else happened," I said. "What was that?"

"Well," he answered, "there was a big split at Fifth Avenue church over something the minister said—basically, he said that Jesus isn't the only way, and that Buddhism or some other religions may be just as good. At the time I thought that was cool, because I didn't know much about it. But when the split took place, I had to come to grips with some things, and one thing just led to another."

"Sounds like God was working on you through all of that," I said. "How did you come to faith?"

"Nancy DeMoss, the widow of a wealthy insurance executive, had a townhouse in the East Seventies at that time, and she had started a program, Executive Ministries, inviting about three hundred people who lived or worked in Manhattan to come to the Plaza Hotel for a black-tie event and a free dinner. We would hear from some famous person who would tell us how they became a Christian—it would be a senator, a football player, someone like Coach Tom Landry, or others. Then someone would speak for a few minutes, and afterward Nancy would invite those in the audience to accept Jesus into their lives. A couple of friends invited me to go, and that's where it began. One night I said the prayer, put my name on the paper, and agreed to participate in a Bible study."

"Did that stop your depression?" I asked.

"It definitely helped. My wife was coming to the same point," he said, "but by different means. Her father was raised in Korea as a Buddhist, but when he came to this country he embraced Christianity. Much later he developed a serious skin cancer, and due to complications it became apparent that he wasn't going to make it. His wife shared with us and the other siblings a most remarkable story. One day she had said to him, with tears in her eyes, 'I know you're in pain but you never speak about your suffering!' and he said the most amazing thing. He said, 'Jesus died for me on the cross; how could this compare to that?'"

"That must have really touched your wife," I said.

"It was the thing that got her on the path, and now we are both fully committed followers of Christ."

"How has that changed your work as a Grammy-winning performer?" I asked.

"For one thing," he said, "it has put me into contact with a lot of Christian performers I would never have known otherwise. But I also think that I'm called to do more now. I have to keep doing what I'm doing in music, but I'm looking for a little more balance in my life, taking more time for myself and my family."

"Looking down the road, into your eighties, do you see yourself still playing an instrument at that age?" I said.

"I don't know," Larry replied. "It's difficult for string players to do that. Isaac Stern played the violin until age eighty, but concertizing wasn't his main focus anymore. His focus was saving Carnegie Hall, which he did, and bringing along great artists like Yefim Bronfman, Itzhak Pearlman,

Midori, Yo Yo Ma, and many others of that caliber. I can see myself teaching more and more; that would be a natural transition for me. A musician's career doesn't ever really end. Music is one of those transcendent spiritual forms, and I'm sure there will be some great music in heaven! So whether I'm performing or teaching, I plan to be at this for a long time to come."

James Surls, Sculptor

James Surls is an artist of a different sort—a fine sculptor whose work is on display in dozens of public collections, commercial centers, and museums in North and South America. He's a former National Endowment for the Arts Fellow and a winner of the Living Legend and Texas Artist of the Year awards. I've collected his work for more than twenty years, and I'm an admirer not only of his prodigious talent but of his remarkable work ethic.

Some of his larger pieces sell for $100,000 or more, which puts him in the front ranks of working sculptors.

James Surls

I interviewed James at the Anderson Ranch Arts Center near Snowmass, Colorado. As we walked around the exhibits, it was clear that other artists view him as a friend and role model. I've known many artists who are pathologically cynical and inward-looking; James provides a refreshing alter-native because he is neither of those things. His winsome personality is appealing, and his enthusiasm and self-discipline are inspiring to those who know him.

When I asked James for a summary of his background, he told me his parents were the ones who encouraged his interest in the visual arts. "My father was a carpenter who built buildings, so he always had blueprints and models and tools around. He wasn't creative in an artistic sense," he said, "but he owned his own construction business and worked with drawings and materials, and he always encouraged me in that way. My mother was off the charts in a creative way," he said, "and she still does things that are unbelievably creative. She makes crosses and other beautiful things out of found materials, using twigs, bark, and leaves."

"When you graduated from college," I said, "were you planning to make a living in art?"

"I think you have to have a deep faith in that possibility," he answered, "or it will never happen. The odds are not good that you'll be able to make a living in art, so most people have a backup plan, which means they go on and get that teaching certificate. But, yes, I knew this was what I'd be doing one day. My backup plan was working as a union welder; I got my union card with Pipeline Local 798 out of Tulsa, Oklahoma. When I finally cashed in that union card, it meant I'd never work there anymore, and my dad wasn't too happy about that. But I knew that if I didn't turn in my card, I'd never make the break."

"Were you able to go full-time at that point?" I asked.

"Well, I taught to supplement my income for the first fourteen years. I could have quit earlier, but I love teaching. Today I survive totally on art."

"You recently turned sixty and you're doing what you love to do," I said. "Did you foresee this when you were, say, forty? What was the horizon like at that time?"

"At forty I didn't see an end," he answered. "I was powerful physically, and I could do whatever I wanted to do. And I've always had a strong work ethic—up early, working hard, putting in a full day—that was the fuel that drove my train. And I think that's paid off."

"Were you working hard for economic reasons or existential reasons?" I asked.

"Mainly fiscal, I would say. I understood that if you don't show up for work on Monday you don't get paid on Friday," he said, "so I think that's the source of my discipline. One time, back in 1979, I needed to borrow $5,000 to make a sculpture, so I went to my bank in Cleveland, Texas, and sat down with the bank president, who had known me for five or six years. I'd never borrowed that kind of money before, but I had a good track record. When I told him what I needed, he said, 'James, I'm probably the only banker on the planet who would say yes to this loan, but I'll do it based on the fact that I know you're a lunch-bucket kind of guy. You'll get out there and put in your time, and you'll do what you say you will.'

"To make a long story short," James said, "he loaned me the money, I made that piece and sold it, and I repaid the loan on time."

"Your self-discipline is unique among artists, I suspect."

"Yes," he said, "I'm afraid that's true."

"What happens when your plans don't work out the way you expected?" I asked.

"Well, I had a giant, major turn in my life that rattled me to the core a few years ago," he said. "My studio in Splendora, Texas, was perfect for my needs, and I thought I'd be there forever. But one day my wife, Charmaine, decided we should move to Colorado where it's cooler and more scenic. I tried to think through this rationally, because I really loved that studio—it was mine, it was paid for, and I didn't want to leave it. So it became a big psychological issue for me, and I basically refused to go."

"What was Charmaine's reaction?" I said.

"She packed her things, got in the truck, and drove off."

"And left you behind?"

"Yes," he said. "And I knew that the most important thing in my life was the woman driving that truck. She was my mainspring. If you'd asked me what was in the box, Bob, I'd say that if I lost my land, lost my building, lost my art, I'd still be me, and I'd still love my wife. And that's what I didn't want to lose."

"You'd already lost two other wives, if I recall correctly," I stated.

"Yes, and I didn't want to cross that bridge again. I'm not sure what would have happened if it had come to that—I'm not saying I'd have cashed in my chips and jumped off a bridge, but it would have been a life-changing event."

"So what did you decide?"

"I walked off and left everything behind," he said. "I still own the studio in Splendora, but I made the move to Colorado because I knew what mattered most was keeping that relationship. To tell the truth, Bob, at sixty that's what I want now. My goal is not land, or possessions, or stuff. My goal now is to have my time mean something."

"Do you feel you're accomplishing that goal?" I asked.

"If a truck ran over me tomorrow," he said, "I would have to believe that I've had a full life, and I'd be ready to go. I don't mean I want to go now, but I'd be ready. The fact is, I'm making plans for ten, fifteen, twenty years down the road, so I'm in no hurry. But I want my presence on this earth to count for something. I'd like to think that my life and work has made a difference."

"What would making a difference consist of for you?" I said.

"I think that to continue to grow, to be creative, to make the best art possible is part of it. I want to be able to exercise my gift as long as possible."

JOHN RUSSELL, SPORTS PHOTOGRAPHER

John Russell is a professional photographer who divides his time between his home on Red Mountain in Aspen, where we met for lunch, and Hawaii. John's long suit is not just his talent and skill behind the lens but also his gift for personal relationships. He has known and photographed some of the most famous people in the world, and he's also very serious about his

JOHN RUSSELL

walk of faith.

When I asked John if he felt his career in photography qualified as ministry, he said, "I don't think I would say that, but I think the old Latin word *vocation* applies in the sense that I'm not sure that I chose taking pictures as my career. God never said to me, 'Go and take pictures,' but I have the sense that this is what I'm called to do."

"When did you begin to see it that way?" I asked.

"I can't say there was a moment when I suddenly knew it, but I recall Oswald Chambers's comments about realizing one day that you're not living for yourself anymore. You're living for a higher purpose. It just dawns on you. You're like an athlete who's in the zone; you're not conscious of what you're doing because you're performing in your giftedness. I think that's what I've felt. I'm not always conscious of what I'm doing, but I know that I'm aligned with God's purposes. As human beings, we have a tendency to say, 'This is my plan.' But the truth is, when we're doing what we're called to do, it's not our plan, it's his plan."

"You're fifty-six now," I said. "What would your life have to be like at seventy-six, twenty years from now, for you to be satisfied with what happens between now and then?"

"I don't see much changing," he said. "I don't know what may be out there health-wise, but I imagine I'll still be doing the same things twenty years from now. I have a married daughter, so I'd love having a bunch of grandchildren around the house one of these days."

"How about retirement?" I asked.

"That's an absurd concept to me," he said. "I read an article about the great photographer Henri Cartier-Bresson, who's now in his nineties, and he's still out taking pictures. He doesn't need the money, and he certainly doesn't need the success, but he loves what he does. I feel that way too."

Clark Esser, Megabuilding Contractor

John has a great life, and a great place to pursue his craft. I was fascinated listening to his stories about the people and places he's photographed over the years. A few days after our meeting, I spoke with Steve Esser, a new friend from California. During our conversation, Steve told me about his father, Clark Esser, an accomplished project manager and builder. At age eighty-six, Clark is still going strong. So I asked Steve for details.

Clark Esser

"One of the most impressive things about my father," he said, "is his unwillingness to retire. He's passionate about his work, which he sees as a great platform for personal ministry. He's an expert in the area of building churches, and at age seventy-eight he took on the task of building Southeast Christian Church in Louisville, Kentucky, which was nearly an $80 million project. He finished that job just before his eighty-third birthday.

"How did he land a job like that?" I asked.

"The church put out a call for bids," he said, "and three firms indicated they wanted to make presentations. The first two were big, wealthy Louisville builders. They came in with PowerPoint presentations and slides and color charts, and they really made an impression on the board. Dad was last and he just had one manila folder and some sketches. When he stood up he made a brief presentation, gave them his credentials, and then asked why they'd want to pay the price those other guys were asking when he could manage the project for less and subcontract the building to other firms. He said they'd save a ton of money and get a better job. Well, it must have been the right touch, because he landed the contract, and he delivered right on time, just as he said he would."

"Did the board realize your dad was in his late seventies at the time?" I asked.

"I don't think it was an issue," Steve said, "but a funny thing happened later. After they awarded the contract, Dad and a group of board members went out to lunch, and as they were driving to the restaurant they passed a big dental clinic. Dad mentioned that one of his sons is a dentist, but had recently retired. When he said that, those men looked at him, wide-eyed, and said, 'Your son is retired? How old is your son?' Dad said, 'He's fifty-five now.' So they said, 'How old are you, Clark?' and Dad said, 'Seventy-eight. Is that a problem?' They looked at him and then looked at each other and said, 'No. Apparently not!'"

"Dad's eighty-six now and is going back to take on a $35 million addition that will occupy him for the next eighteen months. So he's not hanging up his cleats just yet!"

I spoke to three members of that same board after the new construction was completed, and asked if they were satisfied with the job. They said, "Are you kidding? The whole project went like clockwork. We've been begging Clark Esser to move back here and take over all our real estate projects." It was apparent to everyone that Mr. Esser was still up to the challenge, with new projects on the drawing board.

I asked Steve, "What would your father say if you asked him to think about retirement?"

"First of all," Steve said, "he'd tell me the word *retirement* isn't in the Bible. Second, he'd say that staying involved and doing something that's rewarding and contributing to the overall cause of Christ is what gives him purpose in life. It's his reason for living, and that's what finishing well is all about. And," Steve added, "he's going to finish well. He's going to take it all the way to the goal line; he doesn't want to stop short. He's not as fast as he used to be, but he's good at his work and he plans to stay in the game."

CHAPTER EIGHTEEN

It's about Running through the Tape

AND GOD BLESSED THEM SAYING, BE FRUITFUL AND MULTIPLY.
— GENESIS 1:28

FORGETTING THOSE THINGS WHICH ARE BEHIND AND REACHING FORWARD TO
THOSE THINGS WHICH ARE AHEAD . . . I PRESS ON.
— ST. PAUL

Life is a miracle, a precious commodity too valuable to waste. Many of the successful people I interviewed have realized this. Whether they've had a clearly defined Life II experience, or incorporated their significance into their initial careers, the idea of ever stopping to rest on their laurels is unthinkable. They don't intend to waste even an ounce of the precious gifts they have been given. Why should they miss out on the exhilaration of feeling the wind in their face as they sprint toward the finish line? Where's the joy in listening to the creak of the rocking chair while watching the road for the undertaker to arrive? Why turn off the ignition and just rust out? Instead these dynamic personalities choose to let the odometer spin as long as the spark plugs still fire. Each of them is an inspiring example of lives that ignore the culture's expectations of retirement and just keep on being productive. I hope they will inspire you to "just keep on doing it" as well.

IT'S NEVER TOO LATE

Caroline Hunt is a vibrant and attractive woman who is comfortable in her own skin. At eighty-one, she is one of the best examples I know of what marketing expert Faith Popcorn calls *"down aging."* She looks ten to twenty years younger than her age, and she *is* younger, both psychologically and

CAROLINE HUNT

personally. At age sixty-five she found herself divorced from her second husband, the mother of five children, and with no need to work. Yet she has done an enormous amount of work in the last fifteen years. She was a guiding force in the formation of Rosewood Hotels, a chain of twelve luxury hotels anchored by the Mansion on Turtle Creek in Dallas. And she has kept her hand in many civic and charitable interests as well.

When I asked Caroline to explain how all that transpired, she said, "I credit the Junior League with getting me out of the house and into volunteer work. I was always active at church; we had church circles, and I taught Sunday school. But I was very shy, and the Junior League gave me the opportunity to get more involved. I found that I enjoyed volunteer work and enjoyed learning about it. And before I knew it, I was involved in business activities and beginning a whole new life."

Her first hotel, Caroline told me, was actually her children's idea. They started by renovating a famous old home, and because of their mother's interest in historic preservation, they carefully retained architectural elements imported from Europe by the original owners. They added a distinctive nine-story hotel, which was quickly recognized with awards for its ambiance, cuisine, and service—even being named the best hotel in the world by the readers' poll of *Travel and Leisure.* Today there are twelve Rosewood Hotels in six countries. They're great hotels.

When Caroline was asked to design a line of toiletries for the hotels, she created the Lady Primrose product line, which has been enormously successful. So successful, in fact, that she opened a chain of Lady Primrose boutiques adjacent to the hotels. And they do a land-office business. Neiman Marcus contacted her and she had to hold them at arm's length until she could rev up production enough to handle the large commercial orders they wanted. Today Lady Primrose is sold in 1,800 fashionable stores worldwide.

Along the way Caroline formed a partnership with a friend, Vivian Young, who took on the persona of Lady Primrose, and together they have opened an antique shop and tea room in Dallas, provisioned with collectibles from Great Britain and elsewhere. "There's a book by Bruce Richardson," she told me, "*The Great Tea Rooms of America*, and he chose our tea room as one of his twenty-two American great ones. So we have been a success on that level too. It's been a fun time for me," she added, "and I have thoroughly enjoyed it."

Years ago when Caroline was in college, *Life* magazine ran a cover story on her legendarily tight-fisted oil-baron father with the headline: "Is H. L. Hunt the Richest Man in the World?" Recalling that picture, I asked her, "How big a factor was money in your life, Caroline?"

She said, "We never discussed money. In fact that magazine cover came as a great surprise to me. We never thought about our wealth."

Money messes up so many people. They can bury their central core under their fixation on money and never discover the real meaning of what makes them tick. When money stifles deeper values, it makes people cold, suspicious of others, and can rob them of any incentive they may have had to do more with their lives. When I asked Caroline about all that, she said she has encountered a number of people whose intentions were questionable, but she doesn't let that get her down because she has too many other things to think about.

She has served on the board of Tandy Corporation and other companies, but Caroline says the best part of her life now is the time she spends with her family. Her core, she says, is the family business, with a lot more emphasis on *family* than on *business*. She said, "I go to all the board meetings. Now that I'm eighty, I don't feel I have to go to every meeting, but I go to most of them. The reason I go is to create an example for my children that business is a serious matter. And I enjoy being with my family. I meet with them every Tuesday morning."

Then Caroline revealed the core that undergirds everything she does and explains why at eighty-one she still looks forward to each day with joy and anticipation. She told me that people often ask her, "What do you want from the rest of your life?" And she answers, "Well, for one thing, you know you're getting older. You know you're not going to last forever, and what I've always wanted is to be useful. And I think I'm useful being close to my children. As long as I'm feeling useful, I'll keep doing it."

"Has this been a good period of your life?" I asked.

She smiled. "Oh, I think it's the best. It's the best period of my life because I'm happy, and I have wonderful friends, and I enjoy everything I do."

Models That Keep On Keeping On

Someone who means a lot to me, and who has made a world of difference to a great many nonprofits and Christian ministries around the world, is

BILL POLLARD

Bill Pollard. Bill began his career as partner in a Chicago law firm. He was recruited from there, by means of a long-term leave of absence, to serve as an officer and senior counsel to the president of Wheaton College. At Wheaton he helped administer the university's endowments and other business matters, and he also served as an important link to the school's most famous alumnus, Rev. Billy Graham, with whom he has had a lifelong association.

Bill left Wheaton when he was recruited by ServiceMaster as president and CEO. The company has long been famous as an organization that has made faith an integral part of its business. They strive to do their business by the highest ethical standards.

When I visited ServiceMaster, I found the company's four-part mission statement incised in white marble letters six inches high in the lobby of the company's suburban Chicago headquarters:

1. To honor God in all we do
2. To help people develop
3. To pursue excellence
4. To grow profitably

Here's a set of objectives truly etched in stone!

ServiceMaster has enjoyed one of the best profit growth rates of any public company. During his twenty-year tenure, Bill Pollard and his associates took them from two hundred million in revenue to over six and a half billion on the day he stepped down as CEO. He served as chairman for several years after that and still maintains close ties to the organization, but now Bill spends all his time serving others and using his gifts to encourage the encouragers. He's opportunistic and responsive, alert to needs and meeting them in big ways. For example, Bill has been a prime encourager of Frances Hesselbein as she has led the Drucker Foundation these past thirteen years. He serves as chairman of the Trinity Forum,[1] whose mission is to help leaders engage the key issues of their personal and public lives in the context of faith. Founded in 1991 as a nonprofit organization, it fosters strategic programs and publications that further its mission: to contribute to the transformation and renewal of society through the transformation and renewal of leaders.

Work That Isn't Work at All

During a conversation about some of the things Bill Pollard has done since leaving ServiceMaster, I asked if he had any role models for finishing well. "Oh, yes," he said. "Three men clearly represent the kind of model I'd want to emulate: Peter Drucker, Billy Graham, and Ken Hanson, who preceded me as CEO at ServiceMaster."

"Those are great models," I said. "But what's the common thread?"

"The main one is that they've done work all their lives that, for them, wasn't work at all. Their work hasn't been an arduous task for them; it has always been their joy. It's serving God and serving others, and they've loved every minute of it. That's something I really admire.

"Mixed with that," he continued, "is a continuing passion for what they're doing and the gifts God has given them. There's nothing sadder than to sit down with a group of retired people and listen to them talk endlessly about themselves and their own self-interest. I don't think that's finishing well."

"Unfortunately," I said, "our culture tends to reward the egocentric way of thinking. Most of what we see on television or in the newspapers is about 'Me, me, me.' When people retire with not much on their minds, I suppose it's natural for them to think like that."

"Yes, I guess it happens," Bill said. "When you have more discretionary time and some financial resources, it's amazing how fast you can get side-tracked focusing on yourself."

"So that's not what you've seen in these three men you admire?" I asked.

"That's right. They're not focused on themselves but on others, and they keep on going even when it's hard work," he said. "Ken Hanson is gone now; he succumbed to cancer, but he was going strong right up to the end. The other two men are getting older too. Peter Drucker is in his nineties and Billy Graham is in his eighties, but neither of them is allowing physical limitations to slow them down. Sure they have days of depression or weariness, I imagine, but they move through it with endurance, and you won't see any evidence that it's too hard for them."

Despite advancing age, Bill said, his role models have kept up with the times. "They're still relevant in their thinking, their conversations, and in the way they live," he explained. "They're not thinking in the past. If you go to a Saturday night crusade to hear Billy Graham, you'll see all these bright young people; you'll listen to music that's just unbelievable; and you'll see people of every age, race, and background in the stands with you. And then an old gray-haired man stands up, and he's just as relevant to this younger generation as he is to everyone else in the crowd."

Bill's assessment of the evangelist was confirmed in an interview I had with Bob Shank, an ex-entrepreneur who works closely with Billy Graham and his son and heir-apparent, Franklin Graham. Bob told me that he had been in Dallas prior to the crusade there in 2002, and the Graham team was putting out the word to be sure and come to this crusade because it would be Dr. Graham's last. But Graham soon put a stop to that.

"As the mission date approached," Bob told me, "Dr. Graham called the senior team together and said, 'Stop saying that this is my last crusade.' He told them he wasn't done yet, and he wasn't about to quit. He said, 'I want to do two more next year.'"

"Graham was eighty-four that year," Bill told me, "but before the senior team could leave Dallas, they had to get plans in play for two more unexpected additions to his calendar. The first was to be in San Diego and the second in Oklahoma City. It was a stitch to watch Cliff Barrows at age eighty as the emcee, and George Beverly Shea at age ninety-five getting up there to sing before Billy preached! Then Graham got up there and preached for forty minutes each night. And those forty minutes were like turning the clock back twenty years and seeing him as mentally engaging, lucid, and witty as ever. He's looking ahead now to the missions to Kansas City, Los Angeles, and New York City. He plans to finish strong, hitting both coasts at age eighty-five."

Bill sees that same spirit in his other living model, our mutual friend Peter Drucker. He said, "Peter is constantly priming his mind with current events and topics of interest, and he has an uncanny way of relating those things to what has occurred in history. He puts today's topics into a context of what's gone on before. His mind is just continually working, and he has been an important source of inspiration for me."

"I certainly understand that," I replied. "I feel much the same way."

THE WIDOW'S MITE

Frances Hesselbein is an American icon, a genuine hero to me and countless others. A winner of the Presidential Medal of Freedom, America's highest

FRANCES HESSELBEIN

civilian award, Frances resigned thirteen years ago (she most emphatically will not use the word *retired*) as head of the Girl Scouts of America. After leaving GSA, she worked with Dick Schubert and me to start the Peter F. Drucker Foundation for Nonprofit Management (now Leader to Leader Institute). This foundation applies the wisdom of Peter and 350 other management thought leaders to the nonprofit organizations that do so much to fill the gap between business and government for millions of people.

Frances describes her life as *mission focused*. In a recent e-mail she told me:

> Next week I speak in Minneapolis to eight hundred busi-
> ness leaders and clergy together in a "State of Faith: Ethics
> at Work" conference at the Central Lutheran Church down-
> town. They like my belief that ethical, principled business
> leaders are called, just as clergy are called. The title they

gave me for my speech is "We Are Called." They were amazed
to read my book and find I am writing about what they decided was their focus.

Frances lives on her Girl Scouts pension, a modest inheritance (Jesus'
parable of the widow's mite comes to mind), and reimbursement of expenses
paid by the organizations she serves. I, and others on the board of the
Drucker Foundation, have never been able to persuade her to take a salary.
She says she doesn't need or desire it. Even her honorariums go to the
foundation. Her life is focused on serving others. Consequently nobody can
say no to Frances when she asks us to serve. Her powerful personal example
goes before her. She once called Len Schlesinger at Harvard Business School,
one of the 350 management thought leaders who have written and spoken
for the Drucker Foundation, with a request. Before Frances could ask, Len
said, "Frances, the answer is yes. Now, what's the question?" That's typical.

So far, the Drucker Foundation publications number over 500,000 books
published in seventeen languages. Its Web site (www.leadertoleader.org)
had nearly one million visits in 2002. Frances's age is not a topic for discussion, and I'm not going to be the one to put it in print! But let's just say
she's ahead of me in life—in several ways. She isn't rich, but she's persua-
sive, and the focus of her ceaselessly virtuous life does the persuading.

A Matter of Calling

Frances knows who she is, and she understands instinctively that there's a
bigger context to life, career, and occupation that most people recognize.
So when I interviewed her, I got straight to the point. "Frances," I said,
"what do you think of when I say the word *retirement*?"

"I don't understand it," she told me, "because I come from a family that
thought that was an obscene word. My grandfather at ninety-six had not yet
retired. At ninety-four he ran for his last term of office, a four-year term.
At ninety-six he played a pipe organ recital for his friends and family."

"What was the office he ran for?" I asked.

"He was the justice of the peace in Southfork, Pennsylvania, for over
fifty years. When he was a young man, he had a small department store in

that town. They prevailed on him to run for office, so he did. At ninety-six he was working every day, and if you had said retirement to him, he would have thought you very rude. It would be like asking how much money he made. People don't retire, they resign. When I left the Girl Scouts organization, I resigned. I made that very clear. You move, a door opens, and you walk through that door. In time another door opens and you walk through that door too."

"It takes a certain amount of faith to believe in that process, doesn't it?" I asked.

"I have a very strong belief that we are called to do what we do," Frances responded, "and when we're called, we're given the energy. And when we're no longer called, we will not have the energy. My grandfather was called to be justice of the peace in Southfork. He died quietly at ninety-seven, still in office. *Ripley's Believe It or Not* ran an article identifying him as the oldest living Republican officeholder in the United States."

"Looking at your lifetime up to this point," I said, "do you see a pattern to it?"

"Let me tell you this, Bob," she replied. "I've had four jobs in my life, and I've never applied for one of them; they just happened. I got pushed into a couple."

"I think I was one of the pushers," I said.

"Yes," she said with a smile. "You were one of the big pushers. Obviously, I don't know anything about career planning or long-term planning because not one of these career moves was ever planned. Someone else planned them for me. And I think there's something wonderful about that. Whatever you're supposed to do, you find yourself doing it. Speaking to any group, I don't hesitate to say that we are called to do what we do. And I really believe it."

"I once remember asking you, 'How are you doing?'" I said, "and you responded, 'Great.' And I said, 'Frances, you'd say that if you were on the *Titanic*.' Do you recall your reply?"

"Yes," she said. "I said, 'If I were on the *Titanic*, it wouldn't sink.'"

"That's right," I said, probing for the optimism I'd seen so often in her leadership style. "What did you mean?"

"I was being a bit facetious, but I really do believe that attitude has a lot to do with success. My husband, John, used to laugh at my behavior—always bouncing around, being so sure of myself. He'd say, 'If you were drowning, going down for the third time, you'd be shouting, "Today was great, but tomorrow will be better!"'"

"What's the source of that, Frances?" I asked. "Where do you get that positive attitude?"

"I'm doing what I'm supposed to be doing," she said, "and somehow I've been given the direction, and the energy, and the calling to do what I'm doing. It's vastly satisfying. Once a month I fly to Sacramento to be with my children. Someone once said, 'The secret of life is doing good work, being with good people, and learning to give and receive love.' I'm so grateful that all my life I've had the privilege of being with good people, doing good work, and being with people I love. So, obviously, a big part of my attitude comes from that."

A Practical Example

Some people understand that the best way they can serve others is to keep right on making money doing the work they love to do, then "reinvesting" their gains in the hospitals, universities, and seminaries that serve the rest

BOONE PICKENS

of us. Thank God they do! I spent hours as a child in my local Carnegie library, as did millions of others. Andrew Carnegie's life as a pioneering philanthropist has been a major influence on my own Life II.[2] It's inspiring to see others today emulating Mr. Carnegie.

One of the best examples I know of this type is Boone Pickens, my next-door neighbor in a Dallas high-rise. According to a profile on Boone's money-making strategies in the pages of the *Wall Street Journal*, the legendary tycoon has made more money between the ages of sixty-eight and seventy-five than he did in his well-chronicled forty-year career with Texas-based Mesa Petroleum. At this point, he's not making money either to spend it or keep it (he has plenty), but to give it away to causes that matter to him. Boone loves to work! Through the 1980s, he made headlines for virtually inventing "a new way to make money in energy."

As the *Journal* put it, his secret was structuring corporate takeovers to play the value of resources in the ground against the depressed stock prices of the big oil companies.

Along the way, Boone accumulated a fortune, but he hasn't stopped doing what he loves. He told the *Journal* reporters that he's simply "reinventing" the way he operates. Boone has so far found three different ways to make money on oil and gas—drilling for it, buying undervalued companies with reserves, and running a commodities fund.

"I started Mesa Petroleum in 1956," he told me, "with $2,500 in capital. I gave a $2,500 note to my two backers, and they gave me a $100,000 line of credit for three years. If I didn't have them off the line in three years, they had the option of taking whatever assets we had, and I didn't have anything. I studied geology, and I'd only had one three-hour accounting course. So three years seemed like forever to me. But I had them off the note in three years, and everything worked out fine."

Money was never the object, Boone told me, but it was the way he kept score.

"So what do you say to people who call you a big spender?" I asked him.

"I'm not a spender," he said. "If you came up to my ranch, you'd say there's been a lot of money spent here. That's because I like to build things, but I don't like to shop or to waste a lot of time buying stuff for myself. If I buy clothes, I go to the store and stay maybe two hours, once a year, and I'll buy three suits and whatever else I need to go with them. That's it."

When Boone has a plan, he goes after it with a passion. And if he's that way when he buys his suits and blue jeans, you can bet he's the same way in business. "By 1980," he told me, "I was convinced that finding oil and gas was too expensive. You couldn't find it cheap enough to make any money. If we had to drill for it, it would cost us three dollars a barrel, but if we could buy companies with oil in the ground, we could buy it for a dollar a barrel. So that's the approach I decided to take."

Unfortunately, as he told me, the approach wasn't very popular, and pundits and others in the mainstream media gave him a beating.

"Do you remember Lester Thurow?" he asked.

"Yes," I said. "An economist at MIT."

"That's right," Boone replied. "We debated before the MIT business school, and Lester described me as a viking. He said I came in on my ship and plundered the town. I took all the food and vegetables, put them on my boat, and left. So when it was my time to respond, I said, 'Lester, that's the most unusual description of what's going on in corporate America that I've ever heard. It has nothing to do with some guy in a boat and somebody's garden. Gulf Oil had 200,000 shareholders when we came in, and their stock was selling at forty dollars a share. The company sold to Chevron at eighty dollars a share—that's a pretty good profit, I'd say.' And I pointed out that stock valuation went from $6.5 billion to $13 billion. Two hundred thousand people made $6.5 billion in the deal. 'So,' I said, 'where's the piracy in that?'"

No Regrets

Boone has had his ups and downs in both business and life. "How do you get beyond the deal that ate your lunch?" I asked. "Do you ever have regrets?"

"No, not at all," he said. "I'm too busy with other things."

"So you just go on to what comes next?"

"Oh yes," he said. "I couldn't have done what I've done by looking back. I take both the credit and the responsibility for my own actions. I don't give anybody credit for my success, and I don't blame them for my mistakes.

"I know I can learn from my past mistakes," he continued, "but I don't want to dwell on them. I've always felt like a ship leaving the East Coast, headed for Europe. I plot the course, but things are going to happen along the way. I'm not drifting, and I'm not in a sailboat. I've got a motor, but I'm affected by wind, waves, storms, or whatever. All those things may cause me to divert for a while, but I know where I'm headed. I've seen that in my business career. It's important to know where you're going."

"You go to the ranch, the office, and you still like the person you're married to," I said. "You're getting along with your kids, and you're still giving money away."

"Yes, I'm satisfied with that," he said. "I look at all the things that have happened, and I'd change some if I could. But I won't get a chance to do that. So I don't dwell on it. I feel pretty comfortable."

"The amazing thing," I said, "is that you don't seem to have slowed down in recent years. Which raises the question, what's a seventy-five-year-old man doing working as hard as you're working?"

"Why do I like to work?" he responded. "Well, I suppose it's what I know how to do. The other day I spoke at the NYMEX and opened the trading that morning. When I stood up to speak, I said, 'I don't have a speech today; I'm just going to make a couple points, and then I think the questions will take care of the discussion here.' The emcee almost fainted!"

"You were his program," I said, "and you were going to be finished in ten minutes!"

"I imagine that's what he thought," Boone said. "But I talked less than five minutes, called for questions, and immediately there were twenty-five hands in the air, in a room of 150 people. One of the questions was 'I understand that you've given a lot of money away.' I said, 'Yes, I have.' And the man asked me, 'Do you enjoy giving it away more than you enjoyed making it?' My response was that I enjoy both of them very much, but I believe making it is still more fun than giving it away."

I said, "You've given money away and raised money for other people too, haven't you?"

"Yes, I raise money for OSU," he replied. "I had twenty alums out at the ranch a while back for a fund-raising event."

"Why do you do that?" I asked him.

"I think that's what I'm here for," he said.

"Is it a God thing?"

"Yes, it's a God thing. I think that I've been gifted not unlike somebody that can sing, or play sports, or whatever. I feel that I've been given a clear message: I don't have to go to work every day, but I've been given the skills to do some special things, and I want to be sure I accomplish them. It's money that's not really mine, in the end. I made it working with other people, and it all goes back to other people eventually."

"But you're wired to make money," I said.

"That's right, and I don't apologize for it."

"What role does faith play in your life?"

"Well, my grandfather was a Methodist minister and I was brought up in a Methodist home. My grandmother, who lived next door to us, went to the Christian church. She was much more focused on her religion than my parents were. Not that they weren't religious, but when I stayed with my grandmother, she always read the Bible to me every night before I went to bed."

"What do you think God expects of you?" I asked him.

"I'm pretty convinced that I've been given the skills I have, and my job is to produce, so I produce. It's just that simple for me. I think that's it."

From day one, Boone told me, he has always loved to work. I asked him to tell me more about that, and he said, "Well, let me tell you a story. I think this says it pretty well. When I first got married to my wife, Nelda, I told her, 'Nelda, honey, there's something I've got to tell you about me.'

"Nelda said, 'Why, sure, Boone. What's that?'

"I said, 'Nelda, I love to work.'

"She responded, 'Well, that's nice, Boone. I think a man should like to work.'

"So I said, 'Nelda, honey, I don't think you understand. I *really* like to work!' And then I just proceeded to tell her what that would mean."

I asked Boone just what it did mean, and he answered, "Okay, I guess the best explanation I can give you is something one of my guys said a few months ago when someone came in and asked, 'Is Boone still focused on business? Is he engaged in what's going on at the office?' Everybody who knows me was standing around, and one said, 'Like 6-6-6.' So the outsider asked, 'What's 6-6-6?' And my guy told him, 'You see, he starts getting the access market trading on commodities at 6:00 o'clock in the morning; he's still there at the office at 6:00 o'clock in the evening; and he works six days a week.'"

We both laughed, and I said, "I'd never heard that story before, but I really like it!"

As we wrapped up our conversation, I said, "Boone, let me ask you one more question before I go. When I say the word *retirement*, what comes to mind?"

"When my dad retired, he spent all his time down at the YMCA; he just played pool or went fishing and hunting. That was okay for him, I guess, but I'm just not cut out that way. Couldn't do it. I'm doing what I love to do, and I don't see any reason to change it."

"So you're just planning on running through the tape," I said.

"I'll be doing it as long as I can," he said. "People used to say to me, 'Pickens, why don't you just retire and give somebody else a chance?' Well, I thought that was unusual. Give them a chance? Everybody has a chance! I'm not crowding anybody out; I'm creating something. It's like a feed trough. Nobody is standing behind you waiting to get up there and get something to eat. This trough is unlimited. It isn't even crowded. You can walk up anytime you want and feed."

Clearly, Boone Pickens knows what he likes, he knows who he is, and he's happy with that. To use a classic Texas expression, "He's happy as a pig in mud," and he's reinvesting the by-product of his repositioned business activities, pouring his money into the lives of generations of people now and yet to come.

CHAPTER NINETEEN

Finishing Well

COME, MY FRIENDS
'TIS NOT TOO LATE TO SEEK A NEWER WORLD.
PUSH OFF, AND SITTING WELL IN ORDER SMITE
THE SOUNDING FURROWS; FOR MY PURPOSE HOLDS
TO SAIL BEYOND THE SUNSET, AND THE BATHS
OF ALL THE WESTERN STARS, UNTIL I DIE.
IT MAY BE THAT THE GULFS WILL WASH US DOWN;
IT MAY BE WE SHALL TOUCH THE HAPPY ISLES,
AND SEE THE GREAT ACHILLES, WHOM WE KNEW.
THO' MUCH IS TAKEN, MUCH ABIDES; AND THO'
WE ARE NOT NOW THAT STRENGTH WHICH IN OLD DAYS
MOVED EARTH AND HEAVEN, THAT WHICH WE ARE, WE ARE,
ONE EQUAL TEMPER OF HEROIC HEARTS,
MADE WEAK BY TIME AND FATE, BUT STRONG IN WILL
TO STRIVE, TO SEEK, TO FIND, AND NOT TO YIELD.
— ALFRED LORD TENNYSON, *Ulysses*

Finishing well is hard to do. We're new at it.

Twenty years from now, the "rules" for this second adulthood of Life II as a productive season of life may be better known. But for now, we're out across the frontier breaking new ground.

This book has been an exhilarating adventure for me. From the beginning I set out to find out what the pathfinders were doing to "crack the code" on this new season. And I have asked you to come along and learn from their words, not mine. That's why I recorded and transcribed the interviews, to present them here as lively conversations. It is in that spirit, then, that we come now to the final thrust and assessment of this remarkable journey.

THE "GOLDEN YEARS"

Dr. Os Guinness is Senior Fellow of the Trinity Forum in Washington, D.C., a popular speaker and author, and a long-time personal friend. Our mutual

Os Guinness

interest in training Christian leaders has brought us together in common bond on many occasions over the years. When I spoke to him recently about this book, he said that now that he inhabits Life II himself, the subject of finishing well has been very much on his mind.

So I asked him my favorite question: "Os, what does *finishing well* mean to you?"

"I find it very interesting," he said, "that we celebrate the achievements of people like Moses, Sophocles, Michelangelo, Churchill, Freud, Victor Hugo, and others who did incredible things in their sixties, seventies, and eighties. But the fact is, *most people don't finish so well.* There are a lot of euphemisms about the golden years, but there's no question that, for many people, things like physical decline, sickness, financial hardships, the death of friends and loved ones, and the loss of a sense of purpose that often comes with retirement actually turn out to be fairly devastating."

"You're right," I said. "But what do you mean when you say there are a lot of euphemisms about the golden years?"

"They're actually euphemisms," he responded, "that cover up our lack of realism about what actually happens to people when they grow old. Old age to some is a terrible burden and they don't want to deal with it honestly. And I think that tendency is reinforced in this country by a paradox. America is the most advanced society in the world. On one hand, modern medicine gives us more years, a much longer life. But on the other hand, American culture puts so much stress on youth, not becoming obsolete, being innovative, and always being up on the latest technology, that it makes old age seem irrelevant much sooner. We live longer, but we're made to feel obsolete much sooner, which is unfortunate.

"In *The Coming of Age*, Simone de Beauvoir says there are really two secrets to finishing well. One is maintaining continuity between what you do before you retire and what you do afterward. I believe that's true.

Second is having a sense that you have a project or task to pursue in your latter years, so that you don't just drift into uselessness."

"That makes a lot of sense," I said. "It's something I've been saying as well." One of the best books on the subject of vocation and calling is Os Guinness's book *The Call*, which should be required reading for anyone who wants to understand their purpose in life. So I asked Os how he looks at the idea of finishing well in the light of his study of calling.

"When we think about the Christian view of calling," he said, "I think it's important to recognize that *we can retire from our jobs, but we can never retire from our calling.* Calling gives us our sense of task or responsibility, right up to the last day we spend on earth, when we will go to meet the Caller. I think that gives life incredible value, and therefore the prosperity of finishing well is that we continue to have a sense of responsibility and engagement that makes each day we live enormously important. This is also a subject in which the Christian view provides such a compelling contrast with the secular view, which tells you that you're over the hill when you reach a certain age."

"It occurs to me," I said, "that literature has a lot to say about this. Have you considered dealing with any of these issues through your Trinity Forum reading programs?"

"Yes," he said. "We're doing that now. The first one is called 'Entrepreneurs of Life,' and the final section in the curriculum, in fact, is called 'Finishing Well.' We have three readings concerning people who didn't finish well, and then a couple on people who did. And they always provoke some wonderful discussions. The first one is the story of Sebastian Marchmain, from the novel *Brideshead Revisited*. It's the story of someone who becomes the caricature of his greatest weakness, the lovable alcoholic, and his friends have never confronted him about it. That reading always creates an incredible discussion."

"But isn't that the normative case for most sixty-year-old alcoholics?" I asked.

"That's right," Guinness said. "That story is about an alcoholic, but you could look at punctuality or bad temper or any other vice just as easily. Often, if people have flaws, they're not really challenged by their spouses or close friends. People just laugh and make excuses for them. And they become a sad caricature of what they might have been, wasting their gifts.

"Then we have another reading using Henry James's story 'The Madonna of the Future,' about a fine painter who is paralyzed by his perfectionism and never paints the ultimate painting he's dreamed of. I've known many people like that. I was partly released from that myself by a wonderful quotation from G. K. Chesterton, who said, 'If a thing's worth doing, it's worth doing badly.' A lot of us need to know that. If we insist on waiting for the perfect situation, we may never use the gifts or talents we've been given."

Os's next example came as a surprise.

"Another reading we're using is about a man who finished badly—Pablo Picasso. It's the story of someone who was completely driven by his talents, and that's where we try to bring out *the difference between calling and drivenness.* Many people confuse those two, I think, and that's unfortunate, because drivenness is a terrible thing. To know your calling is a wonderful thing, but to be enslaved by some inner compulsion can be maddening."

"I would guess," I said, "that Picasso's compulsion was the main reason he kept furiously painting those increasingly angry canvases."

"At the end of the story, Picasso says, 'Every blank canvas is an affront to me.' He had this manic compulsion to paint more, more, more, but the quality of his work was just going down. He was driven. But he was also an atheist and saw himself as a sort of god substitute. Painting was the only thing he could do to create, so I think there was some pathology there, as well."

OBSTACLES IN THE PATH

As Guinness was describing the readings he's using at Trinity Forum, it occurred to me that what they're developing is a study in *obstacles to finishing well.* As we've seen in several of these interviews, the challenge to use the second half wisely is an obstacle course for some. It can also be a minefield. So I said, "Os, you've just named three of those obstacles. Are there other things that you see as obstacles to finishing well?"

"A big one," he replied, "is regret. I see this especially in people who simply can't ask for God's forgiveness, or who can't forgive themselves for the stains on their copybook. They're eaten up by regret. In that vein, one of the stories we're reading is called *Piper's Tangle*, about a man whose regret has turned into hatred at the end of his life. There's no way he can change himself by that time, and at the end he cries out, 'If only God existed!' What you realize is that apart from God there's no way any of us can ever change."

As I listened to Os it occurred to me that one of the blessings of the second half is that you've grown beyond most of the shallowness and experimentation of youth. You've lived long enough to know what works and what doesn't, so you can make many decisions quicker and better than younger people. The downside, however, is that you can also remember all the mistakes and failings of the past, so unless you know how to deal with that you can end up with a lot of regrets. I asked Os where that would fit in the equation.

"I love the little statement by Borden of Yale," he said, "'*No reservations, no retreats, no regrets.*' In some ways, we all have regrets. If you live long enough, you'll have them. But I find I just have to take the times where I've sinned or failed or not lived up to my own expectations, or where I've not lived up to other people's expectations, and I just have to put those at the foot of the cross and know they're forgiven. That's how I can live without regrets and keep on going."

"Well said," I responded. "I like to think of that as a sort of delegation. I delegate all of that stuff to Christ who, amazingly, volunteered to accept the horrible mess that all of us have made, and he knows how to dispose of those sins and failings for me."

"Yes, I agree," Os said. "Unfortunately, a lot of people have such a hazy view of what awaits us after this life is over, they really don't have a Technicolor faith, and life becomes gray for them at that point."

"When you say 'hazy view,'" I said, "are you talking about the wasted hours in front of the television, or idle chatter over lunch at the golf course?"

"I was really thinking more about life after death," he said. "My father had a tremendous sense of God's presence, and he described the way he finished. He said the home he was in at the end of his life was 'the waiting room for heaven.' I like that image very much. The prospect, the hope, and the joy of heaven were vivid and real to him. And I've seen that with many people who really have a strong faith.

"With so many people," he added, "heaven is just a vague concept, and the prospects are a little gray, uncertain, and nebulous. But what you're

ROSS BUFORD

saying about mindless amusements is right too. If someone just lives for their work, taking their identity from what they do at the company, and for relaxation they go down to Florida to play golf, before long they're going to feel incredibly demoralized due to the pointlessness of all that. Those who have a deep sense of what their gifts are—their purpose in life and their calling—are much more alive. *We never retire from our calling.* I love that. Calling continues right up to the last day. Our work may not last, but our calling never dies."

Those poignant words awakened more memories of my son, Ross, and the words he had written for Linda and me before he died. Ross was only twenty-four when he and two friends went on that river expedition to the Rio Grande. But he had taken the time to write out a clear will in his own hand, on his investment banker's stationery from his office. Strikingly, it was written in the past tense. It was, in effect, a letter from the other side. Here's what he said:

> Well, if you're reading my will, then, obviously, I'm dead. I wonder how I died? Probably suddenly, because otherwise I would have taken the time to rewrite this. Even if I am dead, I think one thing should be remembered, and that is that I had a great time along the way. More importantly, it should be noted that I am in a better place now.

The will directed how he wanted his earthly goods distributed, and Ross concluded the document with this benediction: "In closing, I loved you all and thank you. You've made it a great life. Make sure you all go up instead of down and I'll be waiting for you at heaven's gate. Just look for the guy in the old khakis, Stetson, and faded shirt, wearing a pair of Ray-Bans and a Jack Nicholson smile. I also thank God for giving me a chance to write this before I departed. Thanks. Adios, Ross."

Ross finished well at age twenty-four. It's almost as if he isn't gone; he's just in another place, and he's written Linda and me a letter from that place to say that he's gone ahead for a while. I know he will be waiting for us just as he said "at heaven's gate." Ross's letter drew my mind back to the Old Testament to the time when King David lost his son, Absalom: "Can I bring him back again? I shall go to him, but he shall not return to me."[1] It won't be all that long in the whole scheme of things until I join Ross in that "better place" where he now is. Meanwhile, there's work to do here.

At the end of my conversation with Dr. Guinness, I asked him, "What do you think of when I say the word *retirement?*"

He said, "I have never put much of a premium on retirement, because my sense of calling is bigger than any particular job I've done. I haven't worked for a corporation, so I don't have a great pension fund that would allow me to think of going to Florida! But my plan is to keep working until it's my time to go."

"The idea of cashing out isn't something you'd consider?" I said.

"No," he said. "It's never been part of my thinking, or of my parents, or anyone close to me in that sense. My calling will keep me going until my last breath, and calling to me is far more important than where I get my check from. So, no, I'm not cashing out."

A MATTER OF CHOICE

We've met a lot of fascinating people on this journey, heard their stories, reacted to their insights and observations, and nodded in agreement no doubt more than once. I've been especially impressed by the passion and conviction in their voices. I learned a lot from those who've turned a corner in their lives and found, often to their own great amazement, the answers that were there all along.

Some of them have made breakthroughs, but all of them have broken the code. And what is the "code" for Life II—the life beyond halftime? What are the rules of this new game? This is what we've set out together to discover. Our odyssey is, for the moment, ended. It's up to you now to take what you've seen in these pages and find out how they apply to your own life.

You must decide where you will go from here. We've been given more than one lifetime to live. But the question is, will we live both of them to their fullest or just the first one? Can we finish well? Or is the second half of life meant to be a season of retirement, an end of work, and a turning inward?

Will Life II be about living at the center of an ever-shrinking circle of family, friends, and associates, until it's just you and the endlessly flickering television? Or will it be something more?

You and I have been privileged to engage in conversations "over lunch" with the pathfinders out on the edge of the demographic frontier. What they've told us demonstrates that, unlike our predecessors, we do have a choice in this matter of Life II. Part of that previous lack of choice was simply predisposition—how our culture used to think about age and aging. An industrialized society had created predefined patterns and cycles of life. That's "the way people did things" then. But that was then and this is now.

Life II can be the richest and best season of a long and extended life. Peter Drucker has written twenty-two of his thirty-four books after the age of sixty. Boone Pickens has made and given away more money after age sixty-eight than before. Frances Hesselbein began a new foundation that has attracted 350 top management thought leaders to the nonprofit world in her Life II season. And then there's Wilson Goode, going from church to church recruiting mentors so that the at-risk children of prisoners might have a chance at Life I and some choices for Life II.

The pathfinders show us what *can* be done. In many and diverse ways they show us that the final stage of life goes beyond success to significance and surrender. Beyond self-actualization to self-transcendence. They have overcome inertia and the pull of gravity.

Dallas Willard said when I asked him if he, at age sixty-eight, had retired: "No, I'm going on." That, in large measure, is what cracking the code of Life II seems to be about. Willard has found a "rabbit that won't break down" and he's going to follow it right into the eternity that he says is "in session now."

Most obituaries end with the phrase "He is survived by . . ." The practice is to then list family members. But a person who fully lives Life II is survived by so many more—they live on through the parts of themselves that they have given away and surrendered into the lives of others. Those remain.

And, more than that, they are multiplied. They grow and gain forward momentum like a great river that's fed by a thousand streams as it moves forward toward the sea, where it finally empties itself.

> He is not dead, he breathes in you.
> — Jean Racine, *Phedra*

Where are the lives of the great finishers now? They're not lost. They're not even over. They're still there, hidden away in the lives of those of us they've invested themselves in. Their words and, more importantly, their examples of "lives lived for others" remain long afterward.

Now the Life II pathfinders we've "had lunch" with are part of my consciousness, my guidance system. Yours too, I hope.

TWO PARTING SUGGESTIONS

1. Pass it on. Don't keep this to yourself. If someone's name has come to you as you've read this book, buy him or her a copy. Hand it to the person with an invitation to "do lunch" together and discuss what they have learned. It will be an interesting conversation . . . for both of you. If you are part of a small group, that's also a good place to give and receive feedback.

2. At the very end of his life, Jesus prayed for those of us who would follow him and carry on his work. Turn to Appendix 4, fill your name in the blank provided, and find yourself in this prayer. Even better, load this up on your computer, plug in a friend's name, and e-mail the prayer to him or her.

Appendix 1
Cast of Protagonists

PETER DRUCKER, *94*: Teacher, consultant, and author, specializing in strategy and policy for both businesses and nonprofits, and in the work and organization of top management. A prolific writer on subjects relating to society, economics, politics, and management, Mr. Drucker has published thirty-five books that have been translated into more than thirty-five languages, and he serves as a frequent contributor to magazines. *Forbes* magazine, in a 2001 cover story, called him "Still the Youngest Mind." In 2002 Drucker was awarded the Presidential Medal of Freedom, America's highest civilian award. Since 1971 he has been the Clarke Professor of Social Science and Management at Claremont Graduate University, which in 1987 named its Graduate School of Management after him. He was honorary chairman of the Peter F. Drucker Foundation for Nonprofit Management, now called Leader to Leader Institute.

TOM LUCE, *63*: A founding partner of the Dallas law firm Hughes & Luce, LLP. He has served on the boards or as guest lecturer at a number of schools of higher education including the Kennedy School of Government and the LBJ School of Public Affairs. He is also active on the boards of Dell Inc. and multiple community and charitable organizations. A candidate for the 1990 Republican nomination for governor of Texas, he has been appointed five times to major posts by Texas governors. Mr. Luce has concentrated most of his public service efforts on improving public education, which efforts led to his founding Just for the Kids in 1995 and forming the National Center for Educational Accountability in 2001.

DALLAS WILLARD, *68*: Professor in the School of Philosophy at the University of Southern California in Los Angeles. His philosophical publications are mainly in the areas of epistemology—the philosophy of mind and of logic—and on the philosophy of Edmund Husserl. His popular books include *The Spirit of the Disciplines, Renovation of the Heart*, and *The Divine Conspiracy.*

WALLY HAWLEY, *65*: Cofounder of InterWest Partners, one of the larger venture capital partnerships in the United States. Hawley's prior experience includes seven years as president of SHV North America Holding Corporation, a wholly owned subsidiary of a Netherlands corporation, and seven years as a consultant with McKinsey and Company in their San Francisco and Amsterdam Offices. He is currently devoting the majority of his time to nonprofit (ministry) endeavors. *whawley@interwest.com*

JAY BENNETT, *54*: Managing partner of a Minneapolis law firm through which he has developed other business interests. He operates the Wallestad Foundation, a private foundation supporting Christian ministry, and has launched "Kingdom Oil," a Christian Community Foundation that encourages unity and collaboration across historic barriers of denomination and culture and also facilitates Christian giving. Bennett has been very involved in the Halftime movement in Minneapolis.

LAURA NASH, PH.D., *54*: Senior Research Fellow on the faculty of Harvard Business School in the area of entrepreneurship and service management. In addition to academic work in business ethics, Nash has been a consultant and speaker on corporate values at a number of leading corporations for twenty years. Prior to joining HBS, she was program director of business and religion at Harvard Divinity School's Center for the Study of Values in Public Life. Nash has been a frequent contributor to journals and books on business ethics, corporate culture, and leadership, and has been a regular commentator in the media. *lnash@hbs.edu*

JOHN CASTLE, *61*: Dallas attorney and former executive vice president of EDS Corporation, where his responsibilities included legal affairs, corporate communications, community affairs, government affairs, and public relations. He has served as president of the University of Texas Law School Alumni Association and as trustee of the UT Law School Foundation. In 1998 Castle received the ADL Jurisprudence Award. He serves on the board of directors of the Texas Department of Protective and Regulatory Services (since fall 2001), the Episcopal Seminary of the Southwest, the Dallas Institute of Humanities and Culture, Central Dallas Ministries, Paul Quinn College, and the Dallas Foundation. Castle recently chaired a strategic planning committee for the Episcopal Diocese of Dallas. *jcastle10@cs.com*

JEFF HELLER, *64*: President and chief operating officer, he rejoined EDS in March 2003 after a brief retirement. He serves on EDS's board of directors and its executive committee. Previously he was vice chairman of EDS with more than thirty-four years in the data-processing industry. Heller serves on the board of directors of the Dallas Symphony Association, Mutual of Omaha, Trammell Crow Company, Cotton Bowl Athletic Association, and Guaranty Bank. He is a member of the University of Texas Chancellor's Council, the University of Texas Engineering Foundation Advisory Council, the University of Texas McCombs School of Business Advisory Council, and the Longhorn Foundation, and is a trustee of the Southwestern Medical Foundation. He served in the U.S. Marine Corps as a jet pilot from 1960 to 1966 and attained the rank of captain. *jeff.heller@eds.com*

HON. REV. WILSON GOODE, *65*: Philadelphia's first black mayor. Goode's undeniable intelligence and propensity for hard work, illustrated in his rise from a background of poverty and his successful three years as Philadelphia's city manager, make him a significant role model for the next generation of African American politicians. Goode chronicles his personal and political experiences in his 1992 autobiography *In Goode Faith*. He currently heads Amachi, a program to recruit and train mentors for at-risk kids. *wgoode@ ppv.org*

DAN SULLIVAN, *59*: Cofounder and president of The Strategic Coach Inc. A visionary, innovator, and conceptual thinker, Sullivan has over twenty-five years' experience as a highly regarded speaker, consultant, strategic planner, and coach to entrepreneurial individuals and groups. Sullivan's belief in and commitment to the power of the entrepreneur is evident in all areas of The Strategic Coach and its successful coaching program, which works to help entrepreneurs reach their full potential in both their business and personal lives. He is author of several books and courses.

DON WILLIAMS, *63*: Chairman emeritus of Trammell Crow Company, the commercial real estate services and investment firm. Williams founded the Foundation for Community Empowerment and spends much of his time on a comprehensive renewal initiative in low-income neighborhoods, using the Fair Park/South Dallas area as a model.

DR. KENNETH COOPER, *72*: Recognized for more than three decades as the leader of the international physical fitness movement, Dr. Cooper is credited with motivating more people to exercise in pursuit of good health than any other person. At the Cooper Aerobics Center, as president and CEO, Dr. Cooper is supported by a four hundred-person staff in carrying out his mission to educate and encourage optimum health in as many segments of the population as possible. Stretching his international reach, Dr. Cooper has lectured in over fifty countries and authored eighteen books, which have been translated in forty-one languages and Braille and total more than thirty million copies sold.

STEVEN S. REINEMUND, *54*: Chairman and chief executive officer of PepsiCo. Reinemund also served as chairman and chief executive of PepsiCo's global Frito-Lay business. He led Frito-Lay North America, during which time sales and profits for the unit grew dramatically. Reinemund started his career with PepsiCo at the corporation's former Pizza Hut division, where he served as chief executive officer. A graduate of the U.S. Naval Academy, Reinemund served five years as an officer in the United States Marine Corps, achieving the rank of captain. He served on the National Advisory Board for the Salvation Army, and was chairman from 1996 to 1999. In this capacity, he was honored with the William Booth Award in 1999, and the 1998 Excellence in Board Leadership Award from the National Assembly of National Voluntary Health and Social Welfare Organizations. Reinemund was also awarded the Salvation Army's top volunteer award, the Order of Auxiliary Service Medal. He has served on the National Council of La Raza, which in 1997 honored Reinemund with its President's Award.

MARGIE BLANCHARD, 63: Worldwide compelling motivational speaker, an accomplished management consultant and trainer, a best-selling author, and an entrepreneur. Heads the Office of the Future, the research and development arena of the Ken Blanchard Companies, a proactive think tank that anticipates clients' needs and directs the development of products and services to fulfill evolving demands.

KEN BLANCHARD, 63: Prominent, gregarious, sought-after author, speaker, and business consultant, Blanchard is universally characterized by friends, colleagues, and clients as one of the most insightful, powerful, and compassionate men in business today. He is chairman and chief spiritual officer of the Ken Blanchard Companies, and coauthor of *The One Minute Manager*, which has sold over ten million copies and still remains on the bestseller lists after twenty years.

DR. ARMAND M. NICHOLI JR.: For the past twenty-five years, Nicholi, author of *The Question of God*, has taught at Harvard, where he compares Sigmund Freud's atheist-based reasoning against the atheist-turned-believer C. S. Lewis. He is the editor of *The Harvard Guide to Psychiatry*, used by medical schools and universities throughout the world. *amnicholi@aol.com*

DICK DEVOS, 47: As the president of Amway, DeVos led one of the world's largest direct selling corporations. He and wife, Betsy, cochair the Education Freedom Fund that partnered with the Children's Scholarship Fund in 1999 to award more than 4,000 scholarships to underprivileged children in Michigan. *ddv@windquest.com*

GEORGE GALLUP, 73: Chairman of the George H. Gallup International Institute, chose a secular path for a religious call. When Gallup joined the family polling firm, the church lost a prospective priest, but the world gained a world leader in public opinion research. The Gallup Organization has studied human nature and behavior for more than seventy years. Gallup today employs many of the world's leading scientists in management, economics, psychology, and sociology. Gallup Performance Management Systems help organizations increase customer engagement and maximize employee productivity through measurement tools, coursework, and strategic advisory services. Gallup's 2,000 professionals deliver services at client organizations, through the Web, at Gallup University's campuses, and in forty offices around the world.

JOHN FINDLEY, 57: Spent the last twenty-one years of his working career at Findley Adhesives, Inc. where his last position was chairman, president, and CEO prior to the sale of the business. All of the proceeds from the sale went to establish two Christian foundations. The first, Cedarly Ministries, Inc., supports a group of pastors' retreat centers. The second, Vine and Branches Foundation, Inc., was established for the purpose of helping people effect change in their own lives and the lives of others. The foundation accomplishes this goal by making grants to not-for-profit Christian organizations and grass-roots inner-city organizations serving minority residents. *jfindley@wi.rr.com*

TOM WILSON, 56: President/CEO Leadership Network and the Buford Foundation. Wilson has a lifelong commitment to build and nurture Christian leaders. That passion now translates into the foundation's mission to help innovative Christian leaders be more effective, and move from success to significance. *tom.wilson@leadnet.org*

TOM TIERNEY, 49: Recently stepped down as chief executive of Bain & Company. Tierney is credited with building Bain into a major consultancy. An advocate of "constellation leadership," he is now devoted to building his brainchild, the Bridgespan Group, an independent nonprofit consulting practice designed to "bridge" the gap between the seemingly disparate worlds of corporate management consulting and nonprofit organizations worldwide. He recently launched Bridgestar, an Internet-based charity designed to strengthen the leadership of nonprofit organizations. He is coauthor with Jay W. Lorsch of *Aligning the Stars*. *thomas.tierney@bridgespangroup.org*

HAMILTON JORDAN, 58: Jimmy Carter's White House chief of staff, he authored two best-selling books, started an NFL franchise, was named "Sport Executive of the Year" for founding the ATP TOUR (global men's professional tennis tour), and created numerous other successful companies, many in the health and biotechnology sectors. In inspirational speeches he tells the story of his successful battle to overcome three different cancers. His cancer advocacy and unique point of view are summed up in the title of his book, *No Such Thing as a Bad Day*.

MERLE SMITH, 65: President and chief executive officer of Prism Enterprises, Inc., a healthcare manufacturer and distributor based in San Antonio, Texas. Prior to his affiliation with Prism, Merle was president and CEO of Kinetic Concepts, Inc., a healthcare manufacturer and distributor. He is active in his church and works with young adults.

EARL PALMER, 71: Pastor of University Presbyterian Church in Seattle, Washington. Author of several books and frequent conference speaker.

HOWARD HENDRICKS, 79: Dr. Hendricks is chairman of the Center for Christian Leadership and Distinguished Professor at Dallas Theological Seminary. For fifty-three years he has touched the lives of thousands of students at DTS. A Christian visionary, he provides leadership as a board member for several large Christian corporations, including Search Ministries, Walk Thru the Bible, Ronald Blue and Co., and was a past board member and keynote speaker for Promise Keepers. He handles a rigorous speaking schedule, ministering in over eighty countries personally, and his impact is furthered through books, radio, tapes, and films. He has written or cowritten numerous books including *As Iron Sharpens Iron, Living by the Book*, and his newest release, *Color Outside the Lines*, a book on creativity.

JOHN SNYDER, *61*: Founded Snyder Oil Corporation in 1977 and served as chairman and CEO until its merger in 1999 to form Santa Fe Snyder Corporation. He served as chairman of Santa Fe Snyder until its merger in 2000 with Devon Energy Corporation. John received his BS in petroleum engineering from the University of Oklahoma and his MBA from Harvard.

MIKE KAMI, *82*: Considered one of the best consultants in the world on strategic planning and strategic management for future success of organizations, national or global. He was head of strategic planning for IBM and then for Xerox, and lectured for the American Management Association. He now lives in Pompano Beach, Florida, where he continues to write and consult.

ALLISTAIR HANNA, *59*: His position as executive director of Alpha USA is his third career. Hanna started as a nuclear physicist, then went to business school and joined McKinsey and Company, becoming a senior partner. Alpha is a twelve-week, fifteen-session program designed especially to appeal to the unchurched who have questions about Christianity.

RANDY BEST, *60*: After a successful career as an entrepreneur and venture capitalist (Mason-Best), Best established Best Associates in 1990, a private merchant-banking firm which is responsible for the creation of Voyager Expanded Learning, a national education initiative in partnership with public schools. Best has devoted a substantial portion of time and resources throughout his career to philanthropic pursuits, and has had a longstanding interest in education and the welfare of children. *rb@randybest.com*

VESTER HUGHES, *75*: Mr. Hughes's many years of private practice have spanned all aspects of federal taxation—income, estate, gift and excise, individual, and corporate. Hughes has argued two cases before the United States Supreme Court and participated in several other Supreme Court cases. *vhughes@hughesluce.com*

LARRY ALLUMS, *57*: Executive director of the Dallas Institute for Humanities and Culture since 1997, after nineteen years as professor of English, chairman of the English department, and dean of the College of Arts and Sciences at the University of Mobile. He is editor of and contributor to *The Epic Cosmos* and has extensive experience with public programs. His chief intellectual interests include Southern literature, classical and modern epic, and the works of Dante.

ROGER STAUBACH, *61*: After a storied career in both college (Heisman Trophy winner) and professional football (Pro Football Hall of Fame), Staubach entered the real estate industry in 1970 and formed his own company in 1977. The Staubach Company is a full-service commercial real estate strategy and services firm whose primary focus remains exclusively on the user. The company now has 7,800 real estate professionals in over 50 North American and 179 global offices.

BILL SOLOMON, *61*: Chairman, board of directors of Austin Industries. Solomon's assignments have included a wide variety of operational and administrative positions with Austin since 1956. He holds a degree in civil engineering from Southern Methodist University and an MBA from Harvard Business School. Very active in civic interests in Dallas, Solomon has chaired Dallas Citizens Council, Greater Dallas Chamber, and the 2003 funds campaign for the University of Texas Southwestern Medical Center. *bsol@austin-ind.com*

DR. PAT THOMAS, *69*: Medical doctor and surgeon. Thomas was awarded the Bronze Star for his service in Vietnam. He served as chief of surgery of both major hospitals in Tyler, Texas. He is former president and chief medical officer and currently senior development officer at Trinity Mother Frances Health System Foundation. He is active in church and civic affairs.

JIM COLLINS, 45: Collins is a student of great companies—how they grow, how they attain superior performance, and how good companies can become great companies. Having invested more than a decade of research into the topic, Jim has authored or coauthored four books—including the classic *Built to Last*, a fixture on the *Business Week* bestseller list for more than six years, and *The New York Times* bestseller, *Good to Great: Why Some Companies Make the Leap . . . and Others Don't*. His work has been featured in *Fortune, The Economist, Fast Company, USA Today, Industry Week, Business Week, Newsweek, Inc.*, and *Harvard Business Review*. Driven by a relentless curiosity, Collins began his research and teaching career on the faculty of Stanford's Graduate School of Business, where he received the Distinguished Teaching Award. After seven years at Stanford, Jim returned to his hometown of Boulder, Colorado, to found his management research laboratory. In addition to his day job, Jim is an avid rock climber.

RUDY RASMUS, 47: Beginning with nine members in 1992, St. John's United Methodist, under the leadership of co-pastors Rudy and Juanita Rasmus, has grown to more than 8,100 members over the past eleven years and is one of the most diverse (both socially and economically) congregations in the country. Their Bread of Life program currently serves over 6,000 meals each month to homeless individuals, provides emergency clothing, and offers job opportunities and training. The project also operates the *DayBreak* facility, which provides needed shower, laundry, medical, and HIV services to the homeless in the downtown Houston area. The Reverends Rudy and Juanita C. Rasmus, pastors of the St. John's United Methodist Church in Houston, were named the 1998 Distinguished Evangelists of the United Methodist Church by the Foundation for Evangelism.

MILLARD FULLER, *68*: Fuller's business expertise and entrepreneurial drive made him a millionaire at age twenty-nine. But as the business prospered, his health, integrity, and marriage suffered. These crises prompted Fuller to reevaluate his values and direction. The Fullers decided to sell all of their possessions, give the money to the poor, and begin searching for a new focus for their lives. Fuller founded Habitat for Humanity in 1976 with his wife, Linda, and has earned international recognition for his work advocating decent, affordable housing for all. As of 2004, Habitat is at work in more than ninety countries worldwide. More than 800,000 people now have safe, decent, affordable shelter because of Habitat. *mfuller@hfhi.org*

BOB ROBERTS, *45*: Founding pastor of NorthWood Church. He started the church in 1985, and has seen it grow to currently over 2,200 members. Bob teaches courses on church planting, church growth, and nation building at seminaries and universities across the country. He is also a frequent lecturer to church leaders and strategists, both nationally and internationally, having started over fifty new churches in the past two years. He has done active work in nation building in Iraq and Afghanistan. *texplant@aol.com*

TOM MCGEHEE, *48*: Acknowledged leader in collaborative services. He designs and leads collaborative sessions, conducts training and education and coaches organizations in collaborative work. Prior to establishing his own firm, WildWorks, McGehee was a vice president with Cap Gemini Ernst & Young, where he was a lead global facilitator. In this role, he designed and led collaborative sessions all over the world. McGehee has been an executive with EDS and was an officer in the U.S. Marine Corps. McGehee is the author of *Whoosh—Business in the Fast Lane. wild@wildworksgroup.com*

MIKE SHIELDS, *45*: Chartered financial analyst and a member of the New York Society of Security Analysts and the Association for Investment Management and Research, Shields served as president and chief investment officer of Campbell, Cowperthwait Division of U.S. Trust Company in New York. Prior to that, he was principal and growth equity portfolio manager at Scudder, Stevens, & Clark and held several investment management and investment banking roles at NationsBank. He left the investment world to join Leadership Network as director, Halftime Events and Expansion. *michael.shields@halftime.org*

JOE MIRAGLIA, 67: Miraglia has forty years experience in senior human resources positions in three top Fortune 100 companies and university teaching in three graduate schools of business. Since retiring as senior vice president of human resources from Motorola, his focus is best summarized in his ministry's mission statement: "Through Bible-based teaching and coaching, engage Christians and Christian organizations in transforming vision to action in strategic, career and life planning."

LLOYD REEB, 42: Reeb and his business partner own and operate seniors housing. Reeb is a pastor at Mecklenburg Community Church in Charlotte, North Carolina, where he leads strategy efforts within a large seeker-targeted church. He is actively involved in Leadership Network's Halftime initiative, helping high-capacity people move from success to significance, and is on the board of the Finishers Project, an organization of more than seventy leading mission agencies to help boomers find a significant second career in missions. *lloyd.reeb@halftime.org*

JOHN LEFFIN, 44: Focuses much of his time helping churches around the world create ministries to reach and serve people in Halftime. At his church, Leffin leads a Connections Ministry, which helps people determine their spiritual gifts and how to put them to work. This includes plugging them into known ministry needs or helping them create new ministries. In the fall John spends a portion of his time coaching high school football. *john.leffin@halftime.org*

BYRON DAVIS, 55: Was in the Marine Corps at the height of the Vietnam War. He left Fisher-Price Toys as president to spend more time with his family. Relocated, he began attending Seacoast Church, Mt. Pleasant, South Carolina, where he coached the leadership team in creating eighteen campuses, each with three hundred to five hundred members.

MIKE ULLMAN, 56: As CEO took Macy's from bankruptcy to merger with Federated Department Stores. A senior executive at LVMH (Moët Hennessey Louis Vuitton), the world's largest maker of luxury goods, headquartered in France. Most of his volunteer time now benefits Mercy Ships International, which operates a fleet of ships crewed by doctors, water engineers, teachers, and agriculturists who visit some of the world's poorest cities. The services they offer are given free of charge.

CATHEY BROWN, 54: Founded Rainbow Days Inc. based on her own personal childhood experiences. Her personal mission is to "provide children living in high-risk situations with the skills they need to overcome adversity and stay drug free." Brown is a pioneer in the field of life-skills education for children and families in high-risk situations, and is the developer of the "Curriculum-Based Support Group" model of life skills education. She is the author of a series of award-winning curricula based on this model. Over one million children in thirty-three states across the nation have participated in a Rainbow Days' "life-skills support group." *catheyb@rdikids.org*

DENIS BEAUSEJOUR, 46: Was worldwide vice president of marketing at Procter & Gamble, and left to pursue a dream to attend seminary and to use his considerable marketing, organization building, and teaching skills to build God's kingdom. Beausejour announced his departure in a memo, saying that he had spent the first half of his life achieving success and wanted to spend the rest of it achieving eternal significance. *beausejourdf@aol.com*

JEFF SMALL, *34*: Executive director of Willow Creek Community Church's multisite strategy. After a decade in the corporate world, Small left his director of marketing position to serve as a full-time volunteer, coleading Willow Creek's first capital campaign. Once in the world of ministry, he felt God's call to make this his career. He now spends his time growing teams and mentoring leaders in the three new Willow Creek campuses.

DR. DONALD SELDIN, *82*: Built one of the three or four strongest departments of medicine in the world. When Seldin became chairman of the department of medicine at the University of Texas Southwestern Medical School, he was its only full-time member. When he stepped down, the medical faculty was 125 times larger and numbered four Nobel Prize winners. At the same time, he is a highly productive researcher and one of the world's finest medical statesmen.

STEPHEN CLAPP, *63*: Violinist and winner of the Naumberg First Chamber Music Award as member of the Beaux-Arts String Quartet, Clapp is a violin faculty member and chamber music coach at the Juilliard School, where he is also the dean. A deeply committed teacher of professionally oriented violin students, Clapp has been teaching violin since he was fourteen years old. He has written numerous articles in *The Instrumentalist* and *The American String Teachers Journal*, of which he is a former Violin Forum editor, and has traveled widely in North America giving master classes.

RALPH KIRSHBAUM, *57*: His career encompasses solo performance, recitals, chamber music, teaching, and recording. He has appeared as a soloist with major orchestras in North America, Europe, Asia, and Australia. Each summer, he performs in chamber music festivals throughout the world. Kirshbaum is founder and artistic director of the RNCM Manchester International Cello Festival held every three years at the Royal Northern College of Music in Manchester, England, where he also teaches.

LAWRENCE DUTTON, *49*: Noted as a "poetic violist" (*The New Yorker*), Lawrence Dutton has earned distinction as a recitalist, soloist with orchestras, chamber musician, recording artist, and teacher of viola and chamber music. As violist of the world renowned Emerson String Quartet, Dutton performs over one hundred concerts each season and has won six Grammy awards, most recently in 2001 for "Best Classical Album" and "Best Chamber Music Performance" of the complete string quartets of Shostakovich on the Deutsche Grammophon label. Mr. Dutton is currently a professor of viola and chamber music at the State University of New York in Stony Brook and the Manhattan School of Music in New York City.

JAMES SURLS, *60*: Sculptor. James earned his M.F.A. at the Cranbrook Academy of Art, Bloomfield Hills, Michigan. He has received the 1993 Living Legend Award, the 1991 Texas Artist of the Year, and the 1979 National Endowment of the Arts Fellowship.

JOHN RUSSELL, *57*: Sports photography is a lifelong passion. Starting in 1970 with skier Jean-Claude Killy and tennis player Arthur Ashe, he continues to shoot people like Shaquille O'Neal and Andre Agassi who are at the top of their game. Russell had the good fortune to photograph Agassi when he was only four years old, and now thirty years later, he does most of Andre's still photography, which includes working with wife Steffi Graf and their two young children. *johnrussellhawaii@yahoo.com*

CLARK ESSER, *86*: Master builder. As the interview relates, he was hired to do an $80 million project in his late seventies. He brought it in on time and under budget, just before his eighty-third birthday.

CAROLINE HUNT, *81*: Honorary chairman of Rosewood Hotels. Her creation, Lady Primrose's bathing luxuries, are offered in many hotels as well as in 1,800 stores nationwide. Recipient of many awards for community service, she has been named one of the 100 Most Influential Women in the U.S. and one of the 50 Most Powerful Women by *Ladies Home Journal*. She received the Alexis de Tocqueville Award of the United Way of Dallas and is currently cochairman of the United Way Foundation of Dallas.

C. WILLIAM POLLARD: Chairman emeritus of the ServiceMaster Company. ServiceMaster has been recognized by *Fortune*, the *Wall Street Journal*, and the *Financial Times* as one of the most respected companies in the world, and has been ranked the No. 1 service company among the *Fortune 500*. Pollard speaks, writes, and teaches on management and ethics, and is author of the best-selling *The Soul of the Firm*. He also serves on a number of corporate and nonprofit organizations, including Herman Miller, Inc. UnumProvident Corporation, Wheaton College, Billy Graham Evangelistic Association, and the Trinity Forum.

FRANCES HESSELBEIN: Has devoted herself to changing lives for the better. In 1998 she received the Presidential Medal of Freedom, the United States of America's highest civilian honor. The award recognized her leadership as CEO of Girl Scouts of the U.S.A. from 1976–1990 and her role in leading social-sector organizations toward excellence in performance through her work at the Leader to Leader Institute, originally known as the Peter F. Drucker Foundation for Nonprofit Management, where she was founding president. *frances@leadertoleader.org*

BOONE PICKENS, *75*: Founded the company that became Mesa Petroleum in 1956. From 1956–1996, while Pickens was CEO, the company produced more than three trillion cubic feet of gas and 150 million barrels of oil. Pickens is also known for his high-profile corporate control contests for Cities Service, Gulf, Phillips, and Unocal. Upon leaving Mesa in 1996, Boone founded a fund management company, BP Capital, and in early 1997 launched BP Capital Commodities Fund. An investment of $1 million in that fund at inception had returned value of $18.4 million during a six-year period. The BP Capital Energy Equity Fund was launched in late 2001 to invest in public energy companies. Pickens is an active philanthropist to a variety of medical institutions and institutions of higher education, including his alma mater, Oklahoma State University. Pickens was recently inducted into the Oklahoma Hall of Fame. His recently updated 1987 autobiography, *Boone,* was listed for fifteen weeks on *The New York Times* bestseller list.

OS GUINNESS, *61*: Senior Fellow at the Trinity Forum, writer, and speaker. His deep concern is to bridge the chasm between academic knowledge and popular knowledge, taking things that are academically important and making them intelligible and practicable to a wider audience, especially as they concern matters of public policy.

Appendix 2
The Consequences of Inertia

So what's the downside? What's the harm, the consequence of an inward turning life of self-absorption? Thoreau put it well when he said, "Most men live lives of quiet desperation." It may be quiet, but it is desperate. And perhaps worse, it's deadly. Ask your internist. He or she will say something like this: "I can't quote the research, but it's uncanny how many of my patients go into decline almost immediately after they retire, and die a couple of years later."

Death. Decline. Here are some other "D words"—we don't want to say them. We don't even want to think them (that's called Denial). Here are words that come to mind as the consequence of inertia and a failure to re-engage:

Decline
Death
Despair
Deception
Debauchery
Defeatism
Depression
Disability (giving in to it)
Disinclination
Disrespect
Drift
Disenchantment

The interviews in this book were all intended to teach us *how to* finish well, not how not to. But there's definitely another side to the story. Jim Collins uses "comparison cases" in his best-selling business books to put the great companies in high relief against their not-so-great peers. I know plenty of stories of people whose lives finish with a whimper, not a bang. Some of the best ones can be found in great literature. For years, Ivy League medical schools have incorporated readings in drama into their curricula, because the psychological dimensions that emerge in the course of telling a good story can be particularly informative and enlightening. Dramatists and writers live in this space, so I'll use their examples to spare my friends.

Last year in New York, Linda and I saw a wonderfully performed version of Eugene O'Neill's Pulitzer Prize–winning play *Long Day's Journey into Night*, with Vanessa Redgrave and Brian Dennehy in the leads. Drawing back the curtain on the secrets of his own family to make us peer into our own, O'Neill's play was four hours of acting out of all the "D words."

Brian Dennehy played the drunken father who was swilling in despair after retiring from a meaningless career on the stage. He had acted the same melodrama over and over and over again—each week a new audience in a new city, year after year, dragging his disenchanted family along behind him, to spend days in lonely hotel rooms. The Vanessa Redgrave character had taken to opium as a refuge from boredom and lack of any purpose in life except to "be there" for her husband. O'Neill described *Journey* as "a play of old sorrow, written in tears and blood." He dedicated it to his wife, Carlotta, requesting that the play not be staged until 25 years after his death.

Other stage and fictional versions abound. Here's a short watching and reading list:

About Schmidt—Jack Nicholson's Academy Award–nominated role portraying an insurance actuary who drifts instantly into ennui when he retires. *A Man in Full*—Tom Wolfe's novel of Charlie Croker, the man with "a neck like a jersey bull," an aging former Georgia Tech fullback, now an Atlanta real estate tycoon living a desperately deceptive life at the mercy of his creditors and the shopping and status cravings of his trophy wife. *King Lear*—Shakespeare's great play. Lear is a proud but mind-fogged old king who deeds his kingdom to his daughters in order to live a life of ease.

We then see about two hours of disease and despair acted out on the stage as his daughters put him out into the storm.

The Death of Ivan Illych—Leo Tolstoy's classic tale of a Russian judge 110 percent absorbed in his work, who is disconnected from his role by a mysterious disease. He comes home to be served with the reverence due a "great man" only to find that his wife and grown children have had to fashion lives of their own. It's the "I married you for better or worse but not for lunch" situation most second-halfers will discover if they haven't been around much lately.

The Iliad—Book nine of Homer's great classic. The Greek hero, Achilles, retires from battle and just sits in his tent after being slighted by Agamemnon. All pique, no purpose. In response to emissaries sent by Agamemnon, we are treated to the best argument for retirement ever put into words. Following is my summary of the great warrior's points—my paraphrase, not Homer's marvelous poetry. For those who want the real thing, I have included in parentheses the line numbers from the Richmond Lattimore translation:

THE RETIREE'S LAMENT
- Been there, done that. (line 330)
- My material needs are met. Don't need more fame and fortune. Got plenty already. (line 365)
- I can live a long life of ease back on my farm in Greece. It's dangerous out there. I might get hurt. (His mom, the goddess Thetis, tells him he *will* get hurt if he returns to battle and she got it from Zeus!) (lines 407, 393)
- My country has offended my honor. Why should I work where I'm not appreciated? (lines 313, 334, 368)
- I have a different perspective about battle now that I've come away to meditate. I'm in halftime. I'm not caught up in the fray. (line 185)
- I'm ready to settle down. You should be too. I'm going home. *Hasta la vista,* baby! (lines 393, 400)
- Such honor is a thing I need not. (line 607)
- My heart is no longer in this war. (line 703)

- "A man dies still if he has done nothing, as one who has done much. Nothing is won for me now that the heart has gone through its affliction in forever settling my life on the hazard of battle." (That line's the real Homer—line 320).

Does any of this sound like the self-talk that's been going on inside your head? Most of us in the second half of life could make a version of the same arguments. I felt an uncomfortable resonance myself as I read them—there are plenty of weekends when I'd rather stay at the farm!

A Few More Warning Parables

The Short Happy Life of Francis Macomber by Ernest Hemingway—An aging British playboy and his pretty but promiscuous wife seek happiness through gin and guns on an African safari. They find it briefly, but then . . .

Tennessee Williams—All Williams's plays chronicle desperation and self-absorbed decline.

Cat on a Hot Tin Roof—An aging high school hero whose greatest days are behind him (Paul Newman) marries the rich, beautiful daughter (Elizabeth Taylor in her prime as Maggie, "the Cat") of the town's "big man" (Burl Ives) and thereby becomes a kept man. The desperation in this great movie is of the not so quiet variety.

A Streetcar Named Desire—Aging and broke, Blanche du Bois, a lady with lots of secrets (Vivian Leigh) shows up to sponge off her sister and put on airs. The sister's muscular husband (Marlon Brando at his best) punches through her denial and deception. A miserable time is had by all.

Summer and Smoke—Aging actress (Geraldine Page) tries to keep up appearances. Everybody sees through it.

Night of the Iguana—Aging defrocked priest (Richard Burton) in a seedy Mexican resort with a dissolute woman (Ava Gardner) tries to regain a modicum of self-respect. He fails to do so.

The Long, Hot Summer—Aging drifter (Paul Newman again) versus aging town "big man." (This time it's Orson Welles.)

I could go on, but you get the point. The second half of a meaningless life filled with reminiscence, and void of purpose is not a pretty picture on screen, stage, or in short stories. Rent the movie. Buy the book. All the "D words" are there. Just don't do it.

P.S. The Amazon.com listing for *Long Day's Journey into Night* has a section titled "Customers who bought this book also bought" which lists:

Streetcar Named Desire by Tennessee Williams

Who's Afraid of Virginia Woolf? by Edward Albee

Death of a Salesman by Arthur Miller

Waiting for Godot by Samuel Beckett

Once they get started, people can't seem to get enough of Life II as if it is a soap opera. It's engaging to watch, but is that the way you want to live?

As the kids would say, "Get a life, Dad." And that's what this book is about—getting a life—not just a first life, but a second or third life, and maybe even a fourth. It's not over till it's over. Don't quit early. It gets ugly fast. Rent the video and see.

MUST SEE:

Cat on a Hot Tin Roof—or any Tennessee Williams play.

About Schmidt—No movie nails modern retirement better. In an opening sequence you won't ever forget, Jack Nicholson sits at his desk watching the clock tick down to 5 P.M. on his retirement day. He then emerges to a world of little structure and much unfamiliarity. It's funny. It's poignant and it makes its point.

King Lear—Rent the Lawrence Olivier version and buckle up. It's great drama—some think it is Shakespeare's best—but it's not fun. It's indeed a warning parable. Studying this play kept me from selling my company for about ten years!

Appendix 3

Ten Principles for Life II

GREAT ADVICE DRAWN FROM THREE DIFFERENT
INTERVIEWS WITH PETER DRUCKER

#1: Find out who you are.

One of the lessons Peter has taught me through our long-term personal relationship is to find out what my strengths are and put them to work. "Whenever people are on the road to success," he said, "they tend to think of repositioning as something they do if they're a failure. But I would say that you ought to reposition when you're a success, because that's when you can afford it." Repositioning for significance makes more sense when you know who you are and where you belong.

PETER DRUCKER

#2: Reposition yourself for full effectiveness and fulfillment in life's second half.

Only with this knowledge of ourselves, Peter said, can we reposition ourselves for full effectiveness and fulfillment in the second half. "Early in their careers," he said, "people tend to have a fairly limited time frame, of four years or so. They can't visualize what comes after that." By the time they achieve a measure of success, the time frame expands. "Suddenly they begin to think about options that are twenty, thirty, or more years ahead of them." Imagine how the range of possibilities increases when you add twenty or thirty years to your frame of reference—a whole second adulthood!

#3: Find your existential core.

The most important thing, Peter said, is "to have faith as your existential core." What faith does, he said, is provide the framework for your work, your job, your value system, your personal relationships, and all the other things that make you who you are. "There's a strong correlation between high achievement and the ability to come to terms with life's basic questions." And he added, "I think the most successful people are those who have a strong faith. They're people who all their lives have believed in faith, hope, and charity, and who believe that the greatest of these is charity." If they have faith and hope, he said, "now they're ready to move to charity, and there is a very substantial correlation between religious faith, religious commitment, and success as doers in the community."

#4: Make your life your endgame.

The goal, Peter said, is not just long life or even a prosperous one; it's to make a meaningful life out of an ordinary one. At some point everybody wonders, "What's it all about anyway?" Life is often perplexing, and merely chasing "the dream" may not be enough. The question most halftimers ask themselves is, "What do I do now?" The answer is to set your sights on achievements that really matter, that will make a difference in the world. And set them far enough ahead of where you are today that the journey will be demanding but worth the effort. As Peter put it, "Make your life your endgame."

#5: Planning doesn't work.

Peter said planning doesn't work. You can prepare yourself, learn what you ought to know, and expand your experience and professionalism, but ultimately, he said, "opportunity comes in over the transom," and that means you have to be flexible, ready to seize the right opportunities when they come. "Too much planning," he said, "can make you deaf to opportunity." Knowing what you want to do and being prepared and equipped to do it is more important than the specific "how." Peter said, "Opportunity knocks, but it only knocks once. You have to be ready for the accident."

Early in his career Peter Drucker turned down top jobs at Goldman Sachs, Stanford Business School, and Emory University in Atlanta, not because they weren't good jobs but because he knew they weren't the *right* jobs for him. "One has to learn what to say no to," he told me, "and what to say yes to. One doesn't say, 'No because I didn't plan for it,' but 'No because it's not the right opportunity.'"

#6: You have to know your values.

What questions should you be asking about yourself and your life? Peter said, "If you don't respect a job, not only will you do a poor job of it but it will corrupt you, and eventually it may even kill you." If you are a person of faith, you assume a certain value system. But there's a value system for your work, as well. By way of example, Peter said, "Ninety-nine percent of all physicians should not become hospital administrators. Why? Because they have no respect for the job. They're physicians and they feel that hospital administration is a job for clerks. Most physicians I know, including my brother, don't respect the job." Knowing what you value and what you don't can keep you from making some bad choices along the way.

#7: You have to define what finishing well means to you.

Peter said, "I don't think I ever in my life considered making a lot of money as major success. My definition of success changed a long time ago. I love doing consulting work and writing—I regularly lose track of time when I'm doing those things. But finishing well and how I want to be remembered—those are the things that matter now. Making a difference in a few lives is a worthy goal. Having enabled a few people to do the things they want to do—that's really what I want to be remembered for." Peter's definition is right on track for halftimers. Ultimately success has to be viewed in context, and the best context is knowing what finishing well means to you.

#8 : You have to know the difference between harvesting and planting.

For most of us, the early part of our careers is a time of planting. It's about finding out what we do best and where we get the most satisfaction. During our "warrior" years we spend the majority of our time planting, building, expanding, and tending the farm. But planting season eventually comes to an end, and the time comes to start thinking about harvesting the rewards of what we've sown. Peter said, "For many years I measured my work by my output—mainly in terms of books and other writing that I was doing. I was very productive for many years. I am not so productive today, because these are years of harvesting rather than years of planting." As Solomon says, "There is *a time to plant, and a time to pluck what is planted*," and you need to know the difference.

#9: Good intentions aren't enough. You have to define the results you're after.

There has been a huge expansion in the number of nonprofits and charitable organizations the past several years. A lot of people want to put their resources to work where they can do the most good. Unfortunately, as Peter noted, many of them get poor results, or no results. "The problem," he said, "is that they don't ask about results, and they don't know what results they want in the first place. They mean well, and they have the best of intentions, but the only thing good intentions are for (as the old maxim says) is to pave the road to hell." The best results are achieved, he said, when people ask the right questions and then partner with others who have the expertise, knowledge, and discipline to get the right results.

#10: There's a downside to "no longer learning, no longer growing."

"I see more and more people," Peter said, "who make it to their midforties or beyond, and they've been very successful. They've done very well in their work and career, but in my experience, they end up in one of three groups. One group will retire. They usually don't live very long. The second group keeps on doing what they've been doing, but they're losing their enthusiasm, feeling less alive. The third group keeps doing what they've been doing, but they're looking for ways to make a contribution. They feel they've been given a lot and they're looking for a chance to give back. They're not satisfied with just writing checks, they want to be involved, to help other people in a more positive way." And they're ones who finish well.

Appendix 4

The John 17 Prayer

Instructions

This is a prayer that Jesus prayed for *you*.[1] It was his parting prayer as his work on earth was about to be, at last, finished. That work has now passed into the hands of those of us who followed him.

Before you read this prayer, fill your name in the blanks. (You will note there is a male and female version.) Then make it personal. Make it your own, the prayer Jesus prayed for *you* as he passed his life and his work on to you for completion.

A PERSONALIZED PARAPHRASE OF
THE PRAYER IN JOHN 17
FOR

(Male version. Put your own name in the blank.)

After Jesus said this, he looked toward heaven and prayed:

"Father, the time has come. Glorify your Son, that your Son may glorify you. For you granted him authority over all people that he might give eternal life to all those you have given him. Now this is eternal life: that they may know you, the only true God, and Jesus Christ, whom you have sent. I have brought you glory on earth by completing the work you gave me to do. And now, Father, glorify me in your presence with the glory I had with you before the world began.

"I have revealed you to _____ whom you gave me out of the world. He was yours; you gave him to me and he has obeyed your word. Now he knows that everything you have given me comes from you. For I gave him the words you gave me and he accepted them. He knew with certainty that I came from you, and he believed that you sent me. I pray for him. I am not praying for the world, but for those you have given me, for they are yours. All I have is yours, and all you have is mine. And glory has come to me through him. I will remain in the world no longer, but _____ is still in the world, and I am coming to you. Holy Father, protect _____ by the power of your name—the name you gave me—so that you and he may be one as we are one. . . .

"I am coming to you now, but I say these things while I am still in the world, so that they may have the full measure of my joy within them. . . . My prayer is not that you take _____ out of the world but that you protect him from the evil one. He is not of the world, even as I am not of it. Sanctify him by the truth; your word is truth. As you sent me into the world, I have sent _____ into the world. . . .

"My prayer is not for _____ alone. I pray also for those who will believe in me through his message, that all of them may be one, Father, just as you are in me and I am in you. May they also be in us so that the world may believe that you have sent me. I have given them the glory that you gave me, that they may be one as we are one: I in them and you in me. May they be brought to complete unity to let the world know that you sent me and have loved them even as you have loved me."

A PERSONALIZED PARAPHRASE OF
THE PRAYER IN JOHN 17
FOR

(Female version. Put your own name in the blank.)

After Jesus said this, he looked toward heaven and prayed:

"Father, the time has come. Glorify your Son, that your Son may glorify you. For you granted him authority over all people that he might give eternal life to all those you have given him. Now this is eternal life: that they may know you, the only true God, and Jesus Christ, whom you have sent. I have brought you glory on earth by completing the work you gave me to do. And now, Father, glorify me in your presence with the glory I had with you before the world began.

"I have revealed you to _____ whom you gave me out of the world. She was yours; you gave her to me and she has obeyed your word. Now she knows that everything you have given me comes from you. For I gave her the words you gave me and she accepted them. She knew with certainty that I came from you, and she believed that you sent me. I pray for her. I am not praying for the world, but for those you have given me, for they are yours. All I have is yours, and all you have is mine. And glory has come to me through her. I will remain in the world no longer, but _____ is still in the world, and I am coming to you. Holy Father, protect _____ by the power of your name—the name you gave me—so that you and she may be one as we are one. . . .

"I am coming to you now, but I say these things while I am still in the world, so that they may have the full measure of my joy within them. . . . My prayer is not that you take _____ out of the world but that you protect her from the evil one. She is not of the world, even as I am not of it. Sanctify her by the truth; your word is truth. As you sent me into the world, I have sent _____ into the world. . . .

"My prayer is not for _____ alone. I pray also for those who will believe in me through her message, that all of them may be one, Father, just as you are in me and I am in you. May they also be in us so that the world may believe that you have sent me. I have given them the glory that you gave me, that they may be one as we are one: I in them and you in me. May they be brought to complete unity to let the world know that you sent me and have loved them even as you have loved me."

Endnotes

Introduction

1. Bob Buford, *Halftime: Changing Your Game Plan from Success to Significance* (Grand Rapids: HarperCollins/Zondervan, 1995).

2. See Appendix 3 where I have distilled "Ten Principles for Life II" from multiple conversations with Peter Drucker.

3. For more on this, see the Web site at http://www.leadnet.org/.

4. Bob Buford, *Stuck in Halftime* (Grand Rapids: HarperCollins/Zondervan, 2001), 9.

5. Po Bronson, *What Should I Do with My Life? The True Story of People Who Answered the Ultimate Question* (New York: Random House, 2002).

6. Rick Warren, *The Purpose Driven Life: What on Earth Am I Here For?* (Grand Rapids: Zondervan, 2002).

7. Of course, most of the interviews weren't actually "over lunch," but that's the scene I want you to picture in your mind.

Chapter One

1. For more on Just for the Kids, see www.just4kids.org.

2. For more information on Leadership Network, see www.leadnet.org.

Chapter Two

1. Morris spent fifteen years as a professor of philosophy at the University of Notre Dame. In 1996 he left to start a think tank that applies the wisdom of the ages to modern business and contemporary life.

2. James 4:2 NIV.

3. Philippians 3:12 NKJV.

4. NKJV.

5. Lawrence Dutton's interview is featured in chapter 14.

Chapter Three

1. Richard M. Huber, *The American Idea of Success* (New York: McGraw-Hill, 1987), 1.

2. Morgan Scott Peck, *The Road Less Traveled: The Psychology of Spiritual Growth* (Kansas City, MO: Andrews McMeel, 2001).

3. Peter F. Drucker, *Managing the Nonprofit Organization: Practices and Principles* (New York: HarperCollins, 1990), xiv.

4. FaithWorks was a predecessor organization to Halftime. See www.halftime.org.

5. Luke 12:48, paraphrase.

6. Peter F. Drucker, *The Drucker Foundation Self-Assessment Tool.* Learn more about this from the Peter F. Drucker Foundation for Nonprofit Management at www.pfdf.org whose name has changed to Leader to Leader Institute. See www.leadertoleader.org.

7. See Tom Luce's story in chapter 1.

Chapter Five

1. See Laura Nash's formulation in chapter 3.

2. NKJV.

3. See my interview with Steve Reinemund in chapter 6.

Chapter Six

1. Ken Blanchard, *We Are the Beloved: A Spiritual Journey* (Grand Rapids: Zondervan, 1994), 23–24.

2. Ibid., 27.

Chapter Seven

1. For a good review course on temptations, study Matthew 4. After spending forty days in the wilderness, Jesus is tempted with an obstacle course set up to deter his mission in life. The first temptation was material things ("Turn the stones into bread"), the second was to do something showy and spectacular ("Jump off the temple") and the third was power ("Rule all you see before you"). These are still the "big 3" temptations.

2. See the chapter titled "Adios, Ross" in my book *Halftime.*

3. Mark 12:28–31.

4. Consider, for example, the fact that the Vanguard 500 Index Fund regularly outperforms 75 percent of the active money-management experts.

5. Hebrews 11:1.

6. Romans 8:28 NKJV

Chapter Eight

1. Hebrews 11:8 NKJV.

Chapter Nine

1. Lloyd Reeb, *Halftime for Regular People* (Grand Rapids: Zondervan, 2004). Also, visit www.halftime.org for helpful information on these topics, including a personalized Halftime Coaching Guide.

2. For more on Bridgespan, see http://www.bridgespangroup.com. Bain is a leading employer of graduates from Harvard Business School and other top-tier schools.

Chapter Ten

1. Karl Popper, *The Logic of Scientific Discovery* (New York & London: Routledge, 1992).

Chapter Thirteen

1. Robert A. Caro, *Master of the Senate: The Years of Lyndon Johnson,* vol. 3 (New York: Knopf [dist. Random House], 2002); Caro, *Means of Ascent: The Years of Lyndon Johnson,* vol. 2 (New

York: Knopf, 1990); and Caro, *The Path to Power: The Years of Lyndon Johnson,* vol. 1 (New York: Vintage Books, 1983).

2. James C. Collins, *Built to Last: Successful Habits of Visionary Companies* (New York: HarperBusiness, 1994), and Collins, *Good to Great: Why Some Companies Make the Leap—and Others Don't* (New York: HarperBusiness, 2001).

Chapter Fourteen
1. Luke 19:17 NKJV.
2. Luke 12:16-20 NKJV.
3. Matthew 8:12 NKJV.
4. Exodus 20:3 NKJV.
5. Hebrews 10:25 NKJV.

Chapter Fifteen
1. Lloyd Reeb describes his halftime experience in chapter 9.

Chapter Sixteen
1. George E. Vaillant, *Adaptation to Life* (New York: Little, Brown and Co., 1977).
2. Ibid.
3. NKJV.
4. Romans 8:18–19, 26, 29-30 THE MESSAGE.
5. Robert Frost, "A Servant to Servants" in *North of Boston* (New York: Henry Holt, 1915).
6. Vaillant, *Adaptation to Life.*

Chapter Eighteen
1. http://www.ttf.org.
2. See my reference to Carnegie in Buford, *Halftime,* 121.

Chapter Nineteen
1. 2 Samuel 12:23 NKJV.

Appendix 4
1. John 17:1–23.

Additional Resources

Chapter One

Tom Luce and Chris Tucker. *Now or Never: How We Can Save Our Public Schools.* Dallas, TX: Taylor Publishing, 1995.

Tom Luce. *Why Don't We Do What Works?* To be published in 2004.

Chapter Two

Steven Baglas. *The Success Syndrome: Hitting Bottom When You Reach the Top.* New York: Plenum Press, 1986.

Laura Nash and Howard Stevenson. *Just Enough: Tools for Creating Success in Your Work and Life.* Harvard Business School, 2004.

John R. O'Neil. *The Paradox of Success: When Winning at Work Means Losing at Life: A Book of Renewal for Leaders.* New York: G. P. Putnam's Sons, 1993.

Dallas Willard. *The Divine Conspiracy: Rediscovering Our Hidden Life in God.* San Francisco: HarperSanFrancisco, 1998.

Dallas Willard. *Renovation of the Heart: Putting on the Character of Christ.* Colorado Springs: NavPress, 2002.

Dallas Willard. *The Spirit of the Disciplines: Understanding How God Changes Lives.* San Francisco: HarperSanFrancisco, 1990 (1988).

Chapter Three

The Drucker Foundation Self-Assessment Tool. New York: The Drucker Foundation (www.pfdf.org) and San Francisco: Jossey-Bass Publishers.

Laura L. Nash. *Believers in Business.* Nashville: Thomas Nelson, 1994.

Laura Nash and Howard Stevenson. *Just Enough: Tools for Creating Success in Your Work and Life.* Boston: Harvard Business School, 2004.

Chapter Four

Dan Sullivan. *The Goal Cultivator.* For fifteen years, Sullivan has created and led The Strategic Coach Program, which I personally attended every ninety days for three years. Now his wisdom on how to take greater ownership of your future is available in a CD/workbook-based series. Several modules deal creatively with extended life and the need for difference making. For more information on The Strategic Coach Program and other Strategic Coach products and services, contact 800-387-3206 or visit www.strategiccoach.com.

Chapter Six

Kenneth Blanchard. *We Are the Beloved: A Spiritual Journey.* Grand Rapids: Zondervan, 1994.

Gordon MacDonald. *Ordering Your Private World*, rev. ed. Nashville: Thomas Nelson, 2003.

Chapter Seven

Armand M. Nicholi Jr. *The Question of God: C .S. Lewis and Sigmund Freud Debate God, Love, Sex, and the Meaning of Life.* New York: Free Press, 2002. "The twentieth century produced two brilliant men with two diametrically opposed views about the question of God: Sigmund Freud and C. S. Lewis. They never had an actual meeting, but in *The Question of God*, their arguments are placed side by side."

My Utmost Devotional Bible, New King James Version. Nashville: Thomas Nelson. This excellent volume offers great passages from all of the writings of Oswald Chambers interspersed with Scripture.

Chapter Nine

James C. Collins. *Good to Great: Why Some Companies Make the Leap—and Others Don't.* New York: HarperBusiness, 2001.

Hamilton Jordan. *No Such Thing as a Bad Day: A Memoir.* New York: Pocket, 2001.

Lloyd Reeb. *From Success to Significance: Halftime for the Not-so-Rich.* Grand Rapids: Zondervan, 2004.

Thomas J. Tierney and Jay W. Lorsch. *Aligning the Stars.* Boston: Harvard Business School Press, 2002.

Chapter Ten

Howard Hendricks and William Hendricks. *As Iron Sharpens Iron: Building Character in a Mentoring Relationship.* Chicago: Moody Publishers, 1999. A primer on mentoring, hoping to encourage men to enter into mentoring relationships with a view to sharing what is best in themselves with one another.

Earl Palmer. Teaching tapes. Earl is one of the greatest teachers alive today. His approach is fresh, original, lively, and true to Scripture. Check his Web site at www.upc.org.

Chapter Eighteen

Frances Hesselbein. *Hesselbein on Leadership.* San Francisco: Jossey-Bass, 2002.

T. Boone Pickens. *Boone.* New York: Random House, 1999.

C. William Pollard. *The Soul of the Firm.* Grand Rapids: Zondervan, 1996. This book shows how the biblical truth of man being made in the image of God motivates us to view our work as service to him.

Chapter Nineteen

Os Guinness. *The Call.* Nashville: Word, 1998.

Appendix 3

Jack Beatty. *The World According to Peter Drucker.* New York: Free Press, 1998.

Peter F. Drucker. *Managing the Nonprofit Organization,* reprint ed. New York: HarperBusiness, 1992.

Acknowledgments

I love to be around smart people. I always have. And I can't remember any period in my life when I have had more pure enjoyment than spending time with the 120 people who shared their thoughts for this book. The sixty whose thoughts are quoted at length were amazingly open and free with the learnings of their rich lives. Thanks to each of them. The book seemed to come alive in dialogue. For pure hard labor in distilling well over a thousand pages of single-spaced transcript, I am indebted to four people: to Carol Hobbs for turning cassette tapes, some of them in noisy restaurants, into typescript; to B. J. Engle, my tirelessly cheerful and competent assistant for scheduling and rescheduling all of these interviews and for typing draft after draft; to Jim Nelson Black, a capable author and editor in his own right for his absolutely necessary work in rendering all of the dialogue and otherwise tying it all together; and lastly to Tom Williams, who did the final edit—a truly remarkable judge of what should go and what should stay. Wally Hawley, Robert Lewis, and Rick and Jill Woolworth read the first full drafts and made invaluable suggestions from the readers' perspective, as did my wife, Linda. Byron Williamson and Joey Paul came up with the original idea and convinced me to do it.

Peter Drucker has been the leading wisdom figure in shaping my own Life II. It has been like a playwright having access to Shakespeare or a physicist to Einstein. He is the sort of person who comes along once every five hundred years and who is the seminal thinker for a whole field. Peter told me this was important work, which was what I needed to hear to commit a year's time and energy.

Gayle Carpenter, Dave Travis, and Tom Wilson lead Leadership Network, the primary vehicle for my Life II significance career. My trust in their passion, competence, and skill has allowed me to focus the majority of my energy on this project while producing exceptional results through the church entrepreneurs and halftimers we serve.

I have valuable two-way partnerships in the Halftime movement encouraging midlife people to make the transition from success to significance. Within Leadership Network, I am grateful for the passion of John Leffin, Greg Murtha, Lloyd Reeb, and Mike Shields. We also have invaluable partnerships with Jack Dennison at CitiReach International, Roy King at Columbia Biblical Seminary, Ron Proctor and David Williams at Executive Ministries, Nelson Malwitz with Finishers Project, Tom Spitza and Jane Terry at Focus Over Fifty, David Delk and Pat Morley with Man in the Mirror, Inc., Bob Shank with the Masters Program, Russell Crosson and Brian Shepler with Ronald Blue and Company, Terry Taylor with Second Half Ministries, and John Beehner at Wise Counsel.

And perhaps most of all, to you, the readers who bought over 400,000 copies of *Halftime* and shared your personal significance stories through countless e-mails. I've always said, "The fruit of my work grows up on other people's trees."

And to Linda, my lifelong partner and wife of forty-two years, who I fall more in love with every day. She's the one on the left.